SONGWRITING IN CONTEMPORARY WEST VIRGINIA

SOUNDING APPALACHIA

Travis D. Stimeling, Series Editor

TITLES IN THE SERIES

───────────────

Folk Songs from the West Virginia Hills
Patrick Ward Gainer; Foreword by Emily Hilliard

50 Cents and a Box Top:
The Creative Life of Nashville Session Musician Charlie McCoy
Charlie McCoy with Travis D. Stimeling

SONG
WRITING
IN CONTEMPORARY
WEST
VIRGINIA

PROFILES AND REFLECTIONS

TRAVIS D. STIMELING

West Virginia University Press · Morgantown 2018

ISBN:

paper 978-1-946684-27-1

epub 978-1-946684-28-8

pdf 978-1-946684-29-5

Library of Congress Cataloging-in-Publication Data

Names: Stimeling, Travis D. author.

Title: Songwriting in contemporary West Virginia : profiles and reflections / Travis D. Stimeling.

Description: Morgantown : West Virginia University Press, 2018. | Series: Sounding Appalachia | Includes bibliographical references.

Identifiers: LCCN 2018000783| ISBN 9781946684271 (pb) | ISBN 9781946684295 (pdf)

Subjects: LCSH: Musicians—West Virginia—Biography. | Country musicians—West Virginia—Biography. | Lyricists—West Virginia—Biography.

Classification: LCC ML385 .S735 2018 | DDC 782.42164092/2754 [B]—dc23

LC record available at https://lccn.loc.gov/2018000783

Book and cover design by Than Saffel / WVU Press

For Oran Dale Dean, who first taught me why this place is so special.

CONTENTS

PART I:
CHARLESTON—WEST VIRGINIA'S SONGWRITING CAPITAL

PART II:
THE OHIO VALLEY—RIVERS OF SONG

ACKNOWLEDGEMENTS

This book could not have been completed without the support of a vast community of people. First and foremost, the musicians profiled in this book were generous with their time and their resources, often bringing stacks of recordings for me to listen to and offering their homes as a traveler's rest during my journeys around the state. Additionally, the people profiled here were actively involved in the editing of the final manuscript. Through their participation, facts were checked, statements were clarified, and the writing was greatly improved. Thank you all for your friendship and partnership over these past few years. I look forward to many more years of sharing time and songs with you.

This book was inspired, in part, by the three exceptional books of songwriter interviews: Kathleen Hudson's *Telling Stories, Writing Songs: An Album of Texas Songwriters* (Austin: University of Texas Press, 2001), Marshall Chapman's *They Came to Nashville* (Nashville: Vanderbilt University Press and Country Music Foundation Press, 2010), and Jewly Hight's *Right by Her Roots: Americana Women and Their Songs* (Waco: Baylor University Press, 2011). Their models encourage me to explore the songwriting in my own backyard, and my life has been significantly enriched as a result.

West Virginia University provided financial support for this

x   *Acknowledgements*

projectthrough the WVU Faculty Senate Research and Scholarly Activity Grant program. My student research assistants—Stacey DaBaldo, Sophia Enriquez, Cody Pasden, Joey Rabchuk, Jim Savarino, Kenny Piatt, and Anne Stickley—patiently transcribed and edited hours of oral history recordings, often with greater accuracy than I could have. Derek Krissoff at West Virginia University Press has steadfastly supported this project since I first mentioned it to him, and I am grateful for his interest in it. I could not have completed this book without the support of my amazing colleagues Evan MacCarthy, Jada Watson, Douglas Shadle, and Emily Hilliard; their counsel and friendship have made this experience all the more pleasant. And finally, I am grateful for my family, which has allowed me to gallivant around the Mountain State in search of new songs and new friendships.

•

A NOTE ON THE SOURCES

The recounting of oral histories can be a messy process. Interviews can veer off in unexpected directions, and the resulting transcripts can often prove to be difficult reading material. As such, I have worked—often in conjunction with the musicians who are profiled here—to make the interviews more readable. In other instances, oral reports were elaborated upon or clarified in later correspondence between the research consultant and me. Where the research consultant intervened significantly with oral quotations, I have provided a note indicating such. As well, I have attempted to reduce the number of filler words wherever possible, and other portions have been edited for clarity. Most omissions are not marked with ellipses, and some minor interpolations have not been marked by square brackets. In the spirit of transparency, the recordings and transcripts of each interview will be available for researchers to consult at the West Virginia & Regional History Center, West Virginia University Libraries in Morgantown, West Virginia.

INTRODUCTION

Conjure the mountains of West Virginia, and it probably won't be long until you begin hearing archaic fiddle tunes, clawhammer banjos plunking a dance tune, or an ancient ballad that hearkens back to the British Isles and Elizabethan times. Films, books, and even the state's own vibrant folk festivals and fairs trade on the notion that the Mountain State is brimming with musicians playing styles of music that date back to the first settlements west of the Alleghenies in the mid-eighteenth century. And, for the most part, those representations are accurate, as the annual Vandalia Festival, Aunt Jennie Wilson Days, and West Virginia State Folk Festival attest.

But this view of the Mountain State's musical culture doesn't show the entire picture. Rather, it locates the state in a mythical past, as a place whose soundscape has been captured in amber. But closer examination reveals West Virginia to have a diverse musical ecosystem that parallels the biodiversity of its forests. This book seeks to examine one heretofore neglected aspect of the state's musical life: contemporary songwriting.

In virtually every community around the state, songwriters are trying to capture the experiences of their everyday lives, to tell the rich histories of the state and the broader Appalachian region, and to reframe its potent folklore for contemporary audiences. Nearly all of the songwriters profiled in this collection point to the powerful place that West Virginia has in their imaginations. Even a superficial survey of the output of the songwriters in this volume reveals references to John Henry, coal mining, and the Hatfields and McCoys. Natural imagery abounds, from vague celebrations of the mountains and rivers to poetic reflections on the spiritual messages that we can glean from the forests and mountains that dominate the state's physical landscape. And social get-togethers—from moonshine-fueled jam sessions to rural church prayer meetings—provide the spaces for these narratives to unfold.

Like the music they create, West Virginia's contemporary songwriters are a diverse lot. Some have made a bid for national fame and succeeded; others have chosen to play only for the members of their immediate community. Some consider themselves to be full-time professional songwriters, while others are reluctant to identify as writers at all. Some have recorded multiple albums (often without the financial assistance of a record label), while others have never shown an interest for sitting in a recording studio. Some have little formal education, while others hold multiple graduate degrees. But what holds this community of songwriters together is their common desire to use music to express their perspectives on life, perspectives that are often overlooked by journalists, politicians, and academics who prefer to see Appalachia as a cultural backwater.

West Virginia's contemporary songwriters, for the most part, act as part of a vibrant, geographically dispersed community. Songwriters swap their creations at song circles, get together in their homes to host picking parties, and organize special events to showcase their peers. They play on one another's recordings and share access to their industry contacts. They play benefit concerts for one another when someone has medical bills to pay, and they use their social media presence to promote the shows, recordings, and general goings-on in the lives of their fellow songwriters. And they tend to speak in overwhelmingly glowing terms of their musical compatriots. All in all, West Virginia's songwriters genuinely appear to enjoy one another's company and, for the most part, they believe that a rising tide raises all ships.

The songwriters selected for this survey represent a broad cross-section of writers who call the Mountain State home or point to their West Virginian upbringing as a significant part of their musical coming-of-age. Although it would be virtually impossible to document every songwriter living in or having roots in the state, I have made every effort to contact a variety of songwriters, with particular attention paid to geographic and generational diversity. I have conducted oral history interviews with each of the songwriters profiled here, listened carefully to their recorded output and, when possible, traveled to live performances to get a better sense of how they relate to their audiences. Over the nearly two years that I was conducting this research, I also entered into musical relationships with many of these writers. These relationships have taken a variety of forms, from informal jams to backing them up in concerts and producing recordings of their songs. As such, some of the songwriters profiled here have quickly become dear friends, although I have attempted to maintain a degree of objectivity in my descriptions of their work. At the end of the day, I remain a humble fan who considers himself very fortunate to have witnessed such remarkable creativity firsthand.

This book focuses primarily on songwriters who work in what might be broadly described as "folk," "bluegrass," and "Americana" music, a decision that was made after great deliberation. To be sure, West Virginians are writing songs in a variety of genres, including gospel, rhythm and blues, hip-hop, rock, and pop, and one might expect to see those songwriters in this book as well. My decision to omit writers in those genres was shaped by two principal factors. First, it became clear early in my research that the songwriters profiled here constitute a scene that does not regularly overlap with the state's other music scenes. A more limited study, therefore, more accurately reflects the social, musical, and economic connections of this particular group of songwriters. Second, as there is no doubt that songwriters working in other genres also thrive here in the Mountain State, I firmly believe that the scenes that support them deserve book-length studies of their own, perhaps in the *Sounding Appalachia* series at West Virginia University Press. My omission of songwriters working in genres other than folk/bluegrass/Americana should not, therefore, be seen as a lack of interest in them; rather, it is my hope that more sustained engagement with those scenes will generate the excellent publications they deserve.

Each profile in this book can be read as a self-contained piece focusing on a single musician. Reading multiple chapters in that manner will reveal the close relationships that many of these songwriters have had over the years. That being said, I have organized this book around the broad geographic communities in which these songwriters live and work in the hope that such a structure will highlight these interpersonal relationships still more. Inevitably, in a state as small and interconnected as West Virginia, these songwriting scenes often overlap, giving the appearance of one expansive statewide scene.

I have also provided selective discographies at the end of each profile to point the way to further listening. It is my sincere hope that you will seek out these recordings, as they offer a great introduction to their work. But as is often the case, recordings will offer only a limited view of a musician's work that you can augment by witnessing a live performance. I sincerely hope that, after reading this book, you will seek out these excellent songwriters and visit the venues that host their performances.

PART I:
CHARLESTON

WEST VIRGINIA'S SONGWRITING CAPITAL

• • • •

Figure 1. Ron Sowell
(photo by Chris Dorst, courtesy of Ron Sowell).

• • • •

RON SOWELL[1]

In West Virginia, all musical roads lead to Charleston resident Ron Sowell. In more than four decades in the Mountain State, Sowell has played in two of the state's most musically progressive bands, documented traditional string band music, led the august *Mountain Stage* house band, and mentored dozens, if not hundreds, of aspiring songwriters, guitarists, and record producers, all while writing, producing, and playing prolifically. His musicianship can be heard on the albums of many of the musicians profiled in this book, and he's never far away when a jam session or open mic is underway. And although he is a highly sought-after musician who could afford to be less than generous with his time and energy, Ron Sowell exudes kindness and welcomes new challenges with a mischievous smile and boundless energy. It is precisely this willingness to embrace the next exciting thing that has placed him at the center of some of the most exciting music scenes of the past half-century.

Sowell was born in Rotan, Texas, in 1947, but by his fifth year his family moved to Roswell, New Mexico, the UFO capital of the United States. "So that you know," he warns, "the UFO crashed in 1947, so just a little disclaimer that I was actually *not* brought here on the UFO because I came from Texas first. Although they might have dropped me off in Texas. I don't know."

If he descended from extraterrestrial ancestors, he's not able to recall the music he encountered aboard the spacecraft. But his terrestrial father was heavily involved in music, both secular and sacred. "My father was a wonderful singer. He sang in church and in a barbershop quartet and played the harmonica. I was raised in a [Church of Christ] that had no piano. It was really good for your ear training. And so I grew up singing in my church and sitting beside my dad, and when I got old enough, he would drop down and sing bass and I would sing tenor."

But a musical life was not a given for Ron, especially when basketball and music conflicted. His mother bought him a guitar when he was thirteen years old, but he preferred sports with friends to solitary practice. But once he met a neighbor who wanted to play with him, he couldn't be stopped. "He was younger, a little bit younger than me, but he was more advanced than I was, and we got to be fast buddies. And then all of a sudden, we were playing eight hours a day, and [basketball] was all over."

Ron's newfound love of the guitar coincided with the emergence of a national folk music craze, a movement led by the Kingston Trio and Peter, Paul, and Mary, the first group he ever saw in concert. "A lot of people don't remember how revolutionary the Kingston Trio was, even though it was just three guys and a couple of guitars, and, you know, nothing fancy with them. But all of a sudden me and two of my friends were wearing white striped shirts and singing Kingston Trio songs. So that was a huge influence on me. And then, of course, Peter, Paul, and Mary was the next big thing." Surf rockers The Ventures also appeared on the scene, and Sowell, armed with an electric guitar, was immediately drawn to their electrified, guitar-centered sound. "I actually played in a group that did a lot of rock and roll and old Ventures songs. But the church I was in, you couldn't dance. So I started playing for dances, and my parents freaked out! And so I had to quit the band." But by that point, the die had been cast, and Ron soaked up all of the music he could from the radio—including Wolfman Jack's famous border radio broadcasts—and practiced constantly in pursuit of a professional music career.

After graduating from high school, Sowell enrolled at Eastern New Mexico University in Portales, just twenty miles or so from Clovis, where Buddy Holly recorded some of his biggest hits. A political science major with a choir scholarship, Sowell and his two folk music buddies from Roswell, who also attended ENMU, continued performing around campus as The Coachmen, a name taken from the first Kingston Trio album. Choir concerts, musicals, and opera productions allowed Ron the opportunity to develop his stage presence, albeit in limited ways. "I was in *The Unsinkable Molly Brown*, and I was in at least one opera, *Carmen*. But I didn't really have a big singing role. I had some walk-ons. I was a guide, and I walked on with the lead female and said, 'Here we are!'" His choir experience also allowed him to perform around the world, a big development for someone living in the geographic isolation of eastern New Mexico. "We went on a USO tour. We went to Canada—Nova Scotia and Labrador—Greenland and Iceland and London for a week."

During his senior year, Sowell was preparing for the next step of his education—law school—but music was becoming still more significant to his sense of self. He had even begun to make a key transition from covering the songs of other writers to writing a few of his own, although, he observed, "I didn't really play them for anybody." With years of legal study and a professional legal career ahead of him, Ron was at a crossroads. "I guess it was my senior year, and I was signing up to take my LSATs [law school entrance examinations], and I remember I literally, physically froze. I couldn't write. And I went, 'What's going on?' And I realized that I didn't want to do this, you know? I was thinking, 'Well, when am I going to be able to play my guitar?' And then I asked the most appropriate question that any musician could ever ask themselves: What would I do even if I didn't get paid for it? So I just realized that it wasn't that I *wanted* to be a musician. It's what I *was*, and to do anything, to be anything else was to deny that." So Ron put his law school plans on a permanent recess and decided to do the only sensible thing a musician could do: move to a city where gigs and collaborators were more plentiful.

The summer after he graduated from ENMU, though, Ron stayed in New Mexico to play for a "musical extravaganza" called *Desert Fiesta* in Carlsbad. "I auditioned," he said, "and they hired kids from all over the country and there was this huge cast. We had this orchestra and about thirty or forty people in the cast." At the conclusion of the summer, Sowell moved to El Paso, where he took a job at a Travelodge hotel and found a welcoming audience for his music among the travelers who passed through the hotel's bar. He also met a songwriter whose path would intersect with his again in the very near future. "I met this guy named Allen Ramsey playing at the [campus] coffeehouse. And it was his first gig! And so this mutual friend put us together, and we were so green, both of us. We were going, like, 'Wow! Gosh, this is great! Well, what do we do now?' 'Well, I guess we jam and swap some songs.' 'Yeah, that's what we do!'" Before long, Allen Ramsey added a third name, becoming Willis Allen Ramsey, the songwriter behind the AM radio hit "Muskrat Love," made famous by The Captain and Tenille. But despite a new friend and a secure job, Ron was eager to move on. "I played there [at the Travelodge] for a couple of months, and I was making all of this money, and I thought, 'Well, this is easy.' So I gave them my notice. I thought, 'Well, I've got to get some experience, and I'm going to travel. You know, if it's this easy, I'll just go.' And then I left there, and I almost starved to death for like a year. I didn't realize what a great gig that was."

Loading up his 1956 Dodge with all of his earthly possessions, he set out for the "closest big city, which was not very close. It was Dallas, Texas, which was about five hundred miles." With the help of a friend, he secured a regular job singing at a Steak and Ale that promised sufficient income to allow time to work on his music. The Dallas that he arrived in was far from the sprawling corporate town that it currently is. Rather, the early 1970s found Dallas to be a musical hotbed that supported an eclectic cohort of young songwriters, many of whom went on to become luminaries of the Texas singer-songwriter community that flourished throughout the 1970s. The hub of this activity was a club called The Rubaiyat, named after Kahlil Gibran's influential poem, and such songwriters as B.W. Stevenson, Ray Wylie Hubbard, Michael Martin Murphey, and Willis Alan Ramsey—as well as Mickey Raphael, who has played harmonica with Willie Nelson since the early 1970s—cut their teeth there. Also among the crowd was Sowell's future musical partner and *Mountain Stage* compatriot Larry Groce, although they passed like ships in the night during their Dallas years. "I just missed him," Ron recalled. "It was so weird. You know, he had just left when I arrived, and people would say, 'Oh, you would've loved Larry. I hope you get to meet him someday.' And then, I moved here [to West

Virginia] in 1974, and Larry moved, I think, in like '73, and we didn't meet until 1980."

Sowell auditioned at The Rubaiyat shortly after he got to Dallas, and from 1970 to 1971, he was a fixture there. "That's where I really cut my teeth," he remarked. That's where I started to play my original stuff and learn how to talk to an audience." He and B.W. Stevenson, who had a hit with "My Maria" in 1973, were the appetizer for each night's main course. "B.W. and I opened for people," Sowell recalled. "Seventy-five dollars a week, two sets a night, five nights a week. I mean, seventy-five for the *whole* week! Mickey [Raphael] would come in and play harmonica. And then, when I was through with the Rubaiyat, I would go do my Steak and Ale gig."[2]

During his residence in Dallas, Sowell met his first wife, Sandy, who eventually became a strong vocalist and who also worked at the Steak and Ale as a waitress. In late 1971 or early 1972, they moved to Houston, a folk singer-songwriter center that had nurtured the career of Townes Van Zandt, at the same time that most of the Dallas songwriters in the Rubaiyat circle were moving to Austin, the future home of the Texas progressive country music scene.[3] Upon settling in Houston, Ron reconnected with an old "picking buddy," David Ziems. "He moved down to Houston, and we formed a little duo," he remembered. "And when he got there, we thought we only had about three or four songs. But we said, 'Let's go ahead and audition for an agent, because it's going to be weeks before we get a gig, and by that time, we'll have enough songs together.' Well, this is like Tuesday. Thursday, we get a call from the agent, who said, 'Well, I have this guy in Houma, Louisiana, who got sick, and he can't finish his contract. Could you guys be there by Saturday?' He had a great deal more estimation of our talent and abilities at the time than what was actually the reality. We said, 'Sure.' So we went there to Houma. The guy who we were replacing knew every Neil Diamond song . . . and they loved Neil Diamond, and we did not know one Neil Diamond song! They *hated* us! I mean, they didn't just dislike us; they *hated* us. So after the first week, we went in, and the guy said, 'Here's your money, and we won't be needing your services any longer.' So we were pretty depressed."

To get over the disappointment of their week in Houma, Ron,

Sandy, and Dave decided to spend the weekend apart. Ziems returned from his weekend with a new plan: move to New Orleans. "David went to New Orleans," Sowell recalled, "and when we met up at the end of the weekend, he said, 'Oh, my god! We have to move to New Orleans.' We said, 'Really?' And he said, 'I found the perfect club, and I've got a girlfriend.'" Leaving Houston in their rearview mirror (to paraphrase a song about another Texas city), Sowell embraced the new opportunity, taking up residence in the French Quarter and playing in a club called the Wrong Place Saloon. "It was a pass-the-hat place. They started music—which you can only do in New Orleans and maybe New York—at five o'clock in the afternoon and played to five o'clock in the morning, thirty-minute sets. Pass-the-hat, sing, pass-the-hat. And the best sets were like from ten o'clock 'til two o'clock in the morning. But you had to work your way into those sets, and you had to do them at least five nights a week and get somebody to cover for you the other two nights or they gave them to someone else. So I eventually got a set at eleven-thirty." Following him at midnight was a Tulane student named Steve Hill, who would become a key musical collaborator over the next four decades.

Sowell recalled that the Wrong Place Saloon's audience welcomed original songs, even when the tourists rolled in. "Every night, we would have this collection of songwriters, and every night, somebody was coming in with a new song, you know? And when one would stick we would all sing it in harmony," Ron noted. "These tourists would come in, and one of us would get up on stage and sing this song the tourists had never heard before, and all the people in the bar would be singing along."

Passing the hat after one thirty-minute set didn't pay the bills, though, so Sowell balanced a number of gigs throughout the city. "I had a gig at a happy hour at a hotel; I sang from like four to six. And then, from six to ten, I had a gig at a piano bar where I would just sit behind the piano and play guitar and sing from six to ten. And then I went to play the pass-the-hat places—and there were a couple of them—and I always played the Wrong Place Saloon and then sometimes another one after that. And then we would all get together at somebody's place and swap songs 'til, you know, about five o'clock in the morning. And then we could go to Café du Monde and have beignets and coffee and watch the sun come up and then go home, go to sleep, and get up and do it all over again! And on the weekends, we would busk down on Royal Street and Jackson Square."

Yet, while it "was one of the most magical years of my life," Sowell recognized that this pace was unsustainable. When a jazz guitarist from Cincinnati offered him the chance to manage a coffeehouse there called the Family Owl, Ron took him up on the offer. "Sandy and I went up to Cincinnati and checked it out, and my thinking process at the time was—I mean, I'm having this great time in New Orleans—I thought, 'At the rate I'm going, I can keep doing this and have this much fun, and in about five years, I'll be dead. Or I can space out my fun a little bit and maybe live a little longer." So he and Sandy accepted the offer and moved to the Queen City in 1973.

The always peripatetic Sowell couldn't stay put in Cincinnati for long, though, as he began playing coffeehouses throughout the Ohio Valley to fill his spare time. "I had a gig at Wheeling Jesuit College, and a friend of mine, Bob Webb, who I had met in New Orleans, he and his wife were living out in Putnam County. They had moved here [to West Virginia], and so we came down to visit. I thought, you know, I had a couple days off after the gig and said, 'Let's go visit,' and just fell in love with the land. And Bob said, 'Well there's a little farmhouse down at the bottom of the holler that's up for rent.' So we went and checked it out and said, 'Well, let's just stay for the summer.' And that was 1974." As Carter Taylor Seaton notes in her book *Hippie Homesteaders*, pockets of creative people from out-of-state began to find West Virginia a hospitable place to live and create their music, art, and literature during the mid-1970s, and Sowell fit in immediately with this community.[4] Joining him on the farm were Steve Hill, the guitarist and bassist he had met in New Orleans, and Ammed Solomon, who would go on to be another important musical collaborator to the present day.

Life on the farm was conducive to a musical life, as the homesteaders were living in a place with little else to entertain them. Sowell remembers, "Okay, so I was living in this little house that had electricity, but no running water. It had a great well and some of the people who lived up on the hill didn't have electricity." It wasn't long before the residents formed the Putnam County Pickers, a country music group that mixed solid picking with an ironic take on the trappings of country culture. Ron recalls, "We just got together and played at parties and ended up being a band."

The group would have been at home in the Austin progressive country scene that Sowell's old Rubaiyat buddies were pioneering. But, unlike his Texan counterparts, Sowell and the Putnam County Pickers didn't have an urban infrastructure to help them get work: "The way people would get in touch with us is we would all go down to the Culloden post office to get our mail, and we'd walk in the door, and the postmaster would say, 'You know, there's a guy up in Morgantown that wants you guys to play at a festival, and here's his number.' People literally had to track us down. We finally got a phone in an old chicken coop. But I mean we were living in lean-tos and teepees and treehouses and old farmhouses and stuff."

Despite these challenges, the Putnam County Pickers became a highly sought-after group throughout the region.[5] "Steve and I went out on the road [as a duo] for several months, six months or so, and then eventually came back. And we had so many gigs offered us with the Pickers that we ended up doing that." One of their strongest advocates was Jim Andrews, who was an assistant commissioner for the West Virginia Division of Culture and History. Andrews invited the Putnam County Pickers to audition for a big showcase that he was planning to help promote West Virginia artists of all stripes. As Sowell recounts it, Andrews asked to see them at one of their performances, but "we said, 'Well, we don't really have any gigs right now, but we're rehearsing. You can come to our house if you want.' He said, 'Okay.' So he asked us where we lived. So he came to the house where Sandy and I were living at the time. He had to park his car. He got out in his suit, took his jacket off, put his boots on, walked over this little suspension bridge and through the meadow and halfway up this hill to our place and auditioned us in the living room." After the arduous journey, Andrews was apparently impressed, offering them a spot on the showcase. "We got so many gigs [from that showcase]," Ron observed. "A community would hire us to come in and do some stuff in the schools and then do a concert for the community, maybe do a workshop." The

Commission matched the Pickers' fees dollar-for-dollar, "so all of a sudden, we were able to make a living," Sowell remembered. These concerts took him all over the state, introducing him to many amazing people and places in his new home.

The Putnam County Pickers recorded two albums, *It's About Time* (1978) and *Let the Cat Out* (1980), and began to tour more widely, always knowing that West Virginia school concerts were available to fill in any gaps in their schedule. The band played every couple of months at the Lone Star Café in New York City, and they also worked to gain access to the collegiate and military circuits. "We did the NACA [National Association for Campus Activities], and we got gigs all up and down the eastern seaboard. And then we auditioned for a USO tour. We auditioned, and the guy called us up and said, 'Well, you're accepted! How would you like to go to Greenland? And I'm going, 'Great!' because I had already been to Greenland. We found out that *that* was really an audition for a *bigger* USO tour, so we ended up going to Germany, Greece, Turkey, Crete, and Ethiopia on another tour. So that was fabulous." Toward the end of the 1970s, the Pickers were also hired to play for the largest single audience they'd ever seen at the Jamboree in the Hills festival near Wheeling. "During the end of the Pickers," Ron recalled, "we started playing at the Wheeling Jamboree, and the guy who was booking there at the time just absolutely loved us and he booked us for Jamboree in the Hills. The major acts that year were Alabama, Hoyt Axton, Emmylou Harris, Bill Monroe, and the Putnam County Pickers. We were playing for 70,000 people." But by 1981, just as they were performing in front of the biggest audiences of their career, the band members started to move "away from country" and toward new musical directions, leading to the group's end.

As he was traveling around the state with the Putnam County Pickers, Sowell had the opportunity to meet many of the state's leading traditional musicians, including a previously undocumented fiddler named French Mitchell, whose repertoire brought together some of the standard fiddle repertoire of central West Virginia fiddlers and the flashy contest fiddling associated with such Kanawha Valley fiddlers as Clark Kessinger. Sowell remembers being fascinated with West Virginia's fiddling traditions and enjoyed playing with them when he got the chance: "I was at the Ripley Arts and Crafts Fair, and there was this old fiddler sitting on the side of the hill, and I went up to him with my guitar. And he said, 'Do you want to play a tune?' And I said, 'Sure! So he starts playing, and I really didn't know the tune, but, you know, I've got a pretty decent ear, so I'm playing with him. And then we're playing another tune, and by about the third tune, I look around, and there's about four other people pulling instruments out of their cases. And by the time we got through there were like twenty people sitting there, and they were all playing song after song. Tune after tune."

Ron met French Mitchell at the Mason County Fair, where the Pickers were opening for *Grand Ole Opry* star Porter Wagoner. Mitchell needed a guitarist to back him up for a fiddle contest. "Steve [Hill] backed him up, and we just fell in love with this guy." With the support of the West Virginia Division of Culture and History, Sowell produced an LP, *First Fiddle*, showcasing the vibrant fiddling of the seventy-one-year-old Mitchell and his sixty-nine-year-old brother Auvil, who accompanied him on guitar. Now out-of-print, this LP is one of the most exciting recordings of West Virginia contest fiddling released in the last half-century, proudly displaying a musician who Sowell describes as "the Stephan Grappelli of old-time fiddlers." He notes, "It was one of the proudest things I've ever done."

The demise of the Pickers didn't mark the end of Sowell's partnership with his bandmates, though. Rather, his next project, the progressive folk rock/pop group Stark Raven, included multi-instrumentalist Bob Webb and future *Mountain Stage* bandmates vocalist Julie Adams, fiddler/violinist Deni Bonet, drummer Ammed Solomon, and bassist John Kessler. Sowell took pride in the careful attention that he and his bandmates paid to every detail of their songwriting, arranging, and performance style. "We rehearsed all the time, and we were just meticulous about who played where. We would have separate vocal rehearsals and . . . rhythm section rehearsals. We rehearsed in this friend of ours' garage attic, for like a week or two, just running everything, and then we chose this small little club to kind of preview everything. We put lots and lots of thought into what song followed what and who would speak in between songs. And, of course, you had to get all of your gear together and make sure that you weren't going to have dead space and have smooth transitions and make sure the vocals were balanced. We were very, very meticulous about it."

The group, as Julie Adams recalled, had moderate success at colleges and universities throughout the Mid-Atlantic and southeastern United States. But perhaps their largest audience came from a fledgling radio program presenting West Virginian musicians and leading roots musicians from around North America. *Mountain Stage*, hosted by the former Rubaiyat songwriter Larry Groce. He needed a house band to accompany the visiting artists and to fill any gaps in the program, and Ron—who, in 1980, played on the show's pilot with the Putnam County Pickers—wanted to get involved. When the show went on the air in 1983, Stark Raven members Adams and Bonet performed as the Fabulous Twister Sisters on the very first show, and, as Ron recalls, "Larry loved them and hired them on the spot" to be a regular act. When the original bassist quit, Groce hired Stark Raven bassist John Kessler, and to round out the group, Ammed Solomon took the drummer's throne. But Ron was left out and eager to make a place for himself on the program.

"Well," he reflected, "I'm sitting here, and this is like going into the second year. It started out as one show a month locally, and then they developed a statewide thing. And then it was two shows a month statewide. I remember they had Charlie McCoy on one show, and then had John Hartford on another show, and I started thinking 'This is starting to be pretty cool.' I was actually a guest both as a part of Stark Raven and under my own name. I thought, 'I have to get on this show [as a regular]!' So I had begun scheming a way to weasel my way onto the show. At the time, they were doing a lot of comedy á la *Prairie Home Companion*. They were doing skits. Well, writing good comedy takes time, and I knew that Larry was starting to get real busy. So I wrote about three or four comedy sketches, and they used them all. And so I would go and hang out at the rehearsals just to make sure everything was going okay. At one rehearsal, Larry said, 'We're doing this kids' song with this kids' choir, and I need a harmonica player.' He said, 'Wait, you play the harmonica, don't you?' I said, 'Yes, uh, well, yes, yes, I do.' So he hired me as the harmonica player like twice. And I was still just hanging at rehearsals. Larry was having to learn three songs a week playing guitar and singing. And that's hard to do. So I started playing guitar for him because it doesn't matter on the radio. You can't see who's playing the guitar, but I was never hired to be in the band. I just kind of showed up, and they actually were paying me, and nobody said anything, and I didn't want to rock the boat. So about two months before the show was to go national [in January 1985], they were taking new pictures of the staff and the band. And so I'm hanging off in the wings and Andy Ridenour [one of the show's producers] looks around and said, 'Hey, Ron! Come and get in the picture.' And that's how I knew I was in the band." With more than eight hundred episodes under his belt now, Sowell has secured his place on *Mountain Stage*, arranging songs, rehearsing the house band, and even playing and singing a featured number from time to time.

Even amid a hectic production schedule as the bandleader of a nationally—and later internationally—syndicated radio program and as part of the musically intense group Stark Raven, Sowell maintained his passion for songwriting. As Stark Raven fell by the wayside, Ron began to focus even more on producing recordings of his own songs and those of his favorite songwriting colleagues. Among the folks he's produced are Roger Hunt, Paul Epstein, Jon Wikstrom, and Mark and Micah Atkinson. But one of his biggest production successes was with mandolinist Johnny Staats, a Jackson County native who drove a UPS truck as his day job. Staats came to Sowell's attention in 1999 or 2000, when he won the mandolin and guitar contests and placed third in the fiddle contest at the Vandalia Gathering at the West Virginia Capitol Complex, where *Mountain Stage* was recording a program. "So I'm walking down the hall, and I hear this guy playing," Sowell recalls. "[*Mountain Stage* pianist] Bob Thompson and I are walking down the hall, and we literally went like this [jaw drops]. Who is this guy?"

Staats's music stuck with him as Sowell journeyed to Nashville, where he had been traveling every few weeks to write with John Wikstrom. "He and I would write together," he recalled. "I'd go down, and we'd pitch songs. We'd try and write with other people, and we developed this relationship with this guy at Sony Publishing, John Van Meter. And John loved New Grass Revival. So in one of my pitch sessions at Sony Publishing, instead of playing five songs, I played him three songs, and I said, 'John, I don't know why I'm taking up my valuable pitching time with you to play this, but I know you love this kind of music. You need to hear this.' And he said, 'Well, okay.' So he played it, and his jaw hit the desk." Van Meter begged Ron to bring Johnny Staats to Music City. Ron obliged.

When they got to Nashville, Van Meter arranged a house party where Staats had the chance to play for John Cowan of New Grass Revival and Jim Hurst, who was touring with country artist Sara Evans at the time. "During this party," Sowell recalled, "the three of them sat down and started playing. And I went, 'Oh, my god!' And all the way back home, I was thinking, 'If I got the three of them into a studio, it wouldn't be too long until we'd have something special.'" Van Meter offered Ron the use of Sony's studios for the price of the engineer, and Ron began working with Staats to select the songs and make the arrangements for the session. In addition to several instrumental numbers, the album would include Billy Edd Wheeler's iconic "Coal Tattoo," as well as a new song that Sowell co-wrote with Van Meter, Wikstrom, and Tim Bays. "John Van Meter had the title 'Wires and Wood,'" Ron remembered, "and he and my friend John Wikstrom and another friend Tim Bays, who happened to walk into the office that day, started playing around with it and they had an idea for the chorus. And they called me up and sang it to me on the phone. So they sent me a chorus, and I sent them back two verses." The resulting album, *Wires and Wood*, featured many of Nashville's finest, including Jerry Douglas, Tim O'Brien, Sam Bush, Kathy Mattea, Sara Evans, and John Cowan. It received national media attention for the bluegrass star who drove a UPS truck and captured the imaginations of people across the country. But rather than chasing stardom, Staats decided to stay home in West Virginia, where he remains a mainstay of the state's bluegrass scene.

Like so many of the state's most prolific songwriters, Sowell's recorded catalog is relatively limited. In addition to the four albums he cut with the Putnam County Pickers and Stark Raven, Ron has recorded three full-length albums, *Oil and Water* (1992), *Little Movies* (2014), and a children's album *Opposite Day* (2003). His compositions—sung in Ron's melodious tenor voice—often speak of the pleasures of interpersonal communion and suggest a way for us to live in harmony with one another and the environment. In addition to "Wires and Wood," for example, such compositions as "Mother Earth Blues" and "Best Friend I Ever Had" speak to Sowell's kindness, gentleness, and perceptiveness. At the same time, he peppers his live shows and solo albums with songs exhibiting his wry sense of humor, as heard in such songs as "Gig from Hell," which recounts a terrifyingly bad show he played at a mud bog.

Sowell is also a significant advocate for his fellow songwriters, providing safe and supportive places for them to get together and develop their craft. With Will Carter, the founder of the Appalachian String Band Festival at Clifftop, Gary Reynolds, Gar Ragland, and Charleston *Gazette* columnist Doug Imbrogno, Sowell helped to create the New Song Festival, which held a national contest for original songwriters and offered workshops and showcases. Sadly, the national festival was very difficult to plan and implement, and Sowell left the festival to focus on his other work. Currently, he organizes the Woody Hawley Concert Series, which presents concerts by numerous regional musicians at Charleston's Clay Center for the Performing Arts. Furthermore, for the past eighteen years, Sowell has held an open mic on the second Friday of each month, where many aspiring songwriters have gotten their start.

Now, more than four decades after moving to a Putnam County farmstead, Ron Sowell has made significant contributions to the state's musical communities as a songwriter, producer, session musician, and bandleader. Looking back on a career that is still going strong today, Ron considers himself fortunate. "I feel really, just extremely blessed to be able to do this and to do it in West Virginia. I mean I fell in love with this place. When I first moved here I thought, 'I love the land, I love the people, but I don't know if I'll ever be able to make a living playing music here. How could that happen?' This place has really proved me wrong."

DISCOGRAPHY

With the Putnam County Pickers:
... *It's About Time*, New Orchard Music Rose 14-U (1978).
Let the Cat Out, ACI Records ACI 1001 (1980).

WITH STARK RAVEN:
> *One Hundred Million Reasons*, Vitag SR0001 (1985).
> *Learning to Fly*, Wooly Mammoth SR0002 (1988).

AS A SOLO ARTIST:
> *Oil and Water*, Story Circle Music, no catalog number (1992).
> *Opposite Day*, Wingman Records, no catalog number (2004).
> *Little Movies*, Mountain Soul MSRCD 002 (2013.).

. . . .

Figure 2. Larry Groce
(photo by Todd Cerveris, courtesy of Larry Groce).

. . . .

LARRY GROCE[6]

"There's a spring in the mountains, and it flows down through the town."

Every week, Larry Groce's warm voice intones the familiar words of the *Mountain Stage* theme as "live performance radio from the Mountain State of West Virginia" hits the airwaves around the globe. Evoking a bucolic Appalachian life situated in nature and the culture of a small town, Groce's theme frames one of the state's most widely celebrated cultural exports, a radio program that many musicians identify as either a significant career aspiration or one of their proudest achievements. Creating an environment that allows some of the best musicians from around the world to experience the slow-paced but deeply creative musical community that the region has to offer, Groce has been one of West Virginia's greatest musical advocates for more than four decades. At the same time, he has helped to provide an environment in which audiences around the state can also see leading musicians in a variety of styles for relatively little money and hear them over the public airwaves for free.

"From the beginning," Groce reflected, "*Mountain Stage* was never set up as a show only for West Virginians, because if it was, it'd already be long gone. There's not enough of a pool there, and you'd have the same thing over and over and over again. Frankly, people know their hometown people. They don't want to hear that. They want to hear something from elsewhere. You can mix in some of the hometown people if you do it right, if they meet the standards of artists from elsewhere, too. But from the beginning, *Mountain Stage* has given West Virginia artists an edge. A whole lot more people listen to the show outside of West Virginia than inside of West Virginia. I always want them to know it's *from* West Virginia."

Groce's advocacy for the state's musicians and public image has made him a leading figure in the West Virginia music scene for more than forty years. But many people might be surprised to learn that Groce is not a native of the Mountain State; rather, he was born and raised in one of the few states that can boast more chauvinistic residents than West Virginia: Texas. A native of Dallas, Groce was raised among some of Texas's most exciting and widely celebrated singer-songwriters—Michael Martin Murphey and Ray Wylie Hubbard—as well as blues legends Jimmy and Stevie Ray Vaughan. Born in 1948, he entered high school at a musically auspicious time, the early 1960s.

Groce recalls that his own interest in music developed through the 1960s folk revival and a cohort of older friends who introduced him to some of the era's hippest music. "A friend of mine who was in a choir was into folk music very much. He and his brother. They were older. My friend's name was Robert Lam, and his brother's name was Milton. And his brother was old enough to be, like, of the Beat Generation almost. He had a Peugeot back in 1959 in Dallas. They subscribed to *Sing Out!* magazine back then. And so there were leftist things and Pete Seeger, and that's how I heard about those things, besides from books."

One of those books was Alan Lomax's *Folk Songs of North America*, which provided entry to many of the continent's vibrant vernacular musical traditions. "I'd read those songs. I didn't read music, but I could read the words and heard some of those songs, various versions of them, on the pop-folk albums." And at the same time, he was tracing the pathways of American country music through Woody Guthrie. "I was introduced to Woody Guthrie and all that. I got into Flatt and Scruggs. I got into Bill Monroe. The Carter Family." Flatt and Scruggs, in particular, blew his mind, especially their live albums from Vanderbilt University and Carnegie Hall: "What I liked best were the records where they played live."

Groce began to translate his interest in listening and reading into musical creativity by the end of his junior high years. By the time he was thirteen, he had written his first song, "a folky protest kind of song. I mean, it was serious. 'We must all get together,' you know, that kind of stuff, influenced by Dylan and all of those." He also played acoustic string band instruments, appearing at school assemblies during his teen years alongside future progressive country fixture Ray Wylie Hubbard and taking other low-profile gigs to gain experience and earn spending money. "I started playing for money pretty early," he remembered. "I mean, we didn't have a lot of jobs, but we played at the usual Lions Clubs, and every now and then, we got hired to play at dances in between the rock bands. I played banjo as well as guitar. Later, I played mandolin, too. Matter of fact, with Ray, I played mandolin a good bit. But that's how I started playing. First was at school, you know, like at school assemblies."

Rather than immersing himself in a formal pedagogy, Groce and his classmates at Adamson High School built a community of practice in which everyone shared their discoveries with one another, much as folkniks around the United States were doing in their communities. "I didn't take guitar lessons or anything," Groce recalled, "but the way we learned was that some of us played together. [Future Three Faces West and Texas Fever guitarist] Rick Fowler lived down the street from me, and he was a good guitar player. So we would get together, and that's how we learned. We learned from each other, but mostly I learned from him. Then we would learn from listening to records and watching people, watching their hands, even on TV, like *Hootenanny* and those shows, to watch how they were doing that. So that's how I learned, rather than through any kind of instruction."

One of the most significant places for this community to get together was the Rubaiyat, a folk club that brought national acts to Dallas and that supplied homegrown talent as well. "When I was in high school, we met at the Rubaiyat, which was right in the center of Dallas. And it was an interesting place. It was not an alcohol place. It was a coffeehouse, so, therefore, it was open later than the bars. After hours, people came in. It was pretty interesting. I went to hear [Michael] Murphey and Owens ["Boomer"] Castleman and, you know, different people. Jerry Jeff Walker, actually, and later on, Johnny Vandiver." Groce also played the Rubaiyat, gaining valuable experience and networking with many of the leading songwriters of the mid-1960s.

Upon graduating from Adamson High, Groce moved to Illinois, where he enrolled at Principia College, a small college that had, in Groce's recollection, "only seven hundred fifty people." There, he formed a group with his brother, who left Principia after a year, and later with Berke McKelvey, who would go on to teach at the Berklee School of Music in Boston. While at Principia, he also began to tap into the rock music that was coming out of the San Francisco Bay area. "There, I met a lot of people that were from California. I started getting into a little bit of the Grateful Dead—not a lot, although I went to see the Dead at that time—Jefferson Airplane, Quicksilver Messenger Service, Country Joe [McDonald]." But the folk songwriters of the day were also omnipresent in his musical worldview, especially Tim Harden, Tim Buckley, and Phil Ochs. But the group that excited him most blended the great singer-songwriter compositions of the day with rock and country music: The Band. "The one that hit me hardest," he remembered, "and I can't remember how I first heard it—it might have been Ray [Wylie Hubbard] that introduced me to *Music from Big Pink*. Because the Band has been the big central thing of my music that I love the most." During his college years, Groce took advantage of his connections to make the cultural pilgrimage that so many of his generation were making: "I went to Europe twice. I travelled around America á la *Easy Rider*, except in a Volkswagen, not on a bike. In the Deep South, our car got spit on because we had long hair. But we went to Haight-Ashbury. We didn't go to Woodstock, but friends of mine did. I said, 'Ahhhh, that's too many people!'"

In 1969, Groce had the opportunity to make his first recordings in Nashville, resulting in the album *Peace and Joy and Power*. Created for the Christian Science Church, the album consisted of numerous hymns arranged in a contemporary style. "They had never done any hymns like this with the guitar and stuff. They ended up doing it in Nashville in a studio with a guy named Rick Powell that set it up. I think it was an eight-track studio, which was state-of-the-art then, and we used a Moog synthesizer with the sort [of patch cables] that you had to plug and unplug to get sounds. And you couldn't do polyphonic, you could only do single notes." Groce recalls "some big-time players" in the studio, including guitarist Harold Bradley and bassist Henry Strzelecki, both studio powerhouses who had already left their marks on thousands of pop, rock, and country recordings. Despite the depth of the talent pool on those sessions, though, Groce was not terribly pleased with their results. "I went in and sang with my guitar," he recalled, "and sometimes they'd put another guitar in and stuff like that. I wasn't satisfied really with the results, because the people that were producing it were church bureaucrats who knew nothing about music. These other guys [the session musicians] had their thing, but this was odd for them because they had never done these kinds of songs, these kinds of hymns. They were a little different. They weren't like gospel, you know, Carter Family or something like that. They're not Baptist hymns. They're more quiet. It didn't get fixed until the church asked former big band leader, Kay Kyser, to come in to do a remix. I hit it off with him because he could hear the same problems that I heard. I liked the final remix."

Groce had found a talented intermediary who could help him as he navigated the often-difficult waters of record production. "Kay had helped me prepare to make the recording. I went to his house, and he helped me rehearse in Chapel Hill [North Carolina]. He was a great character. He and I hit it off. He had a great phrase. They were playing this arrangement of one of the songs, and he said, 'No, we've got to turn down these instruments. We're putting a hundred-dollar saddle on a forty-dollar mule.' That's what I was thinking, but because I was a kid with no experience, I was afraid to speak up, I was thinking, 'I've listened to a lot of music, but I'm not a producer. Maybe I'm wrong.' I was trying to be humble, but it didn't feel right, and Kay agreed with me one hundred percent, which was wonderful, because he could say, 'No, get rid of this,' and they'd do it because it was Kay Kyser." The Christian Science leaders must have been pleased with his debut album, because they asked Groce to do a second project for them, *The Glad Sound: Songs about Jesus Christ from the* Christian Science Hymnal (released in 1973).

The Christian Science albums featured Groce as a recording artist, but it was his first two albums on Daybreak Records—*The Wheat Lies Low* and *Crescentville*—that brought Groce's songwriting to the record-buying public. "I got the deal because I know some guys from college whose uncles were in the music business in Los Angeles, and they introduced me to them. They'd been in show business. They were in 'Our Gang' comedy, *The Little Rascals*. They'd been in show business since zero. Their sister, who was my friends' mother who died while we were in college, she was a child movie star," Groce noted. The two albums were recorded at "a little bitty studio" on the corner of Santa Monica and Beverly Glen. Despite the opportunity that Daybreak presented, Groce didn't push for national success. "My career has never made any sense at all, how I went about it. It still doesn't make any sense really. But I don't think I was destined to be a pop star anyway. That's not what I am. I'm not that kind of writer, didn't have that motivation or that kind of talent. I wanted success, but I wasn't driven to be a star like people that I see."

Groce lived in New York from 1970 to 1971 and Los Angeles from 1971 to 1972, but it was a novel opportunity in Appalachia that led him to move to the Mountain State in 1972, a move that was permanent. A grant from the National Endowment for the Arts allowed him to be a musician-in-residence serving audiences in West Virginia for one year. A very limited experimental program, it never took off nationally, but it did pay dividends through Groce's decades-long commitment to the regional music scene. He received a call from Loonis McGloban, a musician known for writing the theme song for Charles Kuralt's *On the Road* television series and a long-time friend of Kay Kyser. "I think they asked him to get involved in trying to find somebody who might be good for this job," Groce noted, "and nobody knew who to look for. They weren't looking for a folklorist per se; they were looking for kind of a hybrid person who—I don't even know what their criteria were, but Loonis called me and said, 'Would you like to do a residency in West Virginia?'" After discussing the opportunity with his wife, they decided to visit the state during a cross-country drive from Connecticut back to Los Angeles. While there, he interviewed with Jim Andrews, the head of music for the West Virginia State Board of Education and consultant for the West Virginia Arts Council. It became even clearer that the program's administrators had very little idea as to who they were looking for—neither teacher nor academic nor folklorist. Groce was offered the position, and "we, meaning my wife and me, defined it."

Moving from Los Angeles to the rural Barbour County community of Galloway would be a shock for most people, but the twenty-five-year-old Groce took to his new environs immediately. After renting a cabin for a couple of years, he bought and fixed up a hundred-year-old farmhouse on nineteen acres. His NEA position also took him to many of the rural communities of Tucker, Barbour, and Randolph Counties. "I would make contacts in each school," he remembered. "Schools were the center. I would go to each school, but then I would also go to community organizations like the Helvetia community band. If they needed an instrument, I had a little budget to buy an instrument for them. And so I did a lot of different things. Some of them were trivial. Some of them were useful. And then I would meet with kids who were trying to write songs and work with them. I would go into classrooms, and that's when I first got to know kids and started writing songs with and for kids."[7]

After completing his first nine-month residency, Groce was asked to return for a second year, this time focusing exclusively on Randolph County and funded locally, not by the NEA. He agreed, staying in the residency for a total of two years. It was during his travels around Randolph County that he met the Currence Brothers, who played bluegrass music around their home community of Cassity.[8] Together, Groce and the Currences made one album, and toured around the state, the District of Columbia, and the West Coast. But despite their musical talents and their camaraderie with Groce, they couldn't maintain the arduous pace required of professional musicians because of serious health issues. "I met them in '72 or '73," Groce remembered, "and we did some touring. And then I realized that because they were all hemophiliacs, they just couldn't do it. We had some shows on the West Coast. We did some other shows. Then they started not being able to show up, but I understood. I enjoyed playing with them, and I had a good time with them. It was about three years that we did stuff together, and then they couldn't do it anymore because of their condition. Finally, the two brothers and their nephew got AIDS from blood transfusions that were not screened at that time, and eventually all three died."

At the end of the 1973–74 school year, Groce found himself at a crossroads. On the one hand, he might have tried to remain in the classroom working with eager students. On the other, Groce still harbored dreams of success in the national music industry. In 1974, he left to make another stab at the music business. He traveled to Los Angeles, where he found a manager. "He wasn't a manager at the time" in the conventional sense, but Groce recalls, "he knew certain things about the music business" and brought a degree of access to Groce's music that would have been difficult to obtain if he worked as an independent. "Having a manager in Malibu was useful. If I wanted to get a job singing at Alderson-Broaddus or Davis and Elkins or [West Virginia] Wesleyan, and say I'm a guy from Barbour County, it's like, 'who cares?' But if I say, 'Talk to my manager in Malibu,' [people responded with an] 'Oh!' It makes a difference." It was this decision that helped put Groce in a stronger position to capitalize on what would be his greatest hit, 1975's "Junkfood Junkie."

Groce had always demonstrated a knack for writing novelty songs, which he claims were a tool to help him entertain as a single performer with no great instrumental skills. "When you don't have a band," he theorized, "you'd better be a great guitar player like Leo Kottke or something so you have another element in your show. Or you must be Randy Newman, where you are the greatest songwriter there is, you know. Or you must have a voice like Joan Baez where somebody just wants to hear you sing. I didn't have any of those three. Now I'm a pretty good singer, but a fairly adequate guitar player. So what could I do to keep an audience interested? What I can do is write songs that were funny sometimes and drop them in. And the way I was funny was to be satirical. I never thought of those songs becoming hits, but they got big reactions from the crowd." His novelty songs took many forms: "I had one called 'Turn on Your TV.' I had one about bumper stickers on cars. I had several, and then I would also do just parodies of other songs that were funny just to get a laugh." But his most famous novelty song was about someone who publicly professed allegiance to an organic ideal but who secretly feasted on processed foods.

"Junk Food Junkie" came to him in 1974 as he was driving from West Virginia to play a gig in Boston. It was based on one of the first places he played when he moved to New York in 1970. "It was an organic coffee-house/food place. They had singing later in the evening, you know, and the room was, my goodness, a hundred at most, and they didn't pay you, but they passed the basket to people to contribute." The venue—known as Focus because the owners "were into photography"—featured Groce along with Peter Thom, Peter Farrara, and Melissa Manchester. "I got the inspiration because I was the hick, hillbilly, the cowboy, the whatever, and I wore cowboy boots back then. They thought you were stupid because of your accent, which was actually not a bad position to be in sometimes. So that's where I got the idea about that. In the daytime, you know, I'm 'Mr. Natural,' but then at night I reverted to the way I grew up in Texas—the frickin' Frito factory was there! Fritos and Cheetos and Dr. Pepper started there. That's the way I grew up eating. I wasn't going to get away from that totally. I was around the people who were all into this, you know, granola, organic, I mean, brown rice and all that stuff. You know, great, I can do that, too, if you want me to. But I'm not going to do it all the time. And so that's how that came about. I just had this funny thing and, of course, in my opinion, no satire is funny unless you're aiming at yourself. If you're saying, 'You people are stupid,' it's not funny. But if you're saying, 'Okay, I admit: this is me,' then it can be funny because everybody else goes, 'Yeah, it's me, too.'"

"Junk Food Junkie" might have remained a live-set novelty were it not for a covert concert recording made at McCabe's Guitar Shop in Los Angeles. His manager acquired the recording and hired musicians to add a bass and drums to it, as well as additional applause and a laugh track ("although it already had plenty on there," Groce remembers). Releasing it on their own label, they hired a record promoter to take the single to radio disc jockeys—the musical tastemakers—with the hope that they would add it to their stations' playlists. The disc jockeys, Groce remembered, embraced the song "because they could play off it, and they did. They'd make jokes about it and everything else. And so it had some weird success in isolated places." They song was perhaps most popular in Denver, where one disc jockey put it alongside current hits by Paul Simon and Michael Jackson in a sort of "Top-40 Death

Match." "This record," Groce observed, "beat 'Fifty Ways to Leave Your Lover,' in fact." Unfortunately, distribution issues—caused by the inevitable financial limitations of a small, independent label—limited the record's availability, and despite its popularity on radio, it couldn't go national or get real sales. As a consequence, Groce and his manager entered into an agreement with Mike Curb, who redistributed the record to a national audience, but not without some complications. "Finally, we made a deal with Mike Curb, but then, because of the deal—legal deals went slowly—he pulled it back off the market, and then he didn't re-release it for a few months. And I thought, 'You're killing it! It's got a start, and now it's not being released again, and this is horrible!' But when he did release it [in 1976], it started going up the charts again."

The wider distribution and promotion helped to draw national attention to Groce, and media exposure followed shortly thereafter. "It got me on a lot of shows and got me in *The New York Times* and *Christian Science Monitor*. If it had just been a song that went to number nine as a love song, no doubt I would've gotten some coverage, but not so much because it was not so odd [to see a love song on the charts]. 'Junk Food Junkie' was easy to talk about, easy for the host to joke about. Made them look good. Made them look funny. So I was on all those shows: *The Tonight Show*, *Merv Griffin Show*, *American Bandstand*, *The Midnight Special*. *Doctor Demento* song of the year. *Prairie Home Companion*." On *American Bandstand*, Groce recalled, host Dick Clark greeted him like any great comedic straight man would: "When I came in, Clark was sitting with a bucket of Colonel Sanders [Kentucky Fried Chicken]. He said, 'Want something to eat?'"

Groce's success with "Junk Food Junkie" led to one of the longest relationships of his recording career. Beginning with the 1976 single *Winnie the Pooh for President*, Groce recorded nine albums for Disney Records and more than two dozen book-records made by Disney from the celebrated Little Golden Books series. The relationship required that he draw not only upon his songwriting skills but also his familiarity with traditional American folk songs in a series of albums called *Disney's Children's Favorites, Volumes I-IV* that mixed a few of his originals with many folk and well known older songs. He recalls that children

sometimes recognized one of his original songs when he visited schools
to perform throughout the 1980s, shocking and surprising him. "It was
in West Virginia," he recalls. "I went to this school and sang a concert
for kids. I got to this one song called 'Carrot Stew' that I had written,
and they all sang along. I said, 'How do you know this song?' They
said, 'It's in our music book!' I didn't even know that Disney had given
permission to the Silver Burdette music book series to use it! It made
me feel good because I remember my books in elementary school. I
learned a lot of songs. I remember songs from those books, you know?"
Recording in Nashville with top session musicians, Groce's recordings
of classic folk songs and original material for children have been sta-
ples of childrearing for the past four decades and have introduced generations of children to the treasury of American folk songs. Along the
way, Groce received a Grammy nomination in the children's category
and earned a place in the hearts of many.

As a tireless advocate for great music-making and as a leader in
the state's entertainment business, Larry Groce has been at the center
of some of the most exciting and long-lasting musical organizations of
the past half-century. A talented songwriter whose wit and willingness
to embrace satire often masks a deep earnestness and conviction of
ideals, Groce's most important roles have been those that create places
for people to be creative, whether a classroom in Tucker County or an
internationally syndicated radio program. As such, Groce has helped
to show the people of the Mountain State the wonderful opportunities and cultural resources that are in their own backyards, while also
exposing the many people who come here to work with him the unique
character of his adopted home.

SELECTED DISCOGRAPHY[9]

Peace and Joy and Power, The Christian Science Publishing Society
    408 (1970).
The Wheat Lies Low, Daybreak Records DR 2000 (1971).
Crescentville, Daybreak Records DR 2010 (1972).

The Glad Sound: Songs about Jesus Christ from The Christian Science
   Hymnal, The Christian Science Publishing Society DRP 7340
   (1973).

Larry Groce & The Currence Brothers (with the Currence Brothers),
   Peaceable Records 2 (1975).

Junkfood Junkie, Warner Bros. Records BS 2933 (1976).

Please Take Me Back, MC Records MC6-515S1 (1977).

Disney Children's Favorites, Volume I (with the Disneyland Children's
   Sing-Along Chorus), Disneyland 1V 8120 (1979).

Green Pastures Are Before Me, Peaceable Records 12 (1979).

Medicine Man, Broadbeach Records 7 (1983).

Live Forever, Quarrier Records (2016).

JULIE ADAMS[10]

Regular listeners to *Mountain Stage*, the internationally syndicated live music program recorded (most frequently) in Charleston, are quite familiar with the voice of Julie Adams, the house band's backing vocalist and a regularly featured artist. Most commonly, Adams is heard performing the songs of other people, whether the guest artists who call on her services to support their performances on the show or drawing from the great American popular songbook in her featured slot. "I get to sing a song on every *Mountain Stage* show, so I'm always on the lookout for a great song to sing, usually in the folk, blues, and folk-pop genres. I work hard to find those songs that have great lyrics—that I feel I can sing and own," she reflected, "because I have a hard time singing songs that I don't feel. Even when I'm only performing it once, I still kind of have to feel like I can really be in it. The band works up a tune a few days before the Sunday performance, so we don't have much time to get it together. Each song has to be simple enough that we can master it quickly, but not so simple that it's boring."[11] Although she is normally heard singing the songs of other writers, Adams has been contributing a stylistically diverse catalog of original songs, many of which are celebrated by music fans in the Charleston area, for the past three decades.

Raised just across the West Virginia state line in Cumberland and LaVale, Maryland, Adams's eclecticism can be traced to the vibrant musical life of her family. Her father, a Presbyterian minister and

. . . .

Figure 3. Julie Adams
(photo by Colleen Anderson, courtesy of Julie Adams).

. . . .

English professor at Frostburg State College (now University), was "a classical music nut" who dreamed of singing at New York's famous Metropolitan Opera, and her mother was a church organist. Her father proved to be a particularly strong musical influence on Adams, introducing the folk singer-songwriters of the 1960s to the family and encouraging her to explore many different musical outlets. "My dad was an English professor," she recalled, "so he loved a good lyric. So we had Bob Dylan, Peter, Paul, and Mary, and Judy Collins. We had some common ground that everybody could enjoy. I think at one point we decided that the only one we all like is Leonard Cohen, which is kind of a weird lowest common denominator, or *highest* common denominator, maybe. But, that being said, the reason that church music was an influence was also that my dad was standing there saying, 'Well, don't you want to sing in the choir?' or 'Don't you want to take violin lessons?' Well, okay! 'Would you want to take piano lessons?' I guess I do."

In high school, Adams began to learn the guitar, studying with a jazz guitarist in Cumberland and poring over a chord book. Studying the songs of Cat Stevens and others in her free time, she began to develop a sense of how songs are constructed. "You would just play the song a hundred thousand times and listen to it and try to figure out what the chords were, which was a great way of learning. And it's punishing," she noted. With that acquired knowledge and an increasing interest in performing, Adams found encouragement from her father, who suggested that she begin writing her own music. As she recalled sentimentally, "I probably didn't even know that you could do that until he was sort of suggesting, 'Well, you could write something.'"

Although she describes her early efforts as "some bad things," Adams found more and more confidence to play her creations in public. "There were lots of people playing music in Cumberland," she remembered of the 1970s. "The first place I ever played live—if you don't count church—was a little coffeehouse that was like a little leftover from the 60s. I thought it was cool because my older brother and his friends played there. 'Noah's Coffeehouse' was in the basement of the Episcopal Church. You could play a half an hour or three songs, so you had the chance to play a short set. You didn't have to have a whole night's worth of songs, and that was really important to people learning how to play. But there were also different groupings—duos and trios, singles and bands. There were all kinds of people playing."

After high school, Adams continued playing in the area as she tried several colleges before landing in Morgantown. "I ended up at West Virginia University, which was an hour from my hometown," she recalled. "That's where my friends were going. And I thought, 'These other things aren't working for me. Maybe this will work for me. And it did." While in Morgantown, she took advantage of the thriving live music scene that centered around the constant influx of young people to the university, appearing most notably with two groups: The Paradise Rangers and the Catfish Bullet Band. Adams recalled that, in the early 1980s, the Morgantown scene was not very focused on original songwriting, although some spaces certainly supported emergent voices: "There was a lot of live music. Every Wednesday, the Paradise Rangers played at the latest hotspot. Every Thursday, the local reggae band played there. Every weekend, there were local bands and out-of-towners in nine or ten venues. Of course, it was a college town, so there was no shortage of people to go out and support all those groups."[12]

In the Catfish Bullet Band, Adams became friends with a talented violinist named Deni Bonet, with whom she moved to the state capital in 1982. Performing as the Fabulous Twister Sisters, Adams and Bonet developed a set composed of cover arrangements and a few original songs. "We played some original songs," Adams recollected, "but we were fairly casual about it. We definitely didn't overthink it. But it was fun to see what we could come up with. We'd mess around with a song until we thought it would pass muster in a live performance."[13]

Shortly after their move to Charleston, Adams and Bonet joined forces with the Putnam County Pickers, who were living on a rural farmstead west of Charleston. Comprising guitarist Ron Sowell, bassist Steve Hill, and drummer Ammed Solomon—the future core of the *Mountain Stage* band—the Pickers had been playing together for nearly a decade. The new configuration—rebranded without Hill as Stark Raven—channeled the sounds of the New Wave movement that was sweeping top-forty radio in the early 1980s. One of the group's great strengths, Adams recounts, was the meticulous nature of their arrangements. The Putnam County Pickers, she remembered, "really constructed their music. Up to that point, Deni and I just played songs. You know, 'Well, let's have a solo there.' I mean, we would have an arrangement, but it was not constructed. It was, you know, 'That'll do.' But with Stark Raven, we had an intro, we had harmonies, we had answering harmonies and woven parts and then the violin and the cello played a duet and then solo parts. We were writing and also trying to identify the strong points of each individual performer in the group." The musical strengths of each band member were always a consideration, whether in constructing a powerful arrangement of Procol Harum's "A Whiter Shade of Pale" that features a trio arrangement of Pachelbel's famous canon as an instrumental introduction, or in an original composition such as "Inertia," which alternates full-band textures during the verses and vocal harmonies and strings alone during the choruses. As Adams observed, "When you write music like that for a group like that, it just comes out differently than it would otherwise, which is cool, but it definitely taught me that aspect of songwriting where you would, for example, construct a drum fill to take you from the chorus to the bridge."

Hitting the road in a repurposed bread truck that had been transformed into a band bus and equipment truck, Stark Raven toured extensively throughout the region for nearly a decade. Adams recalls these travels as a highlight of the 1980s. "We were pretty sure we were going to be the next big thing," she recalled. "We played all over the eastern United States, and we worked pretty hard at it. Yeah, we travelled. I mean, it was our full-time job, and we travelled all the time. We played arts council concerts, colleges, countless bars, and public school shows at 9 AM. Every year, we did a southern tour that took us to Atlanta, Charlotte, and Savannah. We worked hard to break into some music scenes in bigger cities. And we always tried to put on the best show we could. Even though we were playing, say, at some bar, we'd set up all the lights and dress up and give it all the energy we had and be as professional as we could be, as though were we playing at Carnegie Hall in New York City."[14] Like many road bands, Stark Raven often fought with imperfect equipment and far-from-ideal accommodations. Adams noted that the band "had totally piecemeal equipment. This was the '80s. Things were not as tidy as they are now. It was big giant equipment, and we packed it all in a big giant bread truck. And it was so dangerous. I mean, it was just packed completely to the top. And then we would sit on the speakers. We sewed cushion to go on the speakers. And then every now and then, we'd look back behind us and go, 'You know, really, don't stop fast, because we're all dead if you stop fast.'" Playing a homemade magnetic Scrabble game in the back of the truck and listening to an AM radio, Adams and her Stark Raven bandmates made every effort to make inroads in the industry, but they were not met with major label interest after two self-produced albums. After a decade together, Stark Raven threw in the towel; Adams laughs, "We did that classic thing: we made a CD and then broke up."

Although Stark Raven disbanded in 1992, its members continued to make music together on *Mountain Stage*, which they had been doing more or less from the outset of the program. Yet, in stark contrast to Stark Raven's carefully orchestrated compositions, *Mountain Stage* required quick and dirty arrangements—what Adams describes as the "Handi-Wipe" or one-time use method. Furthermore, the *Mountain Stage* band gig allowed her to work with and learn from some of the greatest songwriters in the world. When asked whether the experience of learning a new song every week has influenced her own songwriting, Adams remarked, "Yes, it has. Trying to find a song to put on any particular show, you want it to have some sort of relationship to the other songs or the other musicians that are on the show. After you do that about a hundred times, you start really feeling where people's influences are in their music. This is one of the things I really love about the show. I've learned that all contemporary music has roots in older music, be it blues, Tin Pan Alley, old-time, trippy '60s, bluegrass, etc. Musicians love to mix styles together and create something new. But they always owe a debt to the music they borrowed from. And if you look closely, you can even find some common roots between things as seemingly different as '40s big band music and trippy '60s music."[15] Additionally, Adams learned that "there's a lot of good songs out there, but there's only a few *great* songs," a realization that has encouraged her to cultivate her "editor" personality, which she argues helps her cull the bad from the good in her own writing. The prominent role of this internal editor in Adams's creative process has resulted in a relatively limited recorded output, including two live albums with the *Mountain Stage* band, two compact discs (*Struck by Moonlight* and *I Don't Mind Walking*) with Steve Hill and Ammed Solomon, *Christmas Angel* (with Hill), and a 2007 collaboration with West Virginia storyteller and actress Karen Vuranch and Colleen Anderson called *Potluck*.

One of Adams's favorite songs is "Stella Could Bake." Couched in a light calypso groove, Adams captures the culinary wisdom of an elderly mother before offering a meditation on the spiritual values that emerge from shared meals. "I don't know why other people like that one," she reflected. "I know why *I* like it. It's written about a specific person, but it's one of those examples of the specific turning out to be the most universal. It was written about the mother of the *Mountain Stage* piano player, Bob Thompson. His mom used to come to the show all the time. She died when she was eighty-nine, and every now and then, she would make us cakes and cookies and brownies and all these things and bring them to the show. She was a sweet, very strong lady. When she died, at her funeral, Bob's son gave this eulogy that was so beautiful. We were sitting there listening, and, at some point, I thought, 'I should be writing this down.' And he was using food as this sort of analogy for all the good things that grandma does, right? And so that's what that song is about."[16] The song generated the *Potluck* album with Anderson and Vuranch, both of whom contribute moving meditations on food, love, and spirituality.

Another favorite is "Copper Hill," which she wrote for Karen Vuranch's award-winning play *Coal Camp Memories*. Eschewing the stereotypical sounds of bluegrass and old-time music that many songwriters might turn to in such a setting, Adams offers a medium-tempo rocker that draws on West Virginian imagery to explore the coal camp environment. "*Coal Camp Memories* is about growing up in a coal camp from the 1910s through the '60s. And it paints a picture of what life was like in a coal camp and of early coal mining. Karen likes to have a live musician play music at the beginning and in-between scenes as she changes her appearance to become older. So I wrote that song to go in her play. It's my 'West Virginia song.'"

Julie Adams is constantly surprised that people enjoy her songs, and she is quick to deflect praise and compliments. Living in a town that, as she sees it, prioritizes community over competition, Adams seems to prefer celebrating the talents of her peers and mentors to collecting accolades for herself. "Here, everyone is so polite," she observed, "so they respond to almost everything, and I am never sure which ones they really like." Yet, despite her genuine modesty, Adams is a force to be reckoned with in the Charleston music scene. A prolific writer who lets only a small portion of her output reach the public, each composition is a special treat, providing insights into the vicissitudes of love, loss, and healing in a generally upbeat pop-Americana style. Sung with great skill and passion, Adams's songs stand strong alongside the many great songs by other writers that she has performed on *Mountain Stage*.

SELECTED DISCOGRAPHY

WITH STARK RAVEN:
> *One Hundred Million Reasons*, Vitag SR0001 (1985).
> *Learning to Fly*, Wooly Mammoth SR0002 (1988).

AS A SOLO ARTIST:
> *Julie Adams and the Mountain Stage Band Live*, Gadfly Records (1997).
> *I Don't Mind Walking*, Gadfly Records (1999).
> *Julie Adams and the Mountain Stage Band, Volume 2*, Gadfly Records (2001).
> *Potluck* (with Colleen Anderson and Karen Vuranch), Delectable Records (2007).

JOHN LILLY

―――――

"We always joke that John has another five songs between here and the corner," *Mountain Stage* featured vocalist Julie Adams remarked. John Lilly, who edited *Goldenseal*, the West Virginia Division of Culture and History's folk culture magazine from 1997 until his retirement in 2015, has channeled his passion for the traditional country music of Hank Williams, Jimmie Rodgers, and Bill Monroe into a prolific output of songs that sound like they came right out of the early 1950s. With six solo albums, one album of old-time dance music, and one album by Blue Yonder—a trio he formed with guitarist Robert Shafer and bassist Will Carter in 2014—to his name, Lilly is one of the most-recorded contemporary West Virginia songwriters, commonly investing thousands of dollars of his own money into their production. At the time of this writing, Lilly has embarked on his most ambitious project yet: an expansive collection of songs exploring the unique characteristics of a dozen of the nation's fifty states.[17]

A native of Arlington Heights, Illinois, a northwest suburb of Chicago, Lilly was one of one of eight children, living in a "very crazy, hectic home scene. My mother at one time had six children under ten years old at the house. And it was a three-bedroom house." Music was at the center of the family's entertainment, spurred on by his father, who sang with a barbershop quartet and played piano and harmonica. "I seriously didn't know the radio worked in the car until I was

· · · ·

Figure 4. John Lilly
(photo by John Sellards, courtesy of John Lilly).

· · · ·

sixteen years old," he recalled. "Because every time we'd go anywhere, my dad would be singing, and we would all sing along with him. Just a repertoire of songs that he grew up with in the '20s, '30s, and '40s." As a youngster with a limited repertoire, Lilly learned that he could entertain the carload of family by improvising songs: "I didn't know any songs, so I would just make up songs. 'Thanks for taking us, mom and dad. / Thanks for taking us, folks.' That was my early hit. Family loved that one. I'd sing that one for miles." After learning to play "about two chords" on a guitar that he borrowed from his older brother, he devoted increased attention to songwriting, reckoning that "it would be easier to write songs than to learn them." Forming a group with two classmates named Bill, Lilly began to hit the circuit of coffeehouses, folk festivals, and open mics that popped up throughout the Chicago suburbs in the late 1960s and early 1970s.

Upon graduation from high school in 1972, Lilly set out, like so many other recent suburban graduates, to seek a college degree at the University of Illinois in Urbana-Champaign. Enrolling as a business administration major, Lilly quickly became frustrated by his course of study, which was training students for corporate life but providing little opportunity to learn important skills for someone wishing to build a small business. But for everything that Urbana-Champaign couldn't offer academically, it offered in musical opportunity. "I spent all my time hanging out in bars listening to music, and I got a great education at the University of Illinois. Champaign, Illinois, is on a road not directly, but more or less between St. Louis and Chicago. More or less between Des Moines and Indianapolis. So on a Tuesday or a Wednesday night, you could almost get anybody traveling through. I saw Jimmy Buffett for fifty cents. Saw Charlie Mingus for, I'm sure, less than two dollars. George Benson for, I'm sure, less than five dollars. Asleep at the Wheel, New Grass Revival. Great names in jazz and country. And that was really, as it turns out in the long run, my education. I got involved with the campus radio station, and I was a DJ. I got exposed to lots of music, great musicians."

After two years as a business administration major, he discussed his academic dissatisfaction with his parents: "I said, 'Look, I'm just not getting it.' So they said, 'Well, just take some classes that you want that you would enjoy." So I signed up for home economics so I could learn to cook. I signed up for Shakespeare so I could study some Shakespeare. I signed up for bowling, geography. These things that I thought would be interesting." Unfortunately, over-enrollment issues at the university forced him out of most of these courses, eventually leaving him with a three-credit-hour schedule. At that point, he decided to leave school, traveling with a friend of his to San Diego and eventually landing in the Phoenix area, where he enrolled at Arizona State University for one year, initially as a broadcast major and later, as a consequence of the same over-enrollment issues he encountered at the University of Illinois, as a sculpture major.

Returning to Illinois in 1974, Lilly became increasingly immersed in the old-time music revival that had emerged from the 1960s folk music boom. At the Indiana Fiddler's Gathering in Battleground, Indiana, John was turned on to the rich traditions of old-time fiddle music and, in a strange turn of luck, even made his debut as an old-time musician. "I was playing music with a guitar player, later a really good fiddler, named Tim Wilson," he recounted. "Tim was living in Champaign, and the two of us hitchhiked from Champaign to Battleground, Indiana for this music festival, which I kept calling a bluegrass festival, and he kept correcting me and saying, 'No, it's a fiddlers' convention.' Well, whatever. We show up there about four or five in the afternoon, and we're walking up the pathway to where this fiddlers' convention was. It was at this park, and Tim recognized this fiddler. They greeted one another and immediately put their instrument cases down and got their instruments out. The fiddler had a banjo player with him, and then Tim had his guitar, and I had my mandolin, and I was able to just follow the chords that he was playing, strumming rhythm mandolin. About fifteen minutes into this, my first fiddlers' convention, up comes a guy with a clipboard, who addresses the fiddlers and says, 'Mark, what's the name of your band?' And he says, 'Mike Mumbler and the Stink Creek Stump Jumpers.' He says, 'Okay, you're onstage in fifteen minutes.' So an hour after being at my first fiddlers' convention, I was on the stage, performing in a band. To make it even more remarkable, they recorded it and put it on a record album. So the very next year, out comes a record album with my first exposure to old-time music preserved on vinyl!"

Through the mid-1970s, Lilly became increasingly interested in the history of country music, tracing the sounds of his favorite contemporary musicians through the work of the artists who influenced them. "I was hearing harmonies that I recognized from Emmylou Harris, but here's the Louvin Brothers, and that's where they [she] got it. And from the Louvin Brothers, here's the Blue Sky Boys. That's where they got it. From the Blue Sky Boys to shape note singing. That's where they got it. So I kept getting the thread and following it back as far as I could in various styles." Visits with octogenarian fiddlers and banjo players—including Tommy Jarrell and Fred Cockerham, whom he met at fiddle contests in Mt. Airy, North Carolina, and Galax, Virginia—stirred an interest in dance music, so in 1984, he joined the Green Grass Cloggers, a group founded in Greenville, North Carolina, and with a second group (called "the Road Team") based out of Asheville.[18] "All of the men in the group doubled as musicians," he recalled, "so we would dance and then we would get our instruments out and play. We'd join the support musicians who were playing music for dancing. Sometimes we would do a yodel or a Hank Snow song or something like that, and the other guys had some numbers they would do. It was a real variety. I mean, you can't just dance for two hours." During his four years as a member of the Green Grass Cloggers, Lilly toured across the United States and South America, sharing his passion for old-time fiddle music and dance.

The Asheville cohort was led by fiddler Ralph Blizard, with whom Lilly played extensively after leaving the Green Grass Cloggers in 1988. In 1991, Lilly recorded an album with Blizard titled *Blue Highway: Old-Time Songs & Longbow Fiddle*, which featured such well-worn old-time tunes as "Leather Britches" and "Hell Among the Yearlings," as well as songs made popular by Jimmie Rodgers ("Peach Picking Time Down in Georgia"), the Carter Family ("My Dixie Darling"), and Bob Wills ("Trouble in Mind"). "That was some of the most enjoyable music I ever played," Lilly opined. "Ralph personified what I aspired to be musically. He was rooted in tradition, but he was a creative individual who not only played music from his cultural past, but also used that musical knowledge to create new music. He liked to write songs. He liked to improvise, make up tunes. And it was very stimulating to play music with him because he was always like, 'That's a nice little melody. Let's play with that.' Or he'd see something or hear something and say, 'There's an idea for a song, John. Why don't you write a song about that?' And we wrote some songs together. Mostly, he just inspired me to not be limited by being a traditional musician. I realized that Jimmie Rodgers, Hank Williams, Bill Monroe, all these people were tradition-bearers in a way and creative vanguards in another way."

Lilly left the Green Grass Cloggers in 1988 to pursue a music career in Nashville, using some connections at the Country Music Hall of Fame to land a position as a tour guide and independent researcher. "Looking back on it," he reflected, "I was not as focused as I needed to be. In order to succeed in Nashville, you really need to have a plan. I just wanted a career. I just wanted to work. And although I thought I was leaving my options open, in fact, I was letting a lot of stuff get by me because I wasn't as focused as I should have been." For three years, Lilly performed his songs at songwriter rounds in Nashville, attempted to work with co-writers (a Nashville staple), auditioned at Opryland, and tried to make a mark as a yodeler, a skill that he had developed during his time with the Green Grass Cloggers: "In Nashville, I discovered too late that there was a glass ceiling for yodelers. It was a retro thing. It was rooted in the past. It was not what 'today's hot country' was all about. Plus, honestly, they already had Doug Green of Riders in the Sky, so they had guys that could yodel circles around me." In 1991, he left Nashville to rejoin Blizard, with whom he played for two years, in North Carolina.

In November 1992—on Election Day, to be precise—Lilly moved to Elkins, West Virginia, beginning a nearly quarter-century residence in the Mountain State. Hired as a publicist for Davis & Elkins College's Augusta Heritage Center, his new position came with one stipulation: he was required to work on his undergraduate degree. "Though I'd been to college for three and a half years, I still had a long way to go because I'd changed my major so many times. So I worked full time, and I went to school full time. It was a very stressful time, and I actually set the music aside for those few years. I also married, and we started our family. It was a very busy time for me, but there was no music, and it was not very satisfying for me." Realizing that he couldn't put his music aside to care for his family, it was his two-year-old son who inspired him to return to songwriting. "We were just taking the trash out, and he looked up at the sky and saw this first little sliver of a new moon up in the western sky, and he goes, 'Look, Daddy! A broken moon!' And I thought, 'What a choice of words.' So I went inside and wrote this song called 'Broken Moon.'" The title track of his 2000 solo debut, the song—which evokes the honky-tonk sounds of early Webb Pierce and Faron Young—was a finalist at the prestigious Chris Austin Songwriting Contest at Merlefest in 2002 and was critically acclaimed throughout the United States and Europe.

Lilly's albums—which, he notes, collect only a small fraction of his songwriting output—reveal a songwriter who, like his mentor Blizard, deftly blends the sounds of mid-twentieth-century country music with contemporary themes. In the hands of a less creative musician, such an approach could easily result in poorly executed parody or overweening sincerity. But Lilly's songs tend to steer clear of simplistic gags and overly precious settings. Consider, for example, "She Talks to Me (GPS Song)." Appearing on 2015's *Thinking About the Weather*, the song meditates on the nature of our contemporary relationship with technology as the speaker—a characteristically lonely country music rambler— describes his GPS navigation system as the perfect partner. Even when they disagree over the best route to their destination or when she talks incessantly, the speaker doesn't mind and is quick to forgive the source of the "voice so sweet and low." Like Joaquin Phoenix's Theodore in the 2013 Spike Jonze film *Her*, he finds himself falling in love with an artificial intelligence: "She feels so real every time she speaks, / though I know she's just some fantasy." Set to a plodding guitar accompaniment, the melody of the chorus begs for a high harmony vocal evocative of the Everly Brothers, Emmylou Harris, or, more recently, the Milk Carton Kids. This sensitive musical setting transforms what could easily be the subject of a rather silly novelty song into a thoughtful reimagination of a familiar country music trope.

Lilly left Davis & Elkins College in 1997 to become the editor of the august West Virginia history quarterly *Goldenseal*, where he continued the efforts of previous editors Tom Screven and Ken Sullivan to provide a regular spotlight on, among other topics, the state's rich musical traditions. "When I came to work there," Lilly recalled, "one of the first things I did was to put together articles for the twenty-fifth anniversary of *Goldenseal* in 1999 and put together this book called *Mountains of Music*, which was a collection of stories from the magazine about West Virginia traditional music. And there was so much to choose from. It was a pleasure and a challenge to whittle it down to what would fit in one book. I just think that traditional music is an important part of West Virginia culture. It's one thing that people identify with the state, rightfully so. So many great musicians have come from this state."[19]

Lilly's involvement at *Goldenseal* has exposed him to many interesting stories about the state's past and present, some of which have found their way into his songs. "Cinder Bottom Blues," recorded by his band Blue Yonder for their 2013 debut album *Bittersweet Road*, recounts life in one of the most notorious red-light districts of the state's southern coalfields, the Cinder Bottom neighborhood of Keystone, McDowell County. Couched in a minor-mode Django Reinhardt-inspired jazz feel, Lilly depicts a character who has lost his way amid gamblers, prostitutes, and bootleggers, as well as the coal barons and other hucksters who led the pseudonymous evangelist "Virginia Lad" to describe Keystone as the "Sodom and Gomorrah of Today."[20]

Lilly's recordings feature a wide range of talented supporting musicians, both from the Mountain State and beyond, and he has garnered the respect of musicians and songwriters all across the United States. *Broken Moon*, for instance, features singer Ginny Hawker and fiddler Buddy Griffin, while 2011's *Cold Comfort*, which is steeped in the sounds of a Texas honky tonk, showcases guitarist Bill Kirchen (best known for his work with Commander Cody and His Lost Planet Airmen), pianist Floyd Domino, and numerous other Texas music luminaries. Many of these musicians also participate in his annual Hank Williams tribute concert, which he has hosted since 2002. "He died in West Virginia, New Year's Day, 1953. So as we were approaching New Year's Day 2003, the fiftieth anniversary kind of gave rise to this Hank Williams tribute. A friend of mine named Rob McNurlin from Kentucky and I decided to put this thing together. Just me and Rob and Buddy Griffin the first year. And it grew and grew and grew. It's a five-piece, six-piece band. We've got Kayton Roberts, Steel Guitar Hall of Fame steel guitar player, and Buddy Griffin, Rob, me, Roger Carrol, who played with Hank Snow for twenty years, Ritchie Collins from Ashland, Kentucky. And the audiences come by the busload. We draw about four hundred people."

John Lilly's musical journeys have taken him deep into the rich traditions of American vernacular music, and his work as a scholar, writer, and editor has granted him a particularly keen vision of the special stories that shape the lives of people all around the country. Although he is neither a West Virginia songwriter by dint of his birth or the primary subject material of his compositions, he has developed a storytelling approach that speaks to the lives of the people of the state and beyond, and his high tenor voice—evocative of Hank Williams himself—resonates with the older forms of country music that remain popular throughout the region. Immersed fully in the deep river of twentieth-century vernacular song, Lilly gives us a glimpse of what the honky-tonk greats of the 1950s might sound like if they were writing about our modern lives.

———

SELECTED DISCOGRAPHY

As a solo artist:
Broken Moon, JaveLina JL-2000 (2000).
Last Chance to Dance, JaveLina JL-2003 (2003).
Haunted Honky Tonk, JaveLina JL-2007 (2007).
Cold Comfort, JaveLina JL-2011 (2011).
Thinking about the Weather, JaveLina JR-4585 (2015).

With Blue Yonder:
Bittersweet Road, self-published (2013).

Figure 5. Dina Hornbaker
(photo by Sam Owens, courtesy of Dina Hornbaker).

DINA HORNBAKER

———

Armed with a guitar, banjo (which she plays in the clawhammer style), a tambourine, and a passel of harmonicas in a variety of keys, twenty-seven-year-old Dina Hornbaker writes songs that embrace the contradictions of life in twenty-first-century West Virginia, a state whose residents celebrate centuries of traditions rooted in the natural environment yet lie in a wholly modern society. But Hornbaker's roots in the Mountain State can only be traced back a couple of decades, when her father took a teaching position in the music department of the University of Charleston. Born in Oklahoma City and spending some of her formative years in Croatia, Hornbaker remarked that, "since my roots are kind of all over the place, it was hard to find a place that I call 'home.' I have dual citizenship from Croatia and the States. And my dad's side of the family, my great-grandparents, were like wheat and corn farmers in the Midwest. And my [maternal] grandfather was a really big soccer player and economist." This rootlessness forced Hornbaker to find home through experimentation and experience, leading her to a life dominated by her two principal interests: organic agriculture and music. "When I was kind of learning my place in the world and connecting to the passions that I developed over time, then I really began to understand who I am better by doing the things that I love more."

Music had been an important part of Hornbaker's life from a very young age. "Music was part of my life before I was ever born, because my father started playing piano and learning classical piano at age six in Tempe, Arizona. And throughout his entire childhood, he took piano lessons and just had this passion, and he knew that music was his destiny at a very young age." After undergraduate studies and a master's degree in music, her father received a Fulbright fellowship to study the music of the Croatian composer Livadic, during which time he met Dina's mother, a native of the former Yugoslavian republic. Hornbaker and her sister, she recalls, "would sing at shows with him and little gigs and performances and at weddings and things like that. So it wasn't like child labor, you know, like, 'You have to do this!' It was something that we really enjoyed doing at a young age. And yeah, it kind of blossomed from there, I guess."

Voice lessons—taught by her father—were *de rigeur* through high school, and violin, trumpet, and percussion in public school bands and orchestras allowed her to find the best outlets for her musical creativity. Percussion instruments, especially, captured her attention: "When I was doing marching band in middle school, I played snare, lead snare, and so I would make weird [percussion] instruments. I was really fascinated by the different sounds, too, and tones." Such fascination continues well into the present-day, as Hornbaker can be found using her right foot to tap on a tambourine, keeping time with her lively strumming on the guitar and banjo.

In addition to playing and singing, the Hornbaker house was a listening house, drawing eclectic sounds from rock, pop, and classical music together into a lively backdrop. The radio, she remembers, "was always on NPR [National Public Radio], and Bach and Mozart were constantly playing, you know. And, as a child, you want to hear all kinds of music. My parents definitely listen to the Beatles, the Rolling Stones, things like that. And I really connected to that automatically at a young age."

Finding a laid-aside guitar in the house, she began to explore the instrument's potential in her mid-teens. Before long, she decided that she needed lessons to develop her technique, and she found a teacher at a nearby music store. "It was called Cheap Beats, and they renovated old drum sets and guitars and sold them to community members. So I got music lessons from this man, Ed Fields. He moved away eventually. But I took [lessons] for like two or three years. He really influenced me on classic rock music." Fields provided access to his library of classic rock recordings. "I would just sit there in my room and light incense and listen to it. It was really, like, a spiritual awakening for me, I think. I was about fifteen." Particularly powerful was her discovery of strong female voices, especially that of Janis Joplin.

Although she had received extensive classical training both at home and in school, Dina realized that classical training has its limits for a creative musician like herself. Rigid adherence to notating music was stifling, and Hornbaker found it challenging to connect musically with her peers as a result. "I didn't really play with people because I didn't really know friends in my high school [George Washington High School in Charleston] that played that kind of music [classic rock]. They were mostly classically trained, and that was kind of what I wanted to get away from and try something else."

Upon graduating from George Washington High School in 2007, Hornbaker enrolled at Shepherd University in the state's Eastern Panhandle, where she studied for a year before transferring to West Virginia University. Although her time there was brief, Shepherdstown added further fuel to her creative fire. "I would play on the streets. People are so artsy and open there. Everyone there is an artist at heart, you know. And so you play, and people will just walk by and start talking to you, kind of like an open conversation." Yet, despite her life-long involvement in music and her frequent appearances before a live audience, she didn't view herself as much of a musician. "Music was always in the back of my mind," she reflected, "but I never saw myself as a great musician because I would just pick and play. And, you know, I sang what came out. I wasn't even conscious of the words that came out of me sometimes. It just kind of came out."

In Morgantown, a city with a constant influx of young people who are eager to explore their personal potential and to find their intellectual and personal passions, Hornbaker discovered a deep interest in sustainability and environmental conservation, a student movement that often finds students with a guitar or banjo in hand. Through her involvement with several environmental student organizations on campus, including the Sierra Club Coalition, she met a number of young musicians and, with friends, began to play a mix of covers and originals at parties. Eventually, she began to gain courage as a performer, and she sought opportunities to perform at open mics at the legendary South Park bar Gene's and the Blue Moose Café on the corner of Spruce and Walnut Streets. Conversations with Gene's proprietors Lucy and Al Bonner led to her first solo show. Despite being a virtual unknown, Hornbaker remembers that she "really had a lot of support and great feedback. Gene's is a really small space, so it's not like you can't hear anything [people are saying about you], you know? I think when they saw this young person get onstage with a guitar, they were just like, 'I think we're just going to sit down and listen.'" The Gene's gig demonstrated to her that she was capable of maintaining the energy and attention of an audience, leading her to pursue still more opportunities to share her art: "I felt really proud of myself after that, that I was able to perform just with a guitar by myself on stage." She also met Cody Caswell, a horticulture student who sang and played mandolin; together, they also played at the homes of friends in town and performed at one open mic.

A multidisciplinary studies major focusing on geography, Spanish, and communications, Hornbaker also found time to get involved with the university's organic farm, volunteering for a summer before eventually landing an internship there where she "helped them grow all the vegetables on a one-acre plot. And there was a field day for a hundred and fifty people, so we cooked all the food that we grew, and then we served it to them." Dina also became a co-director of Fairtrade 2.0, a student-run entrepreneurial project that sources fair-trade coffee for university venues. Through that work, she "had the opportunity to go to Nicaragua and see how this coffee is made and grown and harvested and processed. And it was really difficult to see that, because this organization revolves around fair trade, direct trade—really, it's like an environmentally friendly product, yet it's the third largest commodity in the world after oil. And it's like, where is this coffee that I'm drinking from right now, you know?" During the two-week visit, Hornbaker was told of a permaculture farm on Ometope [Island]—"this island where there are two twin-peaked volcanoes," she noted—and she found herself drawn to a community that was focused on environmentally, economically, and culturally sustainable agriculture. Intending to stay there for two weeks, Hornbaker stayed for two months, discovering new talents and a newfound openness to her musical creativity. "I learned a lot about agriculture, and I opened myself up more with my music. This girl, Megan, she played the fiddle, and she played a lot of music in Asheville, North Carolina, so meeting her made me kind of loosen up, I guess."

Hornbaker returned to WVU to complete her bachelor's degree in 2012. But it wasn't long before she moved to Portugal to obtain her Permaculture Design Certification (PDC) with Pedro Valdjiu on his farm, Terra Alta. She lived in a tent for four months. "I read a little bit about it before I went there, but I didn't really know too much about him," the adventurous Hornbaker recalled. "And I lived with his family, and there was also some other people living there. I found out that he [Pedro] was a famous musician in Portugal. He is in a band called Blasted Mechanism, and it is this really eclectic, like different, music." Preparing to host forty students for an intensive two-week permaculture course, Valdjiu took Dina to run an errand in a rural mountainous area. While on the drive, he asked her to state her intentions in coming to Portugal. "I remember getting in his van, and we are on the top of this mountain in a really rural, secluded area. And he just put on the brake, and he looked at me, and he was like, 'Why are you here?' And I was like, 'Ahhhh...' I felt really strange and awkward, you know. I was like, 'Why is he asking this question right now?' And I was like, 'To take the Permaculture Design Certification, you know?' He said, 'No, you're here because of music.' And that's when my heart sank and dropped. I took a big gulp. I thought, 'Maybe he's right. Maybe I'm just trying to find my music within myself. And I think he was right, because that was when everything started happening, and I started really, really pushing more and more of my music and sharing it with other people. And people supported it. People like it, you know? And that feedback made me want to do more and made me really happy."

Her time at Terra Alta cemented a belief she had already been developing for some time: namely, that modern society is one that finds people disconnected from one another and from the land. This theme can be heard in one of Hornbaker's most frequently performed songs, "Mountain Momma," which explores the ways that corporations—especially the fossil fuel industry—has exploited the people and the environment of West Virginia. Calling listeners to "save these old mountains" and "save this land," Hornbaker's composition is not simply focused on environmental protection. Rather, as her permacultural training taught her, she positions environmental protection as a component of cultural preservation, presenting a protagonist who sees corporations privatizing access to riverbanks as "coal is eating us alive" and residents fight for survival.

The song has received public support as a consequence of her performances at a number of environmental rallies in the Kanawha Valley. Her Portuguese permaculture training spurred her to action: "When I came back from Portugal, I came back to Charleston. And I was culture shocked. But I was coming back to my hometown where I was raised, and so it was really weird at the same time. So when I came back, I was like, 'I'm going to learn more about my community. Where are these people that have these similar values as I have right now?'" Taking in the film *Blood on the Mountain* during Charleston's West Virginia International Film Festival, she connected to the Charleston-area environmentalist community and became more active in the local movement, especially following the 2014 Elk River chemical spill, which polluted the drinking water of more than three hundred thousand West Virginians. "Mountain Momma," she observes, was particularly effective among people her own age, an audience that she consciously cultivates: "I hope West Virginia, in general, can really connect to it, but I am trying to reach a different audience, maybe a younger audience that are involved with environmentally conscious students."

In addition to playing rallies and open mics, Dina quickly began to cultivate an identity as a performing songwriter in venues throughout southern West Virginia. She performed at Charleston's Third-Eye Cabaret, which has been a remarkable force in the development of the contemporary Kanawha Valley songwriter scene. There, she met many of the leaders of the Charleston scene, including T.J. King, Matt Spade, and Dave Thomas. A chance encounter with *Goldenseal* editor and That High Country Revival fiddler Stan Bumgardner at Bramwell's

Oktoberfest led to occasional duets with a new mentor. And in 2014, she was invited to perform at the Pollination Festival, a summer solstice celebration held in St. Petersburg, Kentucky. The success of her performance there led her to record her first EP, titled *Day By Day*: "I had two shows there, and I did my solo thing, and I didn't have a CD. And everybody was like, 'Can I buy a CD? Where do I get your music?' And that's when I began to think, 'Shit, I need to have a CD. I need to start marketing myself, I guess, as a musician.'" The EP offers a small glimpse into Hornbaker's potential as a songwriter, revealing a directness and frankness that comes across in conversation with her, as well. Rather than weaving dense narratives or relying on poetic conceits, Hornbaker writes with the voice of someone who is profoundly concerned about the future of her community, her state, and the planet.

A global citizen in every sense of the word, Hornbaker has found the roots she sought in the Mountain State. When she talks about the state's potential as a permaculture leader, she shows the promise of a post-coal economy. "I think there is so much opportunity to create not the next Nashville but the next Asheville. I believe in West Virginia so much, and that's why, as a young individual, I am staying here." New opportunities to work with the Mountaineer Montessori School and to teach children about "the interconnectedness of everything" place Hornbaker in a powerful position to shape the state's future, and through her songs and her activism, she offers hope for a better tomorrow.

————

DISCOGRAPHY

Day by Day, self-published (2015).

MIKE PUSHKIN

As the 37th District's representative to the West Virginia House of Delegates, Mike Pushkin is currently one of the leading young progressive voices in state politics, often sponsoring and supporting legislation addressing issues that face the state's working class, the mentally ill, and minorities. Yet, for this Charleston native, politics were, until quite recently, far from the mind of this bowling-alley-managing, cab-driving, songwriting legislator. Rather, as a musician performing in several of West Virginia's most celebrated bands of the past two decades, Pushkin has been a leader in the West Virginia music scene who explores the intersections of rock, soul, reggae, and folk.

Pushkin's musical life began early in the Kanawha Valley of the 1970s and 1980s. A middle school bandsman who quit the program to play football—"They said that if I didn't march, they didn't want me there for concert season. I really just wanted to play the concerts"—he was inspired to pick up the drums and the guitar after listening to the rock and roll records that his mother and uncle collected. "Music was always my passion from a very young age," he remembered. "I kind of took over my mother's and my uncle's record collection. They had old rock and roll stuff from the '50s, like early rock and roll, and I would sit in my room and play records all the time. I would beat on things, started playing drums when I was very young. And I guess when I was about thirteen, I took more of an interest in the guitar."

As a guitarist, Pushkin was heavily influenced by the great rock guitarists of the 1970s, especially Jimmy Page and Jerry Garcia. "I think why I really switched from drums to guitar was that I snuck out to see the midnight movies and saw, at the Cinema 7, *The Song Remains the Same*, which is a Led Zeppelin movie. Jimmy Page seemed like the coolest person in the world to me. So I decided to start playing guitar instead of drums. So I was influenced a lot at that age by Led Zeppelin. And then, after I got a little bit older, I got more and more into the Grateful Dead."

Lessons with drummer Paul Moore and guitarist Chuck Biel helped Pushkin to develop stronger technique on these core rock instruments, and it wasn't long before he began to seek the musical company of others and to make his first attempts at songwriting. As Pushkin remarked, "As soon as I had an amplifier, I formed a band with other kids in the neighborhood. The songs weren't that great, but we wrote a few of our own. Of course, we did the 'Wild Thing' and 'Louie, Louie,' of course, which was the first thing we all knew how to play. And we would write real simple little songs, too." Such formative songwriting experiences would prove useful as Mike continued to pursue his musical career, as his bands have always featured a substantial catalog of original compositions.

Pushkin's first tastes of musical success came in high school with the group Live Bait, which was quite popular among youthful revelers in and around Kanawha County. "We played any kind of gig. We played keg parties down at Alum Creek. And we even played a fundraiser at Stonewall Jackson's prom." Learning how to entertain an audience would come in handy as he moved to Morgantown to begin his studies at West Virginia University. Known for its sometimes well-earned reputation as the home of a "party school," Morgantown offered numerous opportunities for Pushkin to ply his craft and build a professional reputation in the state's youth center. "Quite honestly, I wasn't all that into school," he reflected. "But my friends—Matt, who was in my band and played bass and was like my best friend, he decided to go to WVU, so I decided *I* would go to WVU. So I went up there and started a band." An English major, Pushkin formed Jolly Gargoyle, "a straight-up rock and roll band. We did some of our own music as well as some Rolling

Stones and Grateful Dead and Neil Young covers. It was kind of like we were part of the Sunnyside hippie scene up there. Our home base was the Stadium Inn" on University Avenue. Pushkin recalls that, although his studies occupied some of his time, he was "completely obsessed with the band. And doing whatever I could to, you know, book gigs, schedule practices, create new music. I was really immersed in the band."[21]

After Jolly Gargoyle broke up, Pushkin played in several short-lived groups before forming the Joint Chiefs, which Pushkin describes as "more of a funk band." Based primarily at Nyabinghi Dance Hall in Sunnyside as well as the Sunnyside Music Garden, and "a lot of places that are now little crackerbox condos," Pushkin opines. Moreover, as music festivals catering to the region's countercultural youth set began to flourish in the region, Joint Chiefs were frequently featured, including most notably at the first two CheatFests in the Preston County town of Albright and the Live on the Levee series in Charleston. The songs that Pushkin wrote for the group blended overt political messages with catchy musical structures. As Pushkin observed, politics were "definitely covered up by an extremely danceable beat, because it was a funk band. It might not be such a great analogy, but when I was a kid, I used to watch *Fat Albert*, and they would have songs and try to have some fun and learn a lesson, too. I figured that, if I'd get people dancing and play like really good music, it wouldn't matter what the lyrics were, but if it had some lyrics that people would pay attention and learn a little bit from it, that's even better. [In the Joint Chiefs,] I was writing about the political climate of that time. You know, a lot of the songs were written during the first Bush administration, you know, the first Iraq War."[22]

Morgantown may have been a thriving music scene that supported creative bands like the ones that Pushkin fronted, but by the dawn of the new millennium, Pushkin was finding the University City to be too young a scene for a musician who had just turned thirty years old. "About the time I turned thirty," he recalled, "I felt like I was too old to be hanging out in Morgantown." Amid some personal struggles, Pushkin moved back to Charleston to get a new lease on life. "I came back with absolutely nothing. I couldn't even tell you if I even had a guitar. And I was really struggling for years, until about 2004, trying to get my act together." Pushkin worked as a solo artist and as a member of "some ill-fated bands," including Bubkes, Mike P and the Lowercase Gs, and Head Salad before forming the longer-lasting group 600 Lbs. of Sin. "I was in a band for a short period of time called Head Salad. I really hated the name, but I was hired to replace their singer, so I didn't have any choice over the name," he noted. "We were booked to play a wedding, and I called for a rehearsal, and a couple of guys in the band felt like they didn't need to rehearse for weddings. So I pretty much told them I was going to get a new band together." During that same time period, Pushkin had connected with Josh Thomas, "one of the best guitar players I've ever played with. So I kept in contact with him, and he and I would play acoustic here and there when I was with Mike P and the Lowercase Gs. He wasn't in that band, and when I had a problem with the rehearsal, I took that as an opportunity to form a band with Josh. Josh and I play very well together, so I wanted to get another band together with him, and that's when I formed 600 Lbs. of Sin." Later, he met Siena Farwell, a Charleston vocalist, at an open mic and "invited her to one of our practices." Shortly thereafter, the 600 Lbs. of Sin lineup was solidified.

600 Lbs. of Sin was, like many of Pushkin's projects, frequently involved in political debates and made itself available for progressive political causes. Of particular importance to him were environmental issues, including the fight against mountaintop removal coal mining in West Virginia. "If you look at some of the songs on the old Jolly Gargoyle album—that album came out in like '90 or '91—there were songs on there about climate change," Pushkin observed. "I've always felt that music is something that can bring people together for something positive, like caring about the water you drink or the air you breathe or the mountains you live on." The other Sinners were in general agreement with him—"the people that I've been around [musically] are always like-minded people," Pushkin noted—and in 2010 agreed to play a benefit for Keepers of the Mountain, a Boone County organization led by the late Larry Gibson that provides education about the effects of mountaintop removal.

Pushkin recalled that he had been asked to participate in the benefit because of a song he had written called "29." "I wrote a song a couple of days after the Upper Big Branch disaster [in April 2010]," he remembered. "I was driving a cab that night. There was a Fox News crew at the airport, and I gave them a ride down to where Upper Big Branch is there in Whitesville. And we were talking about it on the way there. I don't remember the conversation I had with the news crew. I slipped down to Marsh Fork Elementary, which is where all the journalists were staying because they didn't have a hotel down there at the time. So I dropped them off down there, and I got out of the cab, and I walked around, and there were the people of the town. The people that might have had family that worked there in that mine were feeding the journalists because there were no restaurants. There were people bringing covered dishes to the elementary school to take care of the journalists. I mean, these people were going through a tragedy, and they were taking care of the journalists from New York, DC, or wherever they were from. So that struck me. So later on that day, while I was driving the cab, I would pull over and jot down a line and pull over again and jot down a line. And by the end of my shift, I had this song that I wrote about it called '29.'"[23]

"29" was an immediate hit among the coalfield activists gathered at Gibson's home, and a cell phone video of the performance was posted to YouTube, where it came to the attention of Reverend Billy, a progressive activist and performance artist who serves as the spiritual leader of the Church of Stop Shopping. As Pushkin recounted, Reverend Billy "came into town to do like a 'mountaintop revival' or whatever they called it when he was doing his show here. He asked the producer of *Mountain Stage* if he could find us and if we could come play as part of his show. So we did that. It was just Josh, Sierra, and me, and we showed up there at the Cultural Center and performed '29' as part of his little show."

Pushkin's political activism in music may have resonated with committed environmentalists and other progressives, but in 2014, his musical activism merged even more overtly with local and state politics. Meshea Poore, the 37th District's representative to the West Virginia House of Delegates, declared her intention to run for Congress, and Pushkin pondered the possibility of running for the vacant seat. "When I read that she had decided to run for Congress in 2014, I called her and talked to her for a while about it and told her how it was very important to me how this district was represented. My mother grew up on the

East End. My father grew up on the East End. For one hundred years, my family has lived on the East End of Charleston because that was historically the Jewish neighborhood of Charleston, and there aren't a whole lot of Jews in West Virginia anyway. I was living on the West Side, which is still part of that district, but it was important to me who was representing it, and I asked her one night—I was driving the cab, and I pulled over and was telling her about it. I said, 'Well, what would you think if I ran?' And she said, 'I don't know. You might win.' So I went and filed the next day." Although he doesn't believe that he "was really seen as a serious candidate at first because people thought that I was like this hippie cab driver that plays guitar," he launched a serious campaign to meet the people in the district, knocking on doors and talking with the people he hoped to represent.

His musical and political worlds collided on January 9, 2014, when a coal-cleaning chemical called methylcyclohexanemethanol (MCHM) was spilled into the Elk and Kanawha Rivers in Charleston, tainting the water supply for three hundred thousand southern West Virginia residents and threatening water supplies along the Ohio River from Huntington to Louisville. The Elk River flows through the 37th House District, Pushkin observed, and he immediately pitched in to assist his neighbors, filling his 600 Lbs. of Sin van with bottled water and distributing it to shut-ins and other people in need. "I was just so ticked off about the whole thing. It was either sit at home and be furious, or just get outside of myself by going out and doing what I can to be part of the solution. You know, during this time, I thought, 'Would I be doing this if I wasn't running for office?' And I thought that I would be. Maybe not twenty-four/seven like what it turned into, and maybe not have done it so much, but I definitely would've done it."

His observations from his travels around the city, his conversations with residents, and his anger were soon channeled into a song, "We're All a Bunch of Water." "You know, I wrote the song," Pushkin reflected, "and if I said what I really wanted to say, I don't know if it would've been printed in the paper. It was easier for me to say what I thought and just put it in a song and express what I was feeling, which was a whole lot of frustration and anger." The song gained a great deal of attention as Pushkin played it at political rallies and streamed it on his campaign website. But "We're All a Bunch of Water" also garnered national and international attention as news of the spill reached the headlines of major news outlets across the globe, including *The New York Times* and "a couple of the international Jewish newspapers, probably because there's not a lot of us to go around here," Pushkin remarked wryly.[24]

Buoyed by his storefront politicking and "We're All a Bunch of Water," Pushkin won the general election in November 2014, and he became the 37th District's representative in the House of Delegates in 2015. In the two years since, he has remained active as a musician, often playing for community events as both a soloist and with 600 Lbs. of Sin, and he serves as the president of the American Federation of Musicians local in Charleston. A cabbie who, until recently, managed the Venture Lanes bowling alley in St. Albans, Pushkin remains a vital advocate for his musical community, his constituents, and his fellow West Virginians. And, as a songwriter, he continues to craft new music that blends "a deeper meaning [with a musical style] that people might actually want to listen to."

————

DISCOGRAPHY

WITH JOLLY GARGOYLE:
Jolly Gargoyle, self-published (1992).

WITH JOINT CHIEFS:
Joint Chiefs' Greatest Hits, self-published (1995).

COLLEEN ANDERSON

Although she wasn't born in the Mountain State, Charleston song-writer Colleen Anderson, as the old cliché goes, got here as fast as she could. "West Virginia chose me, sure as my own mother knows me," she opines in her song "West Virginia Chose Me." "I don't know any other place that people want so desperately to go back to," she told me. "I mean, I don't want to go back to [my home state of] Michigan. I don't feel that way at all. But if I left here, I would want to come back because of my friends and the mountains and the botanical diversity. Mostly the people, though, I would say. It is a place where people tolerate differences."

Anderson's path to West Virginia was paved by the Volunteers in Service to America program, better known as VISTA, a program that was intended to provide vital services to impoverished communities across the United States. From her dorm room at Western Michigan University, Anderson "heard this ad for VISTA, and they used that quote—I've heard it attributed to Eldridge Cleaver, but I'm not sure if it is—'If you're not part of the solution, you're part of the problem.' And that hooked me. And I sent away for the application and filled it out and sent it in. I kind of forgot about it until summer, when I got my acceptance and a plane ticket to Philadelphia." Following two weeks of training, she was presented with a major decision: to work in a rural area or an urban one. "After two weeks in Philadelphia," she recalled, "I

• • • •

———

Figure 6. Colleen Anderson
(photo by Al Peery, courtesy of Colleen Anderson).

• • • •

decided I'd rather have rural. But I could've gone to an Indian reserva-
tion in New Mexico. I could've gone to, who knows, a lot of places in the
country, but they sent me to Cabin Creek."

Arriving in October 1970, Anderson was initially assigned to monitor water quality along Cabin Creek, a job she quickly learned that she
didn't like. Looking for new opportunities, she landed a new assignment with another VISTA volunteer, James Thibault, who was beginning to organize the quilters along Cabin Creek and to help them find
markets for their creations. This venture—Cabin Creek Quilts—lasted
for nearly three decades.[25] "I had a wonderful, wonderful experience,"
she recalled. "In fact, I prolonged my VISTA service a little bit longer
because I was having such a wonderful time. You know, a hundred and
fifty old ladies who told great stories and made beautiful quilts. What's
not to like?" Anderson recalls that music was an almost constant presence in the Cabin Creek watershed: "One of the things people did was
get together and listen to music. And no matter where you were, there
were always people who played guitar, banjo, fiddle. It was always my
favorite part of a party. If there was a party, you would always find me
sitting on the floor somewhere near the musicians. And if there was
singing, I was trying to sing along."

When her VISTA service ended in January 1972, Anderson found a
job with the West Virginia Commission on Aging, and by the fall of 1973,
she moved to Morgantown to complete a bachelor's degree in English.
It was there that she wrote her first song, "a love song for the person I
was eventually going to marry," although, upon further reflection, she
doesn't recall performing the song for him. "I was completely, totally
shy and interior about my songwriting," she remembered. Throughout
her late twenties, Anderson slowly grew more comfortable singing in
public, thanks in large part to her involvement in the Morgantown
Friends of Old-Time Music and Dance (FOOTMAD). "The first time I
ever performed in public was for a FOOTMAD festival. At that point, I
might've written four or five songs, and it was the most terrifying thing
I had ever done," she recollected. "And, of course, it was a lot of fun.
And I really, really liked it."

In addition to FOOTMAD events, she regularly attended informal jam sessions with her husband's law school classmates: "One of the

things we [my husband and I] did when we first got together was to sing together. And he would play the guitar, and we would both sing. So that's how I started singing, but I didn't other than with him or maybe at a small get-together with friends." Anderson remembers that the repertoire that was performed at these jams—later rechristened "The Agnostic Gospel Band"—was drawn largely from the folk and country-rock songbook of the era. "We'd sing anything by The Band," she noted. "You know, [The Grateful Dead's] 'Uncle John's Band' was a great favorite. And old hymns and ballads. The kind of songs you would find in *Sing Out!* In fact, I think some of us had copies of that, and we would refer to it for the words sometimes." The Agnostic Gospel Band—which included her future guitar accompanist George Castelle, Mark Snyder, Anne Harms, and Bruce Perrone, among others—continued to meet periodically for nearly two decades and has recently been revived by Amy Atkins, the daughter of original member David McMahon.

In 1980, Anderson moved to Charleston, and in 1981 moved into the home in which she currently resides. (This quaint neighborhood provides the backdrop for her whimsical 2012 novella *Missing Mrs. Cornblossom*.)[26] The capital city proved to be a welcoming and supportive home for Anderson, whose creative ventures have included an extensive oeuvre of poetry, short stories, and novellas in addition to her songwriting. An accomplished visual artist, she has also made her mark as a graphic designer, providing logos and designs for arts organizations and other enterprises in the Kanawha Valley. More recently, Anderson has contributed original essays to West Virginia Public Radio, and she currently narrates a series of vignettes about West Virginia history through a partnership between West Virginia Public Radio and the West Virginia Humanities Council.

Listening to Anderson's recorded output, one can easily hear the eclecticism that inspires so much of her creative work. Her 2006 album *Fabulous Realities*, for instance, freely mixes jazz-oriented compositions like "Elderblossom Waffle Time" and the sultry bossa nova "Recycle Me" with songs like "Wing of the Hawk," which draws from the state's deep bluegrass tradition. "Well, I would call myself a 'contemporary folk' songwriter," she theorized, "but obviously, every now and then, I stray into a jazzy—or I guess you could call it 'jazz'—kind of thing."

Anderson credits her accompanists for their ability to pull those various elements into her work. "I can hear chords pretty well," she notes. "I can hear in the way that I think a lot of people instinctively know how a song works. I can usually figure out the chords on the piano, figure out what I'm hearing. And if I can't, I'll ask George [Castelle] to help me. Sometimes Ron Sowell will help us out, because he's good at that. Or our friend [who arranged 'Recycle Me'] Jim Martin, just a wonderful jazz musician, can hear those complicated chords. Those sevenths and ninths and those wonderful mushy chords. I love them."

Like much of her work in other creative media, Anderson's songs are often written in response to a community need. "Recycle Me," for instance, "was written at the request of Helene Rotgin, who is no longer with us," Anderson remembered, "but she was a huge environmentalist in Charleston and a real force for good. She could also be very persuasive. She wanted to have an environmental float in a local parade about something or other, and so she had people dressed up as tin cans and things following the float and riding on the float. And she wanted a song, so she asked me to write a song. And I wrote a song that actually didn't work very well for the parade. So, later, I just adapted it as a love song. I thought it was kind of cuter as a love song."

Anderson's powerful protest song "If You Love My West Virginia" emerged from a community in need, this time in response to the 2014 Elk River chemical spill, which left nearly three hundred thousand southern West Virginia residents without safe drinking water. Initially, she and George Castelle composed "a satirical, silly song about the water" that was played over West Virginia Public Radio's *West Virginia Morning* program, but Anderson felt that the situation demanded a more powerful and direct commentary as well. "I got an email from Chuck Wyrostok about two days before this public hearing that happened [at the State Capitol] in early February. And I had been walking around for maybe two or three days before that. That's where I do my songwriting; I'm just walking, and I'm trying things out in my head. And I was still outraged—and particularly at these so-called 'public servants' in this state because nobody was screaming bloody murder. Everybody seemed to be kind of hiding, not really trying to fix this problem. And I just kept walking around and thinking, 'If I could say what

I wanted to say. If I could call that governor and tell him what I think.' And these words started coming, and they started coming very quickly and easily." A call for the state's legislators to act in support of the state's residents and its environment, "If You Love My West Virginia" received its debut on the floor of the West Virginia House of Delegates during a public hearing about a bill intended to increase regulatory oversight of the kinds of chemical storage tanks that failed in the Elk River spill. Since then, she has been asked to perform the song at a variety of public events, including an evening of poetry and political speeches held at Morgantown's 123 Pleasant Street, for which I served as Anderson's accompanist.

Anderson's compositions are filled with beautiful poetic descriptions of nature and often use natural imagery to address familiar themes of love and loss. "Wing of a Hawk," in a lilting six-eight time, conflates the imagined feelings of freedom that a hawk might feel when it glides over the landscape with the fleeting feelings of romantic attraction. Anderson recalled that this song emerged from a poetry workshop at Robert Frost's New Hampshire home. "It was just a heady time," she noted. "I was with fifty other poets, and it was the first time I had been with that many of my peers. I don't think I slept more than four hours in a night. I was out hiking a lot during the day, because I was in the White Mountains. And it was just like days, mornings of hiking and afternoons and evenings of listening to great poets. I was high on everything, and at the same time, I was sort of also infatuated with someone. On the last day, I wanted to do something that would just fix this week in my memory forever. There was a tiny little airport nearby, and for fifty bucks, you could go up in a glider. And I just thought, 'This will make me remember.' And so I went up in this glider with a pilot, and we floated around for fifteen, twenty minutes. And so the imagery for that song comes from that glider flight. It was just really exhilarating."

A gentle poet, an engaged member of her community, and humble to a fault, Colleen Anderson has been quietly reflecting on *her* West Virginia and seeking new ways to present its beauty to others for nearly five decades. Like so many of the people profiled in Seaton's *Hippie Homesteaders*, Anderson came to West Virginia on a whim and found the place to be transformative. Speaking of her love of the state's natural beauty, she noted that, although she "didn't grow up as a 'nature girl,' West Virginia has been just such a rich place for me." Thankfully, West Virginia chose her.

———

DISCOGRAPHY

Going Over Home (with George Castelle), Edna Records (2001).

Fabulous Realities, Edna Records (2006).

Potluck (with Julie Adams and Karen Vuranch), Delectable Records (2007).

"If You Love My West Virginia," self-published (2014).

MIKE ARCURI

———

For thirty years, Charleston-area songwriter Mike Arcuri wandered the back country of West Virginia as a field biologist with the West Virginia Department of Environmental Protection. But music was never far from his mind. "Music has always been part of my life. I was singing from the age of two years old. I could listen to the radio and memorize a song note per note, right on pitch, and I used to amaze my mom. She used to call the neighbors and have them come over and put me in a rocking chair and turn the radio on, and they would listen to me sing and they got a big kick out of that," he recalled. Although he demonstrated significant musical abilities—and was encouraged by his teachers in elementary school—Arcuri did not receive formal training in music until he sought instruction on the guitar and banjo around the age of thirteen. By the time he graduated from high school, he was able to play cover versions of radio hits from the early 1970s, leading to several performing opportunities on the campus of Marshall University, where he went to college. "When I was really young," he remarked, "I was into some of the rock bands that were out at the time, like Steppenwolf and Led Zeppelin, Jimi Hendrix, Deep Purple—some of those. Now, as I got a little bit older and started playing guitar, I got more into singer-songwriters and kind of got away from the rock and roll groups and got more into people like John Prine and

Dan Fogelberg and John Denver. But Jim Croce was probably my number one influence when I was younger."

While at Marshall, Arcuri studied the banjo with Jim McCown, formerly of the popular Huntington-area band The Outdoor Plumbing Company. Although he has more or less abandoned the genre now, bluegrass fascinated Arcuri at the time. "I bought a banjo before I went to college and just pinked around," he reflected. "I didn't know what I was doing. I learned a few chords, mainly strumming it a little bit. But I learned the Scruggs style three-finger picking when I got into college. And that's when I really started to get into the banjo. And I think for about three years, I was into it pretty heavy. I mean, I was actually getting pretty good. But then, once I graduated college, I got into performing as a solo artist, mainly with guitar, very little banjo."

One of the more popular places for Arcuri to perform during his undergraduate and graduate studies at Marshall in the late 1970s and early 1980s was the campus coffeehouse in the studio union, as well as periodic outdoor venues. "In Huntington," he recalled, "I didn't really play the clubs per se. Now I played a lot on campus. The campus had a coffeehouse at the time. It was in the student union building, and I used to play there. In the springtime, we would have outdoor shows. And I had a friend [Joe Barges] who played guitar, and we used to play together. He had some connections, so he would kind of book us gigs around campus and just outside the dorms. We would just set up a PA system, and people would just show up with very little advertising. So I didn't really play around. I wasn't playing in a band or anything, so I didn't play around, like in clubs or anything like that in Huntington. I didn't start doing that till I actually graduated and moved back to Charleston."

Life in Charleston, though, didn't leave much time for gigging, as his work at the Department of Environmental Protection kept him on the road. "I was a field person," he remembered, "so I didn't have a whole lot of time, really, to devote to music. It was just my number-one hobby." But, by the early 1990s, Arcuri decided to put more of his energy into music, launching a country band called Midnight Rain that "played the southern West Virginia honky-tonk circuit," which he described as "a lot of those little one-room honky-tonk bars in Lincoln County, Boone

County, Kanawha County on the outskirts of town. Specializing in the "hot country" sounds of Garth Brooks, Alan Jackson, and other "hat acts," Midnight Rain comprised Arcuri as the lead singer, his brother Greg on drums, and Boone County natives Mike Holstein and Marvin Gillespie on guitar and bass, respectively. "We kind of alternated as the house band in a place called Spikes in Lincoln County. When you think about it, you kind of say, 'Oh, that sounds kind of rough.' But you know, out of all the years that we've played, we never really experienced any craziness, any gunfights. You know, there were a few little fisticuffs, you know, as you would expect at any bar, late night bar. The people appreciated good music, and we did have a good time. And then a place called the Sumerco Lounge in Sumerco. Billy Jack's, which was in Boone County. Sterno's. Easy Rider. I remember that one. I think that was down towards Logan. We didn't really play much in Charleston because the Charleston club scene, they're more for pop."

After five years or so with Midnight Rain—a period that Arcuri recalls as "probably the busiest I've ever been as a musician"—he was looking for something new to challenge him creatively. Feeling "kind of burned out" on the country bar circuit, he formed a duo called Holy Cow with guitarist and potter Keith Lahti, a former member of the group Big Money, which included *Mountain Stage* guitarist and West Virginia Music Hall of Fame founder Michael Lipton. Arcuri met Lahti at the Unity Church in Charleston, where Ron Sowell held a monthly open mic night. Inspired by their mutual love of the acoustic Delta blues of Robert Johnson, Mississippi John Hurt, and Muddy Waters, the group played along the I-64 corridor for nearly fifteen years, a period that also witnessed Arcuri's first serious efforts to write original songs. "It was all original," he recalled, "and we kind of built up a pretty good reputation, you know, as a group. Played around Charleston. Just about everything that successful musicians played. Like back when the Sternwheeler Regatta was here, we played that a couple of times, and we've done Live on the Levee here a couple of times. We played during Festivall, which is a big music festival here during the summertime. We played at Tamarack. They have a 'Sunday at Two' series. We played at various fairs and festivals around the state. So, you know, we got a little bit of notoriety for ourselves, and it was a lot of fun."

As someone who had made a name for himself as the frontman of a cover band, the move to an all-original group challenged Arcuri to develop songwriting skills that he had never had the opportunity to use previously. He was aware that songwriting required a different set of skills, and that it helped to distinguish Holy Cow from other acts in the region. "I could play cover songs and entertain people and make a little bit of money here and there," he observed, "but if I ever wanted to really, really elevate my craft, I felt that I needed to write." As an aspiring songwriter, Arcuri found mentorship from two Kanawha Valley songwriters: Ron Sowell and Doak Turner. "I think probably where I got inspired to write my own was through Ron Sowell," he recalled. "He's a mentor of mine here, and he just meant so much to me as well as to so many people musically. He has been a big help and a big encouragement. So, when I was going to his open mic initially, I wasn't playing my own songs, but I noticed several people were playing their own songs, so I started—I had written a few—so I started playing my own. And they weren't that good back then. I actually took music lessons from Ron. He also helped me arrange some of my songs. He critiqued some of my songs and helped me make them stronger, musically and lyrically."

Whereas Sowell helped Mike with his craft, Doak Turner introduced him to an international network of songwriters and resources through NSAI, the Nashville Songwriting Association International. "He's from St. Albans. He was the coordinator of NSAI in Charlotte, and he would come in to Ron's open mic occasionally because his parents still lie in St. Albans. If he was in town, he would come in, and he would talk about the NSAI group to the people who were attending the open mic and encouraged us to join if we were interested in learning the craft of songwriting. I said, 'What the heck? I don't have anything to lose.'" When Turner left Charlotte for Nashville, he invited Arcuri to stay with him any time he wanted to come to Music City. "I went down there and started attending songwriting workshops, song camps, and Doak introduced me to a lot of people down there, and I just kind of really got the songwriting bug. And that's where it all started. And I've been going to Nashville ever since."

Arcuri has been a strong advocate for the NSAI in West Virginia, currently serving as the coordinator of the Charleston chapter.

Founded around 2009, the Charleston NSAI chapter "was founded by Kevin Levine, who started the Pied Piper music store in Huntington originally, and then they opened up a store in Charleston," Arcuri said. "I came in and became co-coordinator a couple years ago. Now before that, for about four years, I was the co-coordinator of a Christian songwriting chapter up in Ripley. They had a small chapter up in Ripley that was founded by a lady by the name of Rose Wallen. Even though she was a Christian writer, she invited anybody interested in songwriting to come to the meeting, and then it wouldn't be 100% devoted to Christian writers. It was serious songwriters, because she realized she could probably get more members in there if she didn't limit the style of writing to just Christian songs. So I started going because I had no other option locally. And then when she learned how much experience I had going to Nashville, she asked me to become co-coordinator, which I did. And I did that with her for about four years, and she kind of got burned out, so she phased out the chapter. During that time, the Charleston chapter was started, so I was kind of attending both. I was coordinating one and attending the other. And then when one folded up, I became the co-coordinator of the Charleston chapter of NSAI."

Like many performing songwriters in West Virginia, Arcuri has not made a concerted effort to record his music, cutting a few solo tracks and one album with Holy Cow. Rather, he has focused his energies on getting his songs to major recording artists in Nashville and on supporting the community of songwriters who live in the Charleston area. His efforts in Nashville haven't yielded great results so far, but he is well aware that it can take years of effort before someone with major-label backing and name recognition picks up a song for an album cut. "Obviously, that's the goal of a lot of songwriters," Arcuri remarked. "Not everybody, but we'd all like to have a song cut by a major artist. That's kind of a goal. I did have one song played for Luke Bryant, who was the [2016 Country Music Association] Entertainer of the Year. It was when he was just starting. He was known, but he was just really starting to get popular. And his producer is Jeff Stevens, who is from Alum Creek. If we ever have a song that we feel is strong enough, Jeff's willing to give it a listen. And if he likes it well enough, he may even play it for Luke. So he liked one of my songs well enough to play it for Luke once. Although, you know, Luke probably listens to maybe a thousand songs before he decides which ten to put on a record. So I knew mine, you know, didn't have a real good chance of making the record. But still, that gave me some confidence. It's very difficult for someone on the outside, no matter how good their song is. It's just hard. You've got to make connections."

For Mike Arcuri, songwriting requires dedication, and through the support of a network that he has developed over the past four decades, he has been able to maintain the courage to share his creative gifts while developing them still further. "You can be a great painter and be very artistic in that area, but, you know, there are art classes where you can learn how to harness that. So there's an art and a craft to creativity, whether it's painting or whether it's music. And it's the craft part that most people don't really have a good grasp about, which is why their songs, they may be very musical and some of their lines may be clever, but it's incoherent. So a lot of times, it kind of goes over their heads and people lose interest." As such, Arcuri's community—especially his work with NSAI—allows him to improve constantly: "I would not be anywhere near the songwriter I am today without the things I've learned as a member of NSAI."

————

DISCOGRAPHY

WITH HOLY COW!:
  Driftin', self-published (2006).
  Holy Cow!, self-published (2012).

AS A SOLO ARTIST:
  New Songs from an Old Guitar, self-published (2012).

ROGER RABALAIS

———

Since 2010, Kanawha County's Roger Rabalais—along with occasional co-hosts—has hosted SongwriterStage, a showcase of local, regional, and national songwriting talent at various venues around southern West Virginia. SongwriterStage has become a vital source of inspiration for emerging songwriters, a mark of one's accomplishment in the West Virginia songwriting scene, and a communal gathering place to share songs and learn from the informal mentorship that abounds there. Rabalais, a tenacious promoter who works diligently to sustain the enterprise, is an accomplished songwriter himself. He has found a particular niche in writing epic narratives based on historical events, and he aspires to provide a listener- and performer-friendly environment and to inspire further development of the state's songwriting community.

Rabalais's musical journey began in Baton Rouge, Louisiana, during the Baby Boom years of the 1950s. His older brother, Robert, introduced him to the pop records of the late 1950s, including Marty Robbins's "A White Sport Coat and a Pink Carnation," Elvis Presley's "Love Me Tender," and others. Radio was also an important source of new music, and it wasn't long before Roger was interacting with local radio personalities. He recalled, "My younger brother Russ and I have a vivid memory of the first time I ever actually got up the nerve as a young child . . . to call up a radio station and request a song. The song was

'Bye, Bye Love' by the Everly Brothers." In the pop music boom of the early 1960s, Rabalais found himself constantly attracted to the sounds emerging from the tiny speaker of his radio. "There were some stations that I grew up listening to late at night when you could tune in on the radio either with a crystal radio under your pillow or in the car. KAAY was a strong station out in Little Rock. WWL out of New Orleans. WWL was what they called one of those 'middle-of-the-road' stations, you know. What we would have called, as kids, 'old-folk music.' But the traditional top-forty stations that we, all of my era, grew up listening to on AM radio was where I first heard the likes of Elvis and the Everly Brothers and Marty Robbins."

A member of the junior high band, Rabalais left the band because he wanted to play football and wasn't particularly fond of marching. But when football also fell to the wayside at the end of his sophomore year of high school, he returned to music. Inspired by the hip new band out of Liverpool that was taking the United States by storm, Rabalais joined a local garage band as its lead singer. It was around this time that Rabalais also became aware of the role that songwriters play in creating the material he was hearing on the radio.

After high school, Rabalais enrolled at Southern Methodist University in Dallas and later transferred to Lon Morris College in Jacksonville, Texas. But he completed his studies in Baton Rouge, finishing a degree in general studies at Louisiana State University. For the next thirty-five years, Rabalais worked in broadcasting, where, like most of his colleagues, he lived a rather peripatetic lifestyle. "Along the way," he recalled, "I was always intrigued by local music scenes wherever I lived, which over those years included a first job in Pensacola, Florida, and from there, I moved to Lake Charles, Louisiana. I went to New Orleans; came back to Lake Charles; went to Jackson, Mississippi; wound up back in Lake Charles again." Radio also took him to Beaumont, Texas; Aspen, Colorado; Nashville; and Charleston, West Virginia, for a brief stint in the late 1980s.

In 1990, Rabalais relocated to Colorado, where he began to get involved in the local music scene and to get the urge to write songs for the first time. "I wound up running a station in Granby, Colorado, which is just outside of Winter Park," he recounted. "It was while I was there that, ever mindful of my experience in broadcasting, I would find a way to attach the station promotionally to local music. So I latched onto an open mic that was being presented in town there. And one night, I was up on stage with some guys and, as happens with these kind of events, we just kind of drifted into a jam of 'Can't You See' by the Marshall Tucker Band. And I was new in town." The jam led one observer—the owner of a drug store and president of the local Chamber of Commerce—to invite the "band" to play for the town's Independence Day celebrations. With a gig and no band, Roger went to work assembling a group to play a set of cover songs. The group ended up performing for the next several years. "Songs that were in my repertoire then and now include 'The House of the Rising Sun' and songs by Sam Cooke. Some Rolling Stones and some Beatles and stuff like that that we picked up." Aspen provided the opportunity for him to develop confidence in front of an audience. The band "got me over the hump of getting out in front of an audience myself," he reflected. "Although I had done it in open mic situations and so forth all through the years, I remember being petrified to get in the car and drive downtown to play three songs for an open mic." Furthermore, Rabalais began to explore his own creative voice after listening to remarkable compositions by such prolific songwriters as Guy Clark, John Prine, and Rodney Crowell and recordings by Johnny Cash and Waylon Jennings. Jimmy Buffett, too, was a strong influence. His song "The Eye of the Hurricane" is inspired in part by Crowell's "California Earthquake" and Buffett's "Trying to Reason with Hurricane Season." "I thought, 'What a clever phrase that is, you know?'"

In 1999, Rabalais married his wife Carolyn, whom he had met during his year in Charleston in the late 1980s, and returned to the capital city. Working at a local music store, he became acquainted with Ron Sowell, *Mountain Stage* bandleader and host of a monthly open mic at the Unity Church in Charleston. At that point, Rabalais decided to focus more of his effort on songwriting. Inspired by his deep passion for the history of the Old West, he finished a song cycle that told the story of Tombstone and the shootout at the OK Corral. Dating back to the 1970s, he had loved the storytelling of such Old West concept albums as Eagles' *Desperado* and Willie Nelson's *Red Headed Stranger*, as well as the "Outlaw country" of Waylon Jennings and Jessi Colter. Also important was an album called *White Mansions*, which featured many of the leading country singers of the mid- to late 1970s telling the story of the U.S. Civil War.

The resulting album, *Tombstone, Arizona, 1881: A Piece of the West* (2013), captures the legendary tale of Tombstone from the perspective of its leading figures. "I'm not the kind of guy who sits down and writes songs every day. So over several years, I had written about eight or ten songs that told this story pretty much and had written a song from every major character in the story. Perhaps . . . the exclusion of one or two. But I wrote songs from the point of view of an onlooker, just a witness. There was a song for each of the Earp brothers and Doc Holliday and other elements of what they call the 'Cowboy Faction.' The Clant and McClary Brothers." Rabalais hoped to record the songs, but he knew that a home studio production would not be effective in conveying the story in the manner that he hoped. So in 2013, he traveled to Nashville to record the album, which features Rabalais's rough baritone voice recounting the famous story in both prose narrations and song. The album, from which Rabalais frequently performs, has been embraced by the community he wrote about; the Birdcage Museum—housed in the historic Birdcage Saloon—vied for the right to be the only venue in town to sell it.

Rabalais's storytelling drew the attention of Charleston resident Dick Patton, who was a member of the Coal River Group, a group that was attempting to tell the Coal River Valley's history. Patton recommended Rabalais to the group and commissioned him to write some songs to support their efforts. After a quick internet search, Rabalais found that the Coal River was one with a remarkable, but largely unknown, history. "I found out that the Coal River system is the scene of the nation's first inland lock and dam system," he recollected. "Of course, the remnants of those locks and dams are still there. On the river system at that time, people went by their profession name, like doctor, lawyer, or captain, followed by their first name rather than their last name. And so it just so happens that, on the Coal River, there were three Captains Bill. People would come up with nicknames [to differentiate them from one another]. So one of them was referred to as *Lying*

Captain Bill. The other was *Fighting* Captain Bill. And the other was *Drinking* Captain Bill." From that story, Rabalais wrote about all three Captains Bill, conflating them into a single "Lying, Fighting, Drinking Captain Bill."

Roger Rabalais is a fixture in the Charleston songwriting community whose leadership has helped to support the growth of the local music scene. A frequent participant in open mics and numerous performances, he is quick to speak of the strengths of his fellow writers. His radio background allows him to connect his own music and that of his SongwriterStage colleagues with a broader listening public, most recently through the low-powered Charleston station WSTQ. But perhaps most importantly, he helps to reflect local history in song through the research he conducts on the local communities in which he has lived and worked.

DISCOGRAPHY

Tombstone, Arizona, 1881: A Piece of the West, self-published (2013).

PART II:
THE OHIO VALLEY

———

RIVERS
OF SONG

. . . .

Figure 7. Todd Burge
(photo by Josh Saul, courtesy of Todd Burge).

. . . .

TODD BURGE

If Nashville songwriter Roger Miller of "King of the Road" and "Dang Me" fame had a son in the Mountain State, it would probably be Wood County native Todd Burge, who, for three decades, has been writing songs of both ironic silliness and unflinching sentimentality. Armed with an acoustic guitar, ukulele, harmonica, and a host of gizmos and gadgets, Burge can have you laughing about the antics of his dear dog Lou one minute and leave you weeping about his passing the next, all with a simple turn of phrase or a crack in his falsetto voice. A passionate songwriter who takes the work of songwriting seriously—but seldom takes himself seriously—Burge has built a loyal following around the state and across the United States, building that audience through the yeoman's work of constant writing, performing, and promoting. A rare example of a West Virginia singer-songwriter who makes his living exclusively from his music, Burge sets a standard for professionalism in the Mountain State's music scene that many people try to emulate.

"Born the day JFK was buried," Burge was raised in Vienna, West Virginia, where his mother got him involved in a church choir at a young age. "Music was in the church, you know," he recalled, "and we went to the church that my grandparents went to in Boaz, West Virginia, which is right on the other side of Vienna here. It was Sandhill United Methodist Church, just a really small church. Actually, my granddad helped build the place in the fifties. And my mother, I briefly remember her doing runs here and there as choral director. I think she would fill in. I don't think she was permanent. But, we were expected to sing in choir, and I don't remember really music kicking in any serious way at that time. My mom would play piano around the house, and that was kind of a mystery to me, and I think I was probably a little too lazy to get involved in that."

The piano remained a mystery for Burge, even as he made a desultory attempt at formal lessons. "My brother Max picked up the piano at an early age," he remembered. "You know, the big thing at the time was playing 'The Entertainer' and stuff like that. I remember watching him play and thinking I'd like to do that, you know. And so the church pianist—Virginia Lott was her name—lived there right near the church in Boaz. She gave lessons, so I'd go to her weekly and didn't much care for it," he laughed. "Should be a better story. But I remember distracting her and asking her about movies she had watched the night before, and she would like to talk about that. But I also remember going to recitals, and I would take the recital piece and I would—I always say that laziness or attention deficit led me to songwriting because I didn't have the patience to learn the song—and I'd make up my own thing and then just seemed to like the way I wanted the song to go. And I'd do that in a recital, and then that would disappoint Virginia Lott. And she would report that to my mother that my brother Max had the real musical talent. That was kind of the way my early piano went. I look back on that as kind of being my first attempt at songwriting. I enjoyed making up those little passages from songs that she was trying to get me to learn."

Junior high and high school choir experiences also revealed Burge to possess a quick creativity and an uncanny musical ear. "I went on to junior high, and I did make choir and it kind of took hold. And I remember not paying attention much in class, but still being able to retain melodies. And the teacher would have us sing solo. You know, if we were goofing off, she'd have us sing solo and, you know, catch you at goofing off. That was her way of shining a light on the fact that you were not paying attention. But I'd always know the melody. And I remember my teacher being really, you know, angry that she couldn't catch me on that, so I guess I had that. Some natural sense of melody I suppose. I went to PHS [Parkersburg High School] here in Parkersburg and was really, really wrapped up in music, just as a listener mostly, and was really into about everything that the choir director—her name was Singer, by the way—would lay on us. And I was in the offshoot choir too, the Chamber Choir, which was kind of like an honor choir, and we'd travel and compete. And we'd sing madrigal-type stuff and all that, oh you know, classical stuff."

Burge's musical tastes, even as a young kid, also ran toward the eclectic. "In grade school," he recalled, "I was obsessed with Charlie Rich. That kind of, you know, Memphis songwriter. My dad was really into him and that's what introduced me to his music. My parents split when I was just ten, and so I was connected with my father [through Charlie Rich], and I listened to him all the freaking time. I remember our teacher wanting us to bring something we were listening to for one of our classes. I brought Charlie Rich in, you know?" He laughed, "and she was like, 'What?' You know, *the Silver Fox*! But before that, I remember being obsessed with Roger Miller. And I was really into him when I was like, six, five. He was a big deal, and I listened to it daily, you know? It was like the kids' music in our house was Roger Miller." And he owns more copies of one artist's records than the artist himself probably owns: "I have forty-five Neil Diamond records. He doesn't have that many. He would *never* have that many."

Upon graduating from Parkersburg High School in 1982, Burge moved to Morgantown to pursue studies in psychology and English. There, he entered a community of fans and musicians that thrived in a vibrant live music scene fueled by the energy of the punk rock movement. "I was going to the Underground Railroad, which became a famous music venue. They would have people like Timothy Leary come speak, and Abbie Hoffman came and spoke, and they had Bo Diddley play there. And the Dead Kennedys and the Red Hot Chili Peppers and just on and on. It was a very eclectic, very liberal place. It was an amazing thing that was happening in Morgantown at that time."

Along with the Underground Railroad, West Virginia University's campus radio station, U92, played a key role in supporting the local music scene. "U92 had just started," he recalled, "so we had this really 'tapped-into-the-national-scene' club there, and you had a pretty powerful signal for a radio station and serious people behind it there at WVU. They might argue with this, but I, as a Parkersburg person going in and listening to U92, I was hearing what I would consider *pre*-formatted radio, you know? Maybe there was a format there, and I was missing it because it was so formatted here [in Parkersburg] and everywhere else and all of Planet Earth as far as I know."

Particularly exciting for Burge was the ability to hear local bands on the radio. "I remember watching this band Gene Pool, which was a Morgantown local band, play some songs, and I was really into it. And they had this song called 'Pilots Are Melting.' I remember the melody. I haven't heard it for years, but I remember just being turned on by that tune. And the next day, I'm driving, and 'Pilots Are Melting' came on U92, and it just blew me away because local bands didn't get airplay as far as I knew. I didn't know that happened."

It was this epiphany—combined with the research for a paper on punk rock that he wrote for a creative writing course—that led Burge to form his own band, The Larries. "I knew three chords on my guitar, you know, and I remember thinking I had this idea for a song or two. But anyway, I decided I couldn't even play and sing at the same time. I couldn't play chords and sing. I had my buddy Jimmy Clinton come and sing while I was playing, and that kind of started my songwriting. I mean, we made a little demo tape of like six songs. We took it to a party. A friend of ours was a musician, and he said, 'If you throw a band together, you can open up for us.' And another friend of ours, Wesley Poole, had got a drum kit but he's never played in his life. Six days later, we're playing on stage!"

Burge describes his work with The Larries as "through and through do-it-yourself punk rock. And it wasn't politically charged in any way. Well, sometimes, but, you know, it was the Reagan era. It was a mandate to do a little [political material]. But, for the most part, it was just kind of like really . . . goofy, light-hearted, off-the-top-of-our-heads singing about, you know, making love in the back of a Gremlin. Or we had a song called 'Fun in the '80s.' We had a song called 'I'm So Worried about the Kremlin,' which was a tongue-in-cheek, ironic type song." But even more interesting than the content of their work was seeing audience responses to it. "We'd made a cassette and gave it to a disc jockey," he recalled. "He played it on U92, and we'd go to our shows and people would know our tunes. It was like magic to us, you know? I just think that very first experience—if it weren't for U92 and the Underground Railroad, I wouldn't be sitting here right now, I guess."

At the same time that The Larries were beginning to gain traction, Burge was beginning to develop a more sincere voice in his songwriting that ran counter to the ironic material that he was performing with The Larries. Taking his nickname—Bunj—as a stage name, he signed his own record deal as a solo artist. The Larries, he recalled, "was first called The Grateful Larries, and we were kind of, you know, making fun of The Grateful Dead, which kind of pains me now because I really admire them. But at the time, we were kind of making of fun of that scene that surrounded the Dead. We were naïve. And we toured a little bit. Then I wanted to do some serious songwriting . . . what I called serious, you know, heart-on-my-sleeve type stuff. And so I had all these songs that didn't really fit The Larries. They continued without me. We both got signed to a label in San Francisco, and they toured as a three-piece without me. They were still doing some of my songs, and they had written some stuff and they had a record come out. My band was called Bunj and the Beats. I moved to San Francisco because my new Morgantown bandmates just didn't all want to tour, and so I went to San Francisco to pick a band there after we recorded the album. I worked for the label while I was looking for a band, and what I did was, I booked shows for The Larries and I booked shows for the other artists that they had. And really, it was a great, great learning experience. Just going on cold calls, trying to sell bands." Unfortunately, the Bunj and the Beats album was never issued, despite Burge's efforts to purchase the masters; after more than thirty years, Hardway returned the recordings, and he is now considering releasing them.[27] "I still think it's a good record," he reflects.

After a little less than a year in San Francisco, Burge returned to Parkersburg, where he formed the group 63 Eyes with some of his former bandmates in The Larries. 1987 found Burge practicing in a chicken coop that was owned by a woman named Nell Eckhert, who was the mother of one of Burge's mother's colleagues. "We kind of insulated this chicken coop, and we'd have a place where we could go and practice any time," he remembered. But 63 Eyes wasn't limited to the barnyard. Rather, they were ambitious in their touring efforts. "63 Eyes put out vinyl and toured the college circuit in a much more serious way," he remembered. "Mostly up and down the East Coast. We did CBGB's [in New York] and the 9:30 Club in D.C. And we did some of those type of clubs and did fairly well with it."

Yet, while his work with 63 Eyes was helping him gain some fame among the punk and indie rock crowd, Burge still felt like his participation in these groups wasn't allowing him to showcase his most authentic voice as a songwriter. Those groups, he noted, were part of "a totally different world musically than what I think I'm known for now." Writing everything on the acoustic guitar, Burge "felt that some of the lyrics were getting buried after they became rock songs."[28] Reflecting on 63 Eyes's sound, "What 63 Eyes did was really melodic, but very abrasive, you know. And at the time, I thought of these acoustic ideas. I mean, I had songs that really sounded like they should stay acoustic, and I put out acoustic records, and I just assumed the 63 Eyes [fans] would follow me. It was a pretty strong fan base that we had, but it was like, for the most part, they were just not interested. It wasn't like I was playing 63 Eyes-type songs on acoustic guitar. It was just a totally different world, which is fine now. It frustrated me for years." But despite the frustration that the 63 Eyes fans weren't as interested in his acoustic music, Burge continued to explore the serious things that he was feeling in his own songwriting. Sometimes, the band took his songs on, but in other instances, they passed. "Of course, when you're in a band, you have to make decisions as a band," he remarked, "and if the band's listening to a song and says, 'That's not us,' you've got to live with that. But in that earlier band [The Larries], it was all about getting goofy and being silly when we first started, and I wanted to get serious before they did. I wanted to write about everything, you know? Which at times, you just wonder as a songwriter, 'Who needs it?' You know? And then you realize, 'Oh! *ME! I* need it!' I think I have this need to share something with somebody, you know? So to have somebody say, 'Oh yeah, I've felt that,' or 'I feel that is special.'"

With this internal pressure mounting, Burge began to amass a body of songs for his first album, *Never Say Uncle* (1990). Released as a compact disc—Burge was one of the first to release a CD in Morgantown—the album allowed him to begin playing for a different audience. "I had way too many songs," he reflected. "I wanted to play them all, you know? I wanted to see how the audience would respond. I wanted to play in listening spaces that were dead quiet. I thought, in the rock and roll venues it was about the energy more than the lyrics sometimes. I thought, 'I'm writing these lyrics, and nobody's really getting them.' That was a dumb thing to think, because those people really knew the lyrics."

Although he wanted to perform for a listening audience, it was often difficult for Burge to find venues that were appropriate for his new solo act, especially around West Virginia. "You would play the bars," he recounted, "and it was frustrating. You'd play parties or festivals, and it was hard, too. So, you know, I'd go play at the Empty Glass [in Charleston]. I would play at that place or places in Athens [Ohio] that I could play. A lot of the stuff I was doing because I was known as this guy in this rock and roll band. I'd play the same clubs that my rock bands were playing. And I'd open up for a band, or I'd open for my band, and I'd try to pull it off, and you know, it'd be hit or miss. So it was not until I, you know, decided this is really what I must do—a solo thing—and hit the road doing it. You'd find these places, whether it's a bookstore or a university. I remember playing in Bluefield at lunchtime for the college. And I thought, you know, this is going to be [bad], but it was good! You can get these surprises here and there."

A major turning point came for Burge in 1991, when he made his first appearance on *Mountain Stage*, the internationally syndicated live music program produced by West Virginia Public Broadcasting. Burge had set this as a significant career milestone and made every effort to gain the attention of the show's producers. Burge recalled that he "begged them for—it had to be two years. I would send a postcard every time I was in Charleston playing somewhere. If there was ever a write-up in the paper for anything, I would send it to Larry Groce. And he would say, 'Eh, that's not quite right for what we're looking for right now. Send us your new stuff.' I'd only get three or four songs, and I'd send him a cassette, you know? And I would call and follow up. Occasionally, I'd get a person. But I just kept doing that."

His big break came from Deni Bonet, the fiddler in the *Mountain Stage* band and a long-time member of the Fabulous Twister Sisters and Stark Raven. Burge landed a gig at the Smoot Theatre in Parkersburg, where he was supposed to open for former *Dukes of Hazzard* star and country singer Tom Wopat. Burge hired Bonet to join him—"I basically paid her all the money that I was guaranteed"—so that he could play some of his "country-flavored tunes." The gig went well, and Bonet returned to Charleston singing Burge's praises. About six months after the Smoot performance, he received a call asking him to make his *Mountain Stage* debut, but not without some delay. After being bumped by Bob Mould of Hüsker Dü, he made his debut in 1991, where he played with Pere Ubu and Lisa Germano. That first *Mountain Stage* opened all sorts of doors for him. He noted, "That was a game changer for me. It's a national audience, and you could say in various places, 'I was just on *Mountain Stage* last week.' Some places would just book me because I've been on *Mountain Stage*."

In 1996, Burge moved to Pittsburgh, where his wife was studying at a culinary academy. That was followed by a stint in the "Live Music Capital of the World"—Austin, Texas—after which they returned to the Steel City for a while. During that time, Burge performed relentlessly and wrote nearly as ferociously, resulting in two albums, *Dreams Upstairs* (2000) and *New Year* (2003). *Dreams Upstairs* features a lovely song exploring the experiences of people living in the Appalachian diaspora, "Up in the West Virginia Hills." Recounting the tiresome drives that so many people undertake to return home to the Mountain State from places around the country, the song speaks to a broader theme of longing for West Virginia that runs through many of his songs. He recalled writing his first West Virginia song around 1989: "'Why You Need Me Now.' It's on a recording called *Most Requested*. And I remember writing that around '89. It says, 'I'm going back to West Virginia, / Back to my mom and dad. / And I'll let you pine away here and think / about what we once had.' It's just kind of like a heartbroken song where this guy was going back home to his roots after this love went bad, you know? And I wrote it really just tongue-in-check. Just like as a hicky, hillbilly thing." But it turned out that people connected with the song, much as they have with "Up in the West Virginia Hills" and "Wood

County Man," which appeared on *New Year*. "That song would touch
people," he recalled. "At first, I thought it was silly, you know? And then
years would go by, and someone would bring it up, and I'd play it and
you'd be touched by it. Somebody'd move back to town and want to hear
it because that happened to them in real life."

In the late nineties, Burge and his wife returned to Wood County
so she could become a sous chef at the country club in Vienna. In the
almost two decades since returning to West Virginia, Burge has released
multiple albums, each of which showcases his unique blend of sentimentality and irony. For instance, "I'm a Shark" uses a misunderstood
ocean predator whose shark-like demeanor prevents him from making
friends as a metaphor for "a human, middle-aged man who is going
through a severe mid-life crisis and is no longer desired by the opposite sex."[29] And "Joseph's Prayer to His Baby Son" explores the miracle
of the Immaculate Conception from the perspective of a bewildered
Joseph who can't get over the fact that he "never laid a hand on her." At
the same time, Burge's "Change (for Clean Water)" explores the long-
term effects of the 2014 Elk River chemical spill from the perspective of
people who have lived in the chemical valleys along the Little Kanawha,
Kanawha, and Ohio Rivers, wistfully observing that "Mountaineers are
always free to leave."

Over the last decade, Burge has become a leader in the West
Virginia music scene, and his increasing efforts on behalf of aspiring
musicians, up-and-coming venues, and well-established programs
like *Mountain Stage* have helped to promote West Virginia as a creative destination. These efforts have also brought him into the orbits
of such musical luminaries as Kathy Mattea and Tim O'Brien, both
West Virginia natives and both recorded duet partners. O'Brien also
produced Burge's most recent studio album, *Imitation Life* (2015), and
has frequently appeared as his duet partner in live performances. And,
as a semi-regular guest and a guest host on *Mountain Stage*, Burge has
built a substantial body of live recordings, which he culled to create
a live album of material spanning ten years of his solo career, *Live
on Mountain Stage, 2006–2015* (2016). Today, Burge continues to tour
extensively, playing for audiences small and large around the country. He even offers some unique live performances for small crowds

that gather around his Facebook page, and will write songs for special events, birthdays, and holidays, as well as to raise funds for his favorite charity, F.A.R.E. (Food Allergy, Research, and Education). He also conducts songwriter workshops for children and adults, traveling to schools around the Ohio Valley and hosting events for the Song Colony in Marietta, Ohio. An entrepreneur and a compelling musician, Burge's work—like Roger Miller's before him—is simultaneously comfortable and jarring, serious and sardonic, poetic and prosaic.

———

SELECTED DISCOGRAPHY

Hip About Time, self-published (2006).
My Lost and Found, self-published (2008).
Distraction Packed, self-published (2010).
Building Characters, self-published (2012).
Imitation Life, self-published (2015).
Live on Mountain Stage, 2006–2015, self-published (2016).

———

LIONEL CARTWRIGHT

When Lionel Cartwright thinks of his youth in the Ohio Valley, the radio isn't far from his mind. A child of the transistor radio revolution of the 1960s, Cartwright spent many nights "in bed with a little transistor radio and an earphone and just really falling in love with country music." Born in Mason County, his family moved to the northern panhandle town of Glen Dale in 1968, where the powerful signal of Wheeling radio station WWVA captured his attention. "They'd have a lot of those trucker shows at night where they'd have the guy giving road reports and then playing country music. They were from all over. Of course, Buddy Ray, who had a really popular one there at WWVA—Gus Thomas before him. There was a guy in Richmond, Virginia; St. Louis, and then other stations, too." Inspired to play country music through these programs, Cartwright set out on a path to become a country music great, leading to his 1990 hit "I Watched It All on the Radio."

Cartwright's musical path was anything but guaranteed, though, as he didn't come from a particularly musical family. But, like many children during that time, Lionel received piano lessons ("it never really took with me. The switch never got thrown on"). It was a baritone ukulele, a Christmas gift from his brother, that turned him toward a life of music. "I never really thought [that] music was my thing. But I remember on that Christmas vacation there, picking up his baritone uke, and

· · · ·

Figure 8. Lionel Cartwright
(courtesy of Lionel Cartwright).

· · · ·

there was a Mel Bay chord book by it. I remember opening it, and the first chord in it—I can remember the smell of that instrument; I can remember the felt on the inside of the black speckled case. I remember strumming that chord, and then I learned another one-finger chord. I think it was G and E minor; with just four strings, it takes just one finger. And it really was like the skies parted. I just loved it. That's all I wanted to do." Soon thereafter, he picked up the guitar and focused more attention on the piano, practicing on a player that his parents had "bought off a World War II widow whose fiancé had given it to her as a gift, and then he was killed in World War II."

The emerging musical skills that Cartwright was discovering were further expanded as his ears opened to the wave of roots-inspired, high-quality songwriting that could be heard on the FM dial in the early 1970s. In addition to the country sounds emanating from WWVA and other all-night country stations, Cartwright became enamored with the internationally celebrated pianists who were capturing the attention of radio disc jockeys and popular music journalists on both sides of the Atlantic. "Along the way, my brother tells me about these two piano players: Billy Joel and Elton John. In the seventies, of course, there was all kinds of music, like Leon Russell." Starting out like many novices, "plunking around," Lionel began to emulate the music that he heard on the radio. "I would go into the basement with these instruments and try to copy the songs [I heard on the radio], you know? And that's really how I learned to play."

Lionel did not remain a basement musician for long, though. As a teenager, during the heyday of community opry houses and country music venues in West Virginia and surrounding states, he was offered opportunities to perform and record as a soloist, a band member, and a session musician. "I started playing down around Milton on a show called the Mountaineer Opry down there, and gosh, I guess I was like fifteen years old. Played there about once a month, and from there, I got asked to be on a show in Columbus, Ohio, which was called the *Country Cavalcade*—WMNI over in Columbus, Ohio—and ended up doing some of my first recording sessions there, both as a singer and a session musician, so that was just amazing to get to go to a recording studio. That was a big deal in those days."

From those precocious beginnings, Cartwright was offered an opportunity to join one of the country singers he had heard over WWVA, the legendary Doc Williams. With his wife Chickie, Williams had dominated the airwaves throughout the northeastern United States since before the Second World War.[30] Doc "heard me play and asked me to go on the road with him," Cartwright recalls. "That year—I think I was seventeen that summer—I think I spent the year on the road with Doc. I played Dobro and carried a Wurlitzer piano around with me." Cartwright must have impressed Williams during that year on the road, because when the Jamboree's regular pianist left to join the road band of Nashville-based honky-tonk singer Faron Young, Lionel was invited to substitute as a pianist. "I think Danny White was the name of that piano player, and he was interesting because he had no fingers on his right hand. So he would switch his hands and play the bass—the alternating bass notes, you know—with his right hand which had no fingers, and he'd play the right hand with his left hand. So it was quite an amazing thing to watch this guy play piano. I had filled in for him one night. The second week that I went there and filled in, they asked me to come back, which had always been kind of a dream of mine. You know, living eight miles down the road, I had listened to the Jamboree in bed at night, Saturday nights, growing up with a transistor radio with an earphone."

From that second performance in February 1977 (which included a power outage and a concert hall lit by the fluorescence of a thousand chemical glow sticks), Cartwright became a mainstay at the Jamboree for the next five and a half years, during which time he was also a student at Wheeling College (now Wheeling Jesuit University). "I went to Wheeling College there," he observed, "because I didn't want to walk away from that job." The Jamboree hired him initially to serve as the house pianist, but he quickly rose to become the house band leader and, later, a featured singer, as well. The Jamboree afforded him the chance to meet and work with country musicians from around the region and the United States. "Every week, there would be a regional act at the first hour, which we would back up, and then the headline act, which was somebody having hits at the time. I remember Ricky Skaggs, Emmylou Harris, Ronnie Milsap, Buck Owens. I got to be a Buckaroo one night, which was a pretty big thrill."

After five and a half years with the *Jamboree*, Cartwright set off for Nashville with an untold wealth of valuable firsthand knowledge of country music and its musical and professional demands. Arriving in Music City in the late summer of 1982, he had leveraged his professional network to pave the road to some early opportunities in the city, but he was far from mercenary. Rather, as he describes it, his early national career was the result of being in the right place at the right time. Prior to coming to Nashville, the stage manager of the *Jamboree* connected Lionel with Art Rush, the long-time manager of singing cowboy star Roy Rogers and a former student at nearby West Liberty State College. After a meeting at a Rogers tribute in Portsmouth, Ohio, Cartwright and Rush entered into a partnership that would quickly yield new opportunities in the fledgling cable television scene. "Roy Rogers had a chain of fast food restaurants. Well, the guy that did the advertising for them was in Knoxville, Tennessee, and had just been hired to do a show for the Nashville Network. He had done a bunch of those old Opryland productions shows in the '70s and early '80s. My manager says, 'Hey, go out to this audition.' So I go out to Opryland and the little trailer down there, And I had a demo that I had recorded up in Wheeling—three songs—and sat down. They listened to it. I sat down and told them what I had done, and they hired me. They said, 'Well, do you want to be the music director and a singer on this show?' and I'm thinking, 'Heck, yeah,' you know? So they said, 'By the way, it's in Knoxville.' So that was a little deflating for me because I had only been in Nashville a couple of weeks, but it just sounded like such a great opportunity to do essentially exactly what I did on the Jamboree." The show—*I-40 Paradise*—ran for nearly three years on The Nashville Network and moved at a breakneck pace.[31] "We banged out a thirty-minute sitcom—no, twenty-two minutes, you know—but with two live songs to tape every day, five days a week, and then we went to four days a week."

The show also spawned a spinoff, *Picking at the Paradise*, which dispensed with the sitcom plot and focused instead on musical performances. "*Picking at the Paradise* was six to seven live-to-tape songs. We had two of those shows a day. So we did that during the summer, and we end up doing two seasons of that, which would have been 130 shows times six or seven songs. So it was really some pretty serious training of assimilating music and performing it." In addition to star vocalists Reba McEntire, Hoyt Axton, and John Cowan, Cartwright also championed Nashville's deep pool of instrumental talent, inviting mandolinists Jethro Burns and Red Rector, steel guitarist Buddy Emmons, fiddler Buddy Spicher, and banjoist Béla Fleck to share their talents on the program. But perhaps most important to Cartwright was the opportunity to meet his future wife Cindy, who also worked on the program and to whom he has been married for more than three decades.

Cartwright's Knoxville tapings also brought him face-to-face with one of the most significant songwriting teams to emerge from the Nashville Sound heyday of the 1960s: Felice and Boudleaux Bryant. Known for their celebrated compositions for the Everly Brothers ("Bye, Bye Love") and the Osborne Brothers ("Rocky Top"), the Bryants were fixtures in the Knoxville area, which they called home. For Cartwright, his first encounter with the Bryants was the realization of his boyhood country music dreams. "One day, this couple walked through, and I knew exactly who they were," he remembered. "One of the ways I learned songs when I was growing up in the basement was I subscribed to *Country Song Roundup*, and I remember buying my first copy in Point Pleasant, West Virginia, at Fruth Pharmacy. You know, it's kind of the opposite of *Playboy*. I didn't really buy it for the articles; I bought it for the song lyrics, because they would have, every month, the lyrics to the latest hit songs. I would go to Fisher's Big Wheel—that was up in Moundsville, West Virginia—and for sixty-three cents get a seven-inch single, take it home, learn it, and have the lyrics in front of me. So, anyway, as soon as this couple walks through the set of the TNN show we were doing, I remember their pictures from that magazine. And I thought, 'Oh my gosh! That's Boudleaux and Felice Bryant!' And, of course, I want to make a beeline for them. I mean, if you're going to meet some songwriters, I would think that they would certainly be on the list." From this original meeting, Cartwright worked with the Bryants, first featuring their Everly Brothers hits on the TNN show and later serving as the bandleader for the sessions documenting a musical that the Bryants were writing.

The Bryants' son Del, who worked at BMI and later went on to head it, helped Lionel break into the competitive Nashville songwriting scene. Recommending that Cartwright secure a publishing contract, Del steered him to Silverline-Goldline Music, a publishing house led by Noel Fox and owned by the popular country singing group the Oak Ridge Boys. Reflecting on his time in the Silverline-Goldline stable, Cartwright enthusiastically observed, "I'm telling you, that experience was my best experience in the music business. Period." Alongside Gail Davies, Gretchen Peters, and Steve Earle, he developed his craft and sought a hit. But even as they all chased success in the fast-paced and highly competitive music industry, Cartwright recalls, the Silverline-Goldline writers also found great joy in everyone's songwriting break-throughs and career milestones: "It was just magical. It was in an old house up at the top end of 16th Avenue, and we would go down there and write, or you would get with another person and write. There was a—I think it was a twelve-track—Akai machine where everybody cut their demos. But we would get together at the end of the day in the kitchen—the time of day that Noel referred to as 'beer-thirty'—and play each other's songs, man! We would play each other's songs. And it was about, 'Hey, now what did you write today? What did you write today?' And, oh my gosh, it was so inspiring! You could not *not* be inspired by that."

One of the more inspiring moments in Lionel's memory of this time came courtesy of Steve Earle, a songwriter who was beginning to draw attention for his abilities to tell the stories of working-class people in his 1986 album *Guitar Town*. "I remember one day, I was sitting up in one of the rooms upstairs. Again, it's this cool old house, right? This old two-story house, and I'm in one of those rooms with a desk and working on a song. And Steve Earle comes in, and, you know, he keeps throwing his head back to throw his hair out of his face, right? And he goes, 'Hey, man, can I play you something?' And I said, 'Yeah.' And I know that he and his band, the Dukes, were down in the basement cutting these demos. So he comes in, pops a cassette in the cassette player and plays me the just-mixed demo of 'Copperhead Road.' And he's like—I'm sitting in a chair, right? And he pulls up a chair, and he's like four feet in front of my face. He puts his elbows on

his knees and just stares me down the whole four-minute song. And it
was just the best!"

Unfortunately, the Shangri-La of Silverline-Goldline was short-
lived; after only two years or so on their roster, Cartwright found himself caught up in the wave of media conglomeration that hit Nashville
and the entire media industry in the late 1980s. Silverline-Goldline
was purchased by Lorimar, which was then purchased by Warner-
Chappell. Cartwright recalls that the atmosphere changed dramati-
cally as he and his peers left the creative oasis of their mom-and-pop
publisher for the increasingly corporate world of Warner-Chappell.
"I had some great times at Warner-Chappell, but it was never that
[Silverline-Goldline atmosphere] again because Warner-Chappell had
like eighty writers. So it was a very different, very much more corporate environment. And I don't know, man. That never was a fit for me,
just the whole 'whatever-it-takes-to-get-a-hit' thing. And, hey, we all
want hits. But it's just a mindset shift. Instead of celebrating each other's creativity and just being blown away and cheering each other on.
Had I not had that experience, you know, listening to Steve Earle sing
a song or listening to what Gail Davies was doing, or Harry Stinson or
Gretchen Peters, you know, then I wouldn't have anyone to compare it
to. But I just know that there was so much soul in that environment,
and it wasn't that we were clueless about the business side of the business, but we valued the songs more than we did unit sales or money."

Despite the increasing corporatization of the Nashville music
industry in the late 1980s, country radio was turning away from the
slick productions and pop crossovers that had dominated its playlists
in the years following the national success of the John Travolta-starring
Urban Cowboy. This "neotraditional" movement first emerged around
the "Class of 1986," which included Dwight Yoakam, Randy Travis,
and Ricky Van Shelton and was characterized by an embrace of the
honky-tonk sounds of the 1950s and the Bakersfield Sound that Buck
Owens and Merle Haggard made popular in the 1960s. Cartwright
caught the second wave of the neotraditional movement as part of the
"Class of '89," which included such stars as Mary Chapin Carpenter,
Trisha Yearwood, Travis Tritt, and Clint Black. While he was writing
for Silverline-Goldline, Cartwright had signed a recording contract

with Tony Brown, then the head of MCA Nashville. They had first crossed paths during his Knoxville days on The Nashville Network, but by 1986, Cartwright had become part of the MCA roster, the label for which he recorded three albums: *Lionel Cartwright* (1989), *I Watched It on the Radio* (1990), and *Chasin' the Sun* (1991). But it was the title track of his second album that drew the national spotlight his way.

The song, which explores his deep personal experiences with his transistor radio in the 1960s, emerged from a co-writing session with award-winning songwriter Don Schlitz, who is probably best known as the writer of Kenny Rogers's mega-hit "The Gambler." But, as Lionel recalls, the song had a long gestation period: "I had a little, just a tiny spiral notebook that I would keep in my back pocket, so any time a song idea came along, I'd write it down. Travis, I bet I had that idea on that pad for like eight years." Inspired by the 1965 Connie Smith hit "Tiny Blue Transistor Radio" (penned by Nashville songwriting legend Bill Anderson), he had always wanted to write a song about his own love of the radio. When Schlitz heard Cartwright perform at a TNN taping, he approached Lionel to invite him to a co-writing session: "I've not really been a big co-writer, but, of course, I wanted to write with Don because he was just a legendary writer around town. We got together to write, and, when you do these co-writes, you are expected to bring something to the table. He said, 'Hey, I just wrote with Ronnie Milsap the other day.' And I said, 'Oh, gosh, I've always loved Ronnie Milsap.' He said, 'Yeah, man, you should see the collection of old-time radios he has.' And I'd heard about that collection. I'd heard it's incredible. I said, 'Man, that reminds me of an idea. I've had the idea of sneaking a transistor radio to bed and listening to it with an earphone and, you know, just the world coming to you.' And I kid you not, he picks up the guitar and says, 'Hey, I had one, too. It was a six-transistor.' He said, 'You know what a six-transistor is?' I said, 'No, I just thought you called it a 'transistor radio.' But he strummed a chord and [Cartwright sings] 'Had a six-transistor when I was a kid. / Under my pillow, I kept it hid. / When the lights went out and no one could see, / over the airwaves, the world came to me.' And in two-and-a-half or three hours, that song was done." The song, "I Watched It All (On My Radio)," skyrocketed up the charts as it resonated with many listeners who saw the radio as a window to a much broader world than the ones they inhabited, eventually reaching #8 on *Billboard's* "Hot Country Songs" chart in 1990.[32]

Just as Cartwright's solo career was starting to take off, though, he began to wonder whether the constant search for a hit was something that thrilled him. After three albums for MCA and a number-one single with 1991's "Leap of Faith," Cartwright—always a behind-the-scenes guy who played and sang well and wrote compelling songs—looked at the corporate music industry and the increasing competitiveness of the Nashville scene and opted to step aside at the peak of his popularity.[33] Following the rise of arena country superstar Garth Brooks, whose media juggernaut was fueled in part by the development of more accurate sales reporting figures, Cartwright just didn't feel at home in the business anymore. "When Garth came along, when that kind of level of sales that was absolutely unprecedented [became more common], [the industry] changed, you know? And it became about [sales], and that's fine. But I just, I felt that was kind of a beginning of a kind of separation for me. I don't want to speak for anybody else, so I'll just speak for myself. I missed the heart. I missed some of the soul that had been, to me, so central in artists like everybody from Mary Chapin [Carpenter] to Merle Haggard to James Taylor to, you know, you can go on and on and on. So I started looking in other wells, in other pools of styles for inspiration, and then they were out there."

In 1998, Lionel produced and funded an independent album of ten songs, for which he wrote all the material. Sharing it with radio disc jockeys, he found that one of the songs was gaining some traction. Thinking that he might have something valuable on his hands, he "got the crazy idea that I was going to release it as a single and send it out to the same radio stations I always called [when I was promoting my MCA material]. So I sent a single out, man, and darned if it didn't get picked up by a couple of reporting stations."[34] Mailing gold compact discs with black print to disc jockeys across the United States, he gained the attention of the head of record promotion at Asylum Records, a subsidiary of Warner Brothers, who showed interest in picking up the album. But, seeing that the Nashville industry was focused primarily on sales and not on artistry, he opted to keep it independent.

Since 2001, Lionel has channeled much of his musical creativity into his work at Bellevue Community Church (now HopePark Church), where he serves as the musical director. The Nashville worship center boasts a high-caliber group of musicians, including legendary Nashville multi-instrumentalist Charlie McCoy, another West Virginia native. "We [Cindy and I] stumbled onto this church. It was just a little startup church. It was interdenominational, which I felt pretty strongly about. There's so much about church that had kind of been distasteful and even beyond that. But we tried this little church that was starting up and started going there and made some really good friends there. And they asked me to lead worship, and I said, 'Oh, man, that really not my thing.' But they kept asking." Eventually, Cartwright relented and agreed to sing for a service. Selecting the Don Schlitz-Paul Overstreet song "Like Father, Like Son"—a song that he had been performing live for several years—as his debut, he blanked on the lyrics, which, he recalls, "was only made more humiliating by the fact that Paul Overstreet happened to be sitting in the room."

Having now served in the music ministry for more than fifteen years, Cartwright points to the great fortune that he has to mentor young musicians and to point them down a path toward personal and professional success. "What's been fun is to be able to be kind of a mentor to some of the ridiculous players coming in. A lot of them are young. Not all of them. It's really great to get to be part of their lives and help cultivate and maybe hopefully reinforce some healthy mindsets. But I really resonate with these guys."

Talking to Lionel Cartwright, one gets the sense that he is profoundly grateful for the opportunities that have come his way. Whereas many artists and songwriters might be bitter about the timing of his recording career, Cartwright recalls his excitement for the chance to make three major-label albums. From a dedicated music nut pulling country songs apart in his Glen Dale basement to a dedicated music nut pulling Bon Iver songs apart with teenaged church musicians, Cartwright has chosen to pursue a life in which he can be at peace while creating music on his own terms. Now, as he approaches his sixth decade, the mysteries of music excite him as much, if not more, than they did when he started.

DISCOGRAPHY[35]

Lionel Cartwright, MCA Records MCA-42276 (1989).
I Watched It on the Radio, MCA Records MCAD-42336 (1990).
Chasin' the Sun, MCA Records MCAD-10307 (1991).

TARYN THOMAS

Just as many of the more experienced songwriters in the state did when they were younger, a new generation of songwriters is beginning to emerge among a vast pool of teenagers and twenty-somethings who write songs for their own benefit and the entertainment of their friends. The majority of young songwriters will never leave their bedrooms with their original creations because they may fear that their songs sound embarrassingly personal at a critical time in their social development, or embarrassingly derivative of contemporary popular music. But some, like Ceredo-Kenova's Taryn Thomas, take the first courageous steps to share their songs with others and to make a mark in the regional and national music scenes.

The twenty-three-year-old Thomas moved to Ceredo-Kenova when she was only five years old when her mother moved her family from Leonardtown, Maryland, to start a life with Thomas's stepfather. Music wasn't really an important part of her life growing up, at least until her teenaged years. "There's one person that I can think of [in my family] that plays music, but I was never really around her: my cousin Stephanie. My mom can hold a tune, but she'd probably never tell you that. My grandfather from Maryland loved country music, and he would always play it on his own big boombox out on the back deck, and we'd go swimming and grill out and pick blue crabs, and it was just the best time. And I just always remember listening to, you know, Shania Twain and Tim McGraw, the Dixie Chicks, that kind of thing." But it was the emergence of country-pop superstar Taylor Swift that encouraged her to try her hand at music. "Honestly, I would be a fool if I didn't give the credit to Taylor Swift," she reflected. "I never got the idea to pick up a guitar until I saw her doing it, because no one around me had a guitar. No one was singing. No one was doing that. It was all sports stuff. That's, you know, small town. You're playing football. You're cheering. And I was doing all that, too. But whenever I saw Taylor Swift, that kind of interested me a little bit, and I was like, 'Oh, wow!'" Swift's first single, 2007's "Tim McGraw," resonated particularly well with the then thirteen-year-old Thomas. "I just feel in love with it," she recalled. "First of all because I already love Tim McGraw. And then there's this girl singing about it and playing guitar, and she wrote her own music."

When the opportunity arose, Thomas got her hands on a guitar at a cousin's house and began to learn how to play, first thanks to her cousin showing her a few chords and soon thereafter in lessons with Paul Williamson at the Music Box in Ceredo-Kenova. The first song she learned was Swift's debut single, and as her confidence and musical vocabulary grew, she was soon writing songs of her own and performing them in public, although her peers made her nervous. "The first place that I probably played in public," Thomas remembered, "was at my church. It's a Methodist church. I remember I wrote my first song, and it was a Christian song, and it was called 'You're the Only Way.' And I was saying, you know, 'You're the only way to go, God.' You know, 'This is what I want to do.' And I felt at that moment that God kind of blessed me with that gift and kind of opened that door to me whenever I opened up to him. And so I started playing at church, and I played that song. And then from there, once I got into high school, I didn't make the cheerleading team, and I was really, really bummed about that. But that gave me the opportunity to do nothing but play my guitar and, you know, write songs about not being invited to these parties and that kind of thing."

High school talent shows allowed Thomas to perform for a potentially more hostile crowd of her classmates, but she remembers that they gave her a generally positive response. "I would never want to play there again. It's terrifying," she opined. "You're up there in front of your friends. They all know you, and either you do really well and they love you or they're going to make fun of you for the rest of your high school days. They actually responded really, really well to me even though, if you were to look back on those videos, they would probably be really, really bad." Upon graduation, her classmates demonstrated their appreciation of her talents by naming her the most musical female in her graduating class.

During high school, Thomas also began courting some professional opportunities, submitting materials to talent scouts in hopes of reaching a wider audience. One of the earliest opportunities to arise from this effort came during her ninth grade year, when she was asked to sing the national anthem at a minor league baseball game for the Southern Maryland Blue Crabs. "I remember I was sitting in class in ninth grade in my social studies class, and, over the loudspeaker, they announced that I was going to be singing the national anthem at the Blue Crabs game, and everyone was so excited." By her senior year, Thomas also had a major audition with top-forty country singer Billy Currington, who was scheduled to perform in nearby Huntington. "I was listening to our country radio station, which was 103.3," she noted. "They mentioned, you know, auditioning for Billy Currington to sing with him at his show. And they were saying, you know, call this number and sing with him at his show. And they were saying, you know, call this number and sing us a line of one of the songs and then we'll tell you if you're in or not." She called, sang for the radio host, and was invited to sing an audition for Currington. Unfortunately, she didn't know the song that Currington wanted to hear, so she spent much of the next day and a half trying to learn it for the audition. Ultimately, though, her lack of familiarity with the song doomed her audition, but she walked away with free concert tickets and important critical feedback from a professional country artist. "All of the contestants," Thomas remembered, "got to meet him, and he told us what he liked and what he didn't like, and it was definitely really cool."

After her Currington experience, Thomas formed a duo called Allure with her friend Gabe Smith. Performing current hits of the Civil Wars and similar duos, Thomas and Smith decided to travel to

Cincinnati to attend a concert by the popular rock group Train. On their way there, Thomas received a text message "saying that Train had just tweeted out that they needed a girl for this song as a duet for tonight's show. And we all just looked at each other, and we were like, 'Okay, we've gotta go this!'" To submit the required video audition, they found a Guitar Center store and recorded a performance in the acoustic guitar showroom. "We just sent it in, and it was just for fun. We got there, and then someone calls me, and they're like, 'I am Train's personal assistant or tour manager, and we were just wondering if you'd like to sing for us tonight.'" Rehearsing in the car, Thomas secured the song in her memory and arrived at the venue ready to join lead singer Pat Monahan on stage. As she was asking the backstage crew for an earpiece, she realized that "this is mainly a thing that they do just to interact with their fans, not to, you know, have someone perform, per se. But most of them, you know, get up there, and he just kind of holds the mic in front of you when it's your turn to sing. And most people kind of freeze and don't say anything or sing badly or whatever, and I just got up there and sang the best I could and had the best time. There were about five thousand people there, and that was probably the moment that just confirmed everything for me. Like, 'Wow! If I can do this, this is what I want!'" Later on, Thomas attended a few more Train shows, and, during one concert in Washington, DC, Monahan recognized her and invited her to sing onstage again.

Feeling the desire for wider success and ready to make a move, Thomas followed the path of her original inspiration, Taylor Swift, and decided that the time was right to move to Nashville. In 2014, she moved to Music City with the full support of her mother, who told her, "You can go to school any time. It's always there. If you want to go to Nashville and pursue this, like, I'm totally behind you." Working with producer Ken Wells, Thomas developed a self-titled EP, which was released in 2014 and features several songs that Thomas hopes will help her find success in Nashville.

Twenty years old and in Nashville permanently, Thomas took a waitressing job on Lower Broadway before moving to the Commodore Grille at the Vanderbilt Holiday Inn, which hosts songwriter rounds each night. Before long, she leveraged her waitressing gig into a professional music-making opportunity. "We didn't have any music starting until about eight o'clock [on Tuesdays]. And so I thought, even though I was new to town, maybe I can do something for those couple of hours and, you know, bring in more people. It'll give me the opportunity to play. And so I asked my boss one day, you know, kind of pitched that idea to him, and he said yes!" Since March 2015, Thomas has hosted the "Artist Round" to support developing songwriters.

Thomas has quickly learned the lessons that come to many aspiring Nashville musicians: writing by yourself won't get you far, and writing with others can be the key to success. One of her earliest co-writing experiences was with prolific Nashville songwriter Bill DiLuigi. Thomas recalls that, "still to this day, I love looking back at that write. We wrote a song called 'When You Were You,' and it was just about, you know, one of my old, so-called boyfriends that acted where I thought he was a different person, basically. So we wrote a song about that. It was awesome. And so, from there, because Bill was such a nice guy, he started introducing me to some of his songwriting friends in town. And that's kind of how it works. You write with one person, and they have a circle of writers that they write with. If they like you and, you know, you guys have a good write, then they're going to introduce you to these people."

As Thomas continues to make progress as a writer and an artist, she has set her sights on a sustainable life in Music City. "If I make money at what I do," she theorized, "that's really, really, really cool. And if I don't, this is all I know, so this is all I can do. And so I'm going to keep doing it because I love it."

DISCOGRAPHY

Taryn, Go Time Records (2014).

· · · ·

———

Figure 9. Patrick Stanley
(photo by Melissa Stillwell, courtesy of Patrick Stanley).

· · · ·

PATRICK STANLEY

In the past few years, Huntington, West Virginia, has become the epicenter of an energetic indie rock scene that is heavily influenced by the Americana music movement. One of the principal bands in this scene is The Horse Traders, a group that blends the hard rock sounds of the more recent Drive-By Truckers releases with Muscle Shoals soul and the more introspective songs from the John Prine catalog. Key to The Horse Traders' recent success is the songwriting of Patrick Stanley, a native of Ona and Huntington and an English teacher at Huntington Covenant School. "Essentially, The Horse Traders is the merging of songwriters who just happen to play different instruments, and so all of us are writing songs and all of us are singing, which is really fun, having three-part, four-part harmonies. So we play a lot of my songs," Stanley notes. "We play a lot of the other guys' songs, too, and it's really fun to sort of transform them, messing around that way."

Stanley's songwriting is deeply influenced by the rich veins of American literature, especially the writing of some of Appalachia's most significant novelists and poets. He immersed himself in this tradition during his undergraduate studies at Marshall University, where he majored in journalism. "Studying English here made me self-aware of why I was doing what I was doing," he recalled. "I took an Appalachian fiction and poetry course, and that course sort of let me step back from my life and see the influence of story in my own growth and in my family heritage and traditions and things like that. So that's when I suppose that my writing took a direction that was mainly focused in stories and ultimately, I guess, Appalachian stories because everything that I have to say—even though it's not directly about the area—is inherently also about being from here." The course was an especially powerful tool in helping Stanley appreciate his family's storytelling traditions. He reflected, "More than specifically appreciating the authors in that class, it made me appreciate the culture of my family and the storytelling that was involved in that. I have these memories of this sort of annual pseudo-family reunion that we have, and through my childhood, we would always go to my grandmother's house. And both of my uncles would be in. My mom and my great-aunt would be there, and just family friends. So every year, it would be this big group of people, and it would be the same stories that we told every year, but like a different person would tell it each year, so being able to see that as something that is super important in my upbringing and my identity."

Appalachian stories abound in Stanley's songwriting, ranging from the dark and tragic to the warm and uplifting. "Even Mountains Can Fall," for example, is a meditation on the exploitation of Appalachian people and land in an era of late coal that draws upon a long tradition of mine disaster songs. Yet, rather than sentimentalizing the noble miners who perish needlessly in pursuit of the valuable fossil fuel or the devastated families of those left behind at Sago, Upper Big Branch, Farmington, and Monongah, Stanley approaches the subject matter-of-factly, almost as if the constant experience of death and near-death in the coalfields is as banal as the day's high school sports scores. Emergency phone calls are placed, families come together to pray for their loved ones, and preachers offer familiar bromides about dead fathers, brothers, uncles, and sons being "in a better place." Transformed from a plodding narrative in his 2014 solo EP *Dirt* to an out-of-control overdriven rocker in The Horse Traders' 2016 EP *I Don't Mind*, "Even Mountains Can Fall" explores both the superficial stoicism so often depicted in reportage about Appalachian people and the emotional turmoil and grief that rages just beneath the surface. Inspired in part by Jeff Ellis's driving "The Men of the Sago Mine" and the stories of Coalwood friend Emily Buckberry and celebrated Coalwood author Homer Hickam, Stanley set out to explore the "costs" of coal in contemporary West Virginia. "Is it [coal] something that we need to take pride in?" he asked. "Is it something that we need to get over? Is it both? So that song, it's sort of enigmatic in a way because it's a relatively upbeat song. The music of it is relatively jovial, but it's a heavy one. I guess that was my exercise in tribute to a truly West Virginian song."

Being a native of the Huntington area, Stanley's view of the Mountain State is shaped as much by the Midwestern landscapes that expand westward from the city as by the mountains to his back. "Mark Twain," for instance, explores the riverboat culture that connects Huntington to the vast inland riverine superhighway that provided an invaluable asset to the United States as it industrialized the nation's midsection in the nineteenth and early twentieth centuries. An effort in "rewriting and fictionalizing Mark Twain's personal history," the song also explores the complex and sometimes turbulent relationship between a father and his son, especially as the father—a symbol of strength and authority—begins to cede power and control to the next generation. Examining the fragility of masculine façades and the vulnerability that becomes all the more common as we age, "Mark Twain" also treats the river as a vehicle to escape the limitations of a life bound by a lack of economic opportunities. As Stanley observed, rivers played a significant role in his own life from an early age, including helping him conceptualize his own father's masculinity: "Where I grew up in Ona was right on the Mud River, so it was just this tiny dirty little river. But you sort of live and die by the flooding of that and, you know, playing by the banks, so that's an important thing. And the Ohio River stories my dad always used to tell stories about. When he was young, he would take his sailboat out and lose it in the water during a storm."

In addition to writing songs and playing throughout the Kanawha and Ohio Valleys with The Horse Traders, Stanley has committed a substantial amount of his energy to encouraging the younger generation to develop their own creative voices. As an English teacher at Huntington's Covenant School, Stanley engages students in discussions of poetry, novels, and songs. "I do a poet a week," he explained, "so every week, we'll come in and there will be a new poet and, at the end of the class—sort of as a way to get everybody together—we just read the poem together and talk about it for ten minutes. So last year [2015], I started with the poet Robert Zimmerman. I was like, 'Has anyone ever heard of Robert Zimmerman?', and they were like, 'No, we don't know who this is.' And so I told them that it was Bob Dylan. A lot of them had heard of him, so we listened to song versions of all the poems that we had read all week. That was the coolest experience because, in my seventh grade class, it was just this ornery little group of kids [who], to the last day of school, would come in singing 'Who Killed Davy Moore?'"

Stanley sees his collective work as an opportunity to challenge prevailing notions of the state and its people, and to provide alternative narratives for his generation and the kids that he teaches every day. "I don't think the great Appalachian story has been told," he reflected. "I don't think it's possible. I think, because of the nature of this area and the attitudes of the people here, that any sort of introspection into any sort of problems, or just any cultural evaluation, is a sort of treason to the area, and you see that in a lot of different ways. We had *Jamie Oliver's Food Revolution* [a television series intended to teach healthy eating habits to Huntingtonians] here, and without even knowing what the implications of that were going to be, without ever knowing the ideologies behind it, people were like, 'Get out of here! We don't need you to come in here and tell us about ourselves.' And I think that's the thing that comes out of this sort of inferiority complex, and it comes out of a place of hurt. We're taken advantage of in the cultural sense because we're depicted as this no-toothed hillbilly-with-overalls kind of character as an entire community, and there's a lot of hurt and there's a lot of resentment. I think that even the sweetest songs that come from here still hold that. That's why I feel like West Virginia music doesn't feel like it needs to stretch its borders: because you don't need validation from anyone else to say 'That's great' or 'That's good,' because your hurt is your hurt."

DISCOGRAPHY

WITH HORSE TRADERS:

Did You Forget to Leave This in Durango?, self-published (2014).

Take It, self-published (2015).

I Don't Mind, self-published (2016).

In Between (split EP with Reverend Hilton), self-published (2017).

AS A SOLO ARTIST:

Dirt, self-published (2014).

• • • •

———

Figure 10. Jim Savarino
(photo by Bob Durbin, courtesy of Jim Savarino).

• • • •

JIM SAVARINO

Wheeling native Jim Savarino has had a curious life, one shaped by external forces that have pushed him toward new adventures and that have been guided by an innate curiosity about the major problems of the world and a desire to find ways to contribute to their solution. A former Marine with extensive graduate training, Savarino is a bona fide rocket scientist who has worked on a variety of projects for NASA. He has developed interests in a number of disciplines and has worked with university professors to understand their research. (In fact, he served as a research assistant on this book because he was curious about the work that I do.) But if you were to ask him about his deepest passions, music would be at the top of his list. As a professional songwriter, Savarino has joined communities of successful songwriters wherever he has lived in order to develop his craft, build his network, and enjoy the companionship of other troubadours around the United States.

Savarino's earliest musical memories are of the *Wheeling Jamboree*, which he heard from the time he was an infant. Born in 1954, Savarino was literally raised at the *Jamboree* thanks to his mother, who worked at Capitol Music Hall, the program's home. "My one sister is ten years older than me," he observed, "so she remembers me as a baby and a toddler. And she said that my mother often took me, and I would be hanging around on Hank Williams, Jr's lap and other people. They've got to hold the baby, right?" When he was a bit older, Jim was drawn to his father's Harmony guitar, which he used to pick out "Wildwood Flower" and some of the main riffs from pop radio of the day. He also recalls the influence of a particularly musical mail carrier, Mr. Paxton, who would occasionally ask to borrow the guitar so he could regale young Jim with a rendition of "Ghost Riders in the Sky."

Music was primarily a solitary endeavor for Savarino, who left home at fifteen and joined the Marines in 1972 at age seventeen. Stationed in El Toro, California, he worked as a radar technician end even earned a backseat license so he could fly the jets he worked with. "But after six flights and three in-flight emergencies," he noted, "I quit. And two of my bosses were killed, and this is not in combat. This is accidents." When he wasn't working on base, Savarino immersed himself in the Southern California country rock and singer-songwriter scene. "Toward the end of the Marine Corps, I actually had a band that was headquartering in my house," he said. "It wasn't my band. I wasn't doing music. I'd go see them all the time. The bandleader moved in with me because he needed a place to stay. And they'd have rehearsals at my house. They were folk-y, and each of them kind of brought their own talents, and they were from all over California. So I started getting into that acoustic music and more folk music at that time." Although he didn't play in public during the six years of his military service, he did play a lot in his spare time, leading one colleague to give him a guitar. He remembered, "Someone heard me playing guitar and gave me this guitar and took my crappier guitar and said, 'You need this.'"

When he left the Marines, Savarino completed an undergraduate degree in physics at California State University, Long Beach. Toward the end of his studies, he ventured into the music department, where he met two professors who were struck by his musical abilities. "I went to the music department," he recalled, "and knocked on a door, and there were two professors and a piano in there. And I went into the room, and I was like, 'Hey, can you guys tell me if I have any talent as a singer?' And they were laughing just like you are, and they said, 'Why would you want to do that?' And I said, 'I may want to do this one day, but I don't want to do it if I don't have talent.' And they laughed some more, just like you, and they said, 'Okay, I'll play. You sing. Just sing what I play.' And I did. And he said, 'Well, not only do have you have talent. You have perfect pitch!' and I said, 'I don't have perfect pitch.' And he said, 'What's that note?' And I said, 'C.' And he said, 'See, you have perfect pitch.' And I said, 'No, I memorized that from my piano at home.' So they said, 'We want you in our program,' and I said, 'No, I'm graduating this month.' And they said, 'What are you doing?' 'Well, I told you, I came to find out if I have some talent.' And they said, 'Well, this was *very* crazy!'"

Savarino graduated from Cal State, Long Beach in 1983 with a B.S. in physics, and he began working as a staff physicist at Delco Systems Operations.[36] After a couple of years, he decided that he wanted to pursue his education further, so he applied and was admitted to the PhD program in physics at Purdue University in Indiana. There, he met a graduate student in English who lived in the same dormitory as he did. After hearing Jim sing in the shower one day, the student encouraged him to sing at an open mic held at the campus coffeehouse. Savarino played open mics when he could, collaborating with fellow physics student Stewart Burnett until coursework got in the way. After two years at Purdue, Savarino decided that he had enough of graduate school and returned to California with a master's degree in hand.

His return to the Golden State in 1987 coincided with the rise of heavy metal and glam rock in southern California, and Savarino began to audition to sing in the bands that proliferated in the region's vibrant club scene. "I wasn't writing yet," he recalled, "but I started auditioning as a singer. They couldn't find enough singers for the bands. And I was trying to avoid heavy metal, and I would just ask them when they called on the phone, 'Well, what kind of music do you do?' And they would respond, 'We can't really explain it.' And it's *all* heavy metal. I finally got into a band called Razor Sharp, where the Zs were in opposite directions, and they really were more alternative than most of the heavy metal things I'd been bumping into. And so I was their singer for a while." That gig lasted until one day when the group brought Savarino a new song. "They handed me the lyric sheet of a new song, and it said, 'The headsman wields his bloody axe.' And I said, 'I'm sorry. I can't do this with a serious face.'" After finding a new singer for the group, Savarino left Razor Sharp behind.

By 1989, Savarino—who described himself at that time as "pretty much a ballad person"—had quit his job at Rockwell Aerospace to devote his full attention to music, despite his fiancée's skepticism. To convince her of his sincerity, he struck a deal with her. "I foolishly promised her that, if I did music," he recalled, "I would try it for a year, and if I didn't make thirty thousand dollars, I would quit and go back to physics. After three months, I had spent about thirteen thousand dollars in recording costs and things and realized that not only was I not going to make thirty thousand, I wasn't going to make anything. So I went and started getting part-time jobs." Thankfully, friends and fans continued to encourage him—and his wife Shirley—to keep up the fight, which he continues to do to this day.

As Savarino was developing his musical career, he began to write some of his own songs for the first time. With the help of guitarist Tim Long, he learned to accompany himself. As he built a catalog of original material at the close of the 1980s, he cut a few demos and played the open mic circuit, often accompanied by guitarist Josh Balbien, who has appeared on two of Savarino's albums. "We met at an open mic, and he played for the Diamonds, and they traveled around the world," Savarino remembered. "He was an excellent guitar player, and he just sort of latched on to me at an open mic and said, 'I'm going to help you. I like your songs.' And we became fast friends, and we did a lot of work together. And at that time, I hadn't written a lot. He would play a little bit, and I would pick up the hard work and be the lead guitar, too." As part of the acoustic music community, Savarino was asked to participate in a Fast Folk album focused on Los Angeles. Through Fast Folk, organized by the New York songwriter Jack Hardy, Savarino's song received some radio airplay, which encouraged him to continue his efforts.[37]

For much of the middle of the 1990s, Savarino was playing paying gigs, such as the National Traditional Country Music Association's gathering in Iowa, while also working part-time to make ends meet. By the start of the new millennium, Savarino had returned to the Mountain State "to raise our daughter in nature."[38] As he built a network of venues to perform around the region, he also sought support for his burgeoning songwriting efforts by participating in two significant songwriting communities. The first of these was the venerable Kerrville Folk Festival, established in the 1970s by Austin, Texas, venue owner and music enthusiast Rod Kennedy.[39] There, he had the opportunity to rub elbows with dozens of exceptional writers, including Michael Elwood and Mike Williams. Since his first Kerrville Folk Festival in 1989, Savarino hasn't missed one, having attended his twenty-seventh gathering as of this writing. Savarino credits Kerrville with pushing him to write constantly. "There were so many good writers at Kerrville that it just kicked me in the pants, and I just did nothing but write. I would write twelve hours a day." The second was a songwriters' circle led by Jack Hardy, the Jack Hardy Songwriters' Exchange, which Savarino began to frequent after moving to New York in 2012. When he returned to Morgantown in 2014, he attempted to recreate the circle's spirit of mentorship, but found comparatively little interest.

Savarino has been a prolific songwriter over the past two decades or more, and unlike many of the state's singer-songwriters, he has committed many of his compositions to recording. Often filled with deeply spiritual lyrics and delicate accompaniments, Savarino's songs frequently deal with community, nature, and our individual and collective places in relation to them. A number of his songs have been written for the benefit of his community, from his song "Where Have All the Mountains Gone?," which he wrote for the West Virginia chapter of the Sierra Club, and "Far from Home," which was commissioned by the Prickett's Fort Foundation to become the theme song for the historic fort and state park in Marion County.[40] As of this writing, Savarino has returned to California to begin his retirement. Yet, during his two decades in the Mountain State, he worked to cultivate a degree of professionalism in himself and those around him.

SELECTED DISCOGRAPHY

The Man in the Street, self-published (1997).
Don't Let the World Get You Down, self-published (2002).
Sun Dreams, self-published (2009).

PART III:
THE EASTERN PANHANDLE

ROOTS
AND
BRANCHES

Figure 11. Adam Booth
(photo by Katelyn Stoneberger, courtesy of Adam Booth).

ADAM BOOTH

Adam Booth—known to his friends and colleagues as "Ad"—is a masterful storyteller. The Huntington native and Shepherdstown resident can be heard at festivals, fairs, and workshops around the state, as well as the National Storytelling Festival held in Jonesborough, Tennessee, presenting his own spirited tales of life in contemporary Appalachia. A student of folklore as well as a classically trained composer and musicologist, the thirty-five-year-old Booth creates original musical compositions that are filled with narrative richness, poetic symbolism, traditional simplicity, and carefully planned structure. Although he is not a songwriter in the same sense as many of the artists profiled in this book, Booth crafts memorable short compositions that distill the best elements of Appalachian songwriting and present them in a profound and moving manner.

Booth's interest in narrative and storytelling began early on in his childhood as he spent time with his paternal family in Wayne County. "My dad's family is from Wayne," he recalled. "My dad grew up in Wayne, and his mother grew up in Wayne, and his grandmother grew up in Wayne. I knew her and one of her sisters until I was in my early twenties. Family history was very important, and storytelling was very much a part of my upbringing. My dad's family has a pretty prominent place in the history of Wayne County, at least in the early twentieth century. My dad's great-grandfather, whom he knew, was the warden of the state penitentiary and had been the sheriff of Wayne County before he became a warden up in Moundsville. So my great-grandmother and her sister and my grandmother and her sister told me a lot of stories about what it was like because this relative of theirs was kind of a celebrity in Wayne County as the sheriff, and then a celebrity of the state because he worked with the governor. So these stories and others like them were very important to my upbringing and knowing what it was like to be from Wayne. We spent a lot of time, as they say back home, 'goin' out Wayne.' We'd go out Wayne to see some family. We would go out Wayne to Geraldine's to have a meal, the Wayne restaurant. Place was very important to my upbringing, knowing where you were from and what that meant, what it meant to be from this area." He reflects, "They really, like, took a needle and thread and sewed that into my upbringing."

On his mother's side of the family, Booth learned about the West Virginia experiences of his Jewish family, which came from Cincinnati and Philadelphia to Huntington, where they established a furniture business in the city's downtown. "I guess I had more of a sense of what it meant to be from a particular family [from my mom's family] because I think it was so important to them to retain their Jewish identity because they were like a little island of people. The congregation was in the midst of a bunch of people who weren't like them. There weren't as many stories on that side, but there was more of a reverence and an attitude about what it was like to be Jewish in West Virginia. Although they didn't really say 'Jewish in West Virginia.' It was just what it was like to be Jewish. On my mom's side, it was important to keep your culture and be aware of who you were, and practice and observation were important parts of my upbringing, even though I wasn't really raised religiously as Jewish. I was raised just culturally that way."

One of the rare music-oriented stories from Booth's extended family came from the Wayne County side. As he outlined his family genealogy for me, Booth recounted, "So my dad's mom is my grandmother. Her mother—who we call 'Mam-maw'—that's Hester Quimby. Her parents were Menis Ketchum and Granny Adkins, and their parents, they called him Wes Ketchum and his wife. They came from Lincoln County, and he had inherited a bunch of land. This is in the

1880s. He had inherited a bunch of land, and the timbering industry was bad for a couple of years because the winters were very mild, and so he had to sell his land to pay off the man. There is a story that was told in my family many times—I heard it from many different people—that they built a raft, what they called a long boat, and they put it in the Guyandotte River, and they sailed it down to the Ohio River, and they went down the Ohio until they got to the Big Sandy and got to Wayne. That's how we got to Wayne. But they had an organ, and they put it on the raft, and they took it with them because his wife—so that's my dad's mom's mom's dad's mom—played the organ, and they would stop every night and have a campfire and cook and everything, and she would play the organ, and they would tell stories that people would come out of the hills because they heard a pump organ playing, and they would sing hymns with her."

Although storytelling was an important part of Booth's early family life, music was not. Ever the folklorist, he has sought out information about music-making on both sides of the family, but musicians were hard to come by in his family. His paternal grandmother was a concert pianist who, Booth said in a follow-up email, "received a scholarship to attend CCM [Cincinnati Conservatory of Music], but didn't go because she married my grandfather."[41] Aside from his uncle Phil Booth, who attempted to build a songwriting career in Los Angeles, musicians were hard to come by in his extended family. "When I later realized . . . what a wealth, what a treasure it is to have Appalachian ballads passed down," Booth recalled, "I went seeking them, and I asked old people on both sides of the family to also try to get some of the Jewish things. 'Well, Uncle Jerry could sing,' my grandmother would tell me. That was my great-grandmother's brother, but he died way before I was around. 'Did anybody play violin or fiddle or anything?' 'No.' On my dad's side: 'Did anybody play banjo in the family or did anybody sing songs?' 'No, nope, no one really sang. No music.'"

Even if music wasn't an important part of family life, Booth recalled, he found himself powerfully moved by musical sounds, especially those that resonated with his emerging sense of self. "I can also recall one time when I was young," he reflected. "There was a concert of the *Sacred Service* by Ernest Bloch that was happening. I read about it in the paper, and I wanted to go. I don't know why we went, but I remember asking my dad if he would take me, and for some reason, he did, which is weird, because we never did things like that when I was young, especially to have my dad take me to the temple for that. But I remember it happened at temple in conjunction with Marshall University, and that's really a standout memory of hearing Jewish music as a kid."

Despite the dearth of music in his background, Booth notes that, "at a very young age, I decided that I wanted to be a composer. Young for, I think, the community where I grew up. I didn't do the Mozart thing. I was about eleven when I started writing music." Like many composers of his generation, Disney films provided the inspiration for his musical endeavors. "I wanted to write music for Disney movies," he remembered. "And I think what attracted me to it was that's it's a spectacle, you know? It's an amalgamated art form: you have the imagery, you get the drama, you hear the music. Sometimes, the music is in the foreground. Sometimes, it's underscore. All these beautiful things that come together just make people happy and sad and just experience storytelling. I was really captivated by that." In addition to Disney films, Booth learned about classical music through his sister's high school marching band experiences. "I'm not one of those that took piano lessons from a young age and learned Czerny and Mozart and Hanon and Beethoven, going through it that way. I came into it from a band route. My sister was in the marching band. I learned about entertaining an audience through marching band. Because my sister is seven years older than I am, I actually learned a lot of Romantic [nineteenth-century] orchestral repertoire that was covered by the marching band. So like *Damnation of Faust*, I learned through the marching band and drum corps."

Something of an autodidact and a self-described "geeky" person, Booth delved into the vast world of classical music during his free moments in middle and high school, encountering along the way some of the leading avant-garde composers of the twentieth century, including Charleston native George Crumb. "Because of my schedule in middle school, I had a free period. So [during] that free period, three of my friends and I just got together in the library, and they had this book of instruments of the world. I just devoured it, and somehow in there, I got turned on to these other composers because, when you get to the electronic instrument section, then you learn about Edgard Varèse and John Cage and the early innovators in tape and electronic instruments and so on. And somewhere along the way, George Crumb was in there. I remember hearing a piece of music at a concert at Marshall, and I want to say that it was part of *Music for a Summer Evening* [Booth later noted that it was *Makrokosmos*] by George Crumb. And then I went to the Governor's School of the Arts, and I found a few pieces by Crumb and Steve Reich and Varèse and just was so into them. But Crumb really stood out to me."

Like Crumb, whose works frequently evoke Appalachian sound-scapes by manipulating the timbre (or character of sound) of the instruments he uses, Booth too found himself attracted to non-standard sound combinations. "My dad and my grandfather, when I was growing up, just could identify birds [aurally], and that was a big part of my childhood, listening to birds. And even today, if I go back home with my dad, he can just listen to birds and pick them out. And I guess I've learned some of that, and I wanted that sound in my music." One instrument that stands out to Booth is the organ, an instrument with seemingly endless sonic possibilities. "I'm infatuated with the organ, and it's an instrument that I just don't fully understand. They are just such an enigma to me because they can do so much, you know? And also, from a young age, I've been fascinated by carousel organs. Endlessly fascinated by them. Like if I'm anywhere and there is a carousel, if I know there is a carousel nearby, I'll go out of my way and ride it if there is an authentic organ on it and not just a recording of an organ. I love them! I love them! Like the only bass drum that sounds like a bass drum on a carousel is the bass drum on a carousel, you know? It doesn't sound like a real bass drum, you know? It's just so fantastic to me. There's like a built-in Doppler effect, you know? It comes and then it goes and then it comes and then it goes. If you pay attention to it, you can almost catch a quarter-step difference in pitch when you're on the far side of the carousel. I just love those things!"

Upon graduating from high school, Booth moved to the University of South Carolina in Columbia, where he enrolled in the undergraduate composition program and began a serious study of music theory. But it was during his graduate studies in musicology at Case Western Reserve University in Cleveland that he began to understand fully the complexity of some of the vernacular musics around him. "I went to school in Cleveland," he remarked. "Case Western Reserve was where I did my graduate work, but they have a partnership with the institute of the Cleveland Institute of Music. So I took a lot of like, theory and, like, twentieth-century harmony applications at CIM, like improvisation and jazz. I'm very theoretical. I understand theory really well, music theory. I was getting into that like in piano playing. And then I was attending a church up there that was an international church, and the music was led by a woman who had grown up basically in an African American musical tradition. It wasn't gospel, and it wasn't spirituals, but it was somewhere kin to that, and I started playing second piano to her. And man, she blew my mind! She was doing things that they wouldn't even begin to teach me at CIM. CIM taught me the theory behind it, so I understood, like, sliding chords and octatonic replacements and things like that for substitute chords. But man, playing next to her? We'd be playing along, and she'd just shout out 'A-flat!' and we would have like, you know, two beats to modulate to A-flat from whatever key I was in. You know, you learn a whole lot about that. . . . When I came back here and started listening to Ethel Caffie Austin play, I was like, 'Oh! I get what she's doing!'"

Also during his graduate studies, Booth further explored a musical repertory that had fascinated him since his undergraduate days: twentieth-century American opera. "I was just really infatuated by American opera," he recalled. The University of South Carolina "had an extensive library of opera scores and opera recordings, and I just devoured them. I listened to so many by, you know, all these composers. Like operas that have never been mounted since the first time, composers that we don't even hear about anymore. And some of them are so good, you know? It's really interesting, the stories. You can divide them into three categories: American literature turned into opera, operas based on American folktales, or operas based on American identity. And I was just so intrigued by that, and I wrote a few small chamber operas while I was in undergrad. So I go to college and get my master's degree, and I'm still interested in John Cage. I really like minimalists. I still like opera. What am I going to do? I had found this opera on a recording by the New York Philharmonic, and it was one of Lukas Foss's operas they had done in concert called *Introductions and Goodbyes*. And it's so basic. It's like a crescendo-decrescendo form, if you will. These guests show up at a cocktail party, and they meet each other, and they have ridiculous names, and then they leave and say goodbye to each other. It's about nine minutes. There was something about the construction that intrigued me, and so I ended up working on Lukas Foss. And it just so happened that my advisor's friend worked with him, so I got to interview him, and I was able to contact some of the people who had premiered the piece who remembered it and remembered working with Foss and Bernstein in like, 1960, and it was a great experience."

Although Booth is quick to note that Foss's music was not a direct influence on his own compositions, his largest musical composition to date, the album-length sage *The Mountain Came Alive* (2013), certainly bears the traces of intense compositional forethought. His first compact disc, the Storytelling World Award-winning *The Mingo Black*, showcased his professional storytelling, which he had been doing since 2006, and introduced him to the particular challenges of compact disc production. While driving to a National Storytelling Festival in Jonesborough, Tennessee, he began to develop a vision for a new album that showcased his many creative strengths. "It's a long drive from where I live to Jonesborough, and the best way I can describe it is that I just had a vision of this album, and it was one of those moments where all these ideas just creatively came to me. And it was all I could do get them jotted down quickly before I lost it all, you know? I know I was going to create an album. I knew it was going to be called *The Mountain Came Alive*. Like, the title was there. I had an idea for what the project was going to look like, that it was going to be some sort of calendar year and that there were certain tone colors that were going to help portray the seasons of the year." Inspired by his recent work in support of efforts to stop mountaintop removal coal mining in Appalachia, *The Mountain Came Alive* draws upon the vibrant musical traditions of the people inhabiting the mountain communities directly affected by the invasive coal mining technique, especially the sounds of balladry and the mountain dulcimer. "I'm thinking that it's going to be Appalachian, so I want to use roots music in it. I want each of the parts to have some elements of roots music. So I started drafting what the roots styles were going to be, and I made a big list, and some of them didn't even make it into it."

Even as the ideas came quickly, Booth was careful to consider the nuances of formal structure and counterpoint, two of the major hallmarks of classical composition. "Each of the sections of this album, I'm just talking about places I've been," he observed. "And so there's a part where I'm describing Helvetia. Now, it's not Helvetia in the story, but to me, that's what it looks like. And there's a part—and this is close to the beginning—where I tried to do a bit of a Percy Grainger thing on the piano, and, you know, he took all those folk songs and arranged them for piano. So what I did was, I took the dance rhythms of flatfooting and also I took the West Virginia state song ["The West Virginia Hills"] and tried to make a Percy Grainger version of the West Virginia state song." Booth also explained that a central melodic motive that he composed, when layered with "The West Virginia Hills," united the entire album. Similarly, a formal process of expanding a chorus helps to give shape to the album's form. "If I were to map the whole thing out and you were to go about one-sixth from the beginning and one from the end, there's an idea that happens where each of the songs has an expanding chorus where, each time a new line of the chorus comes back, it's a little bit longer, and that's just like a mirror thing. You know, I'm very formally oriented because that's how I work. I make sense out of a piece by giving it that structure."

Booth has continued to write compelling stories enhanced with song since the success of *The Mountain Came Alive*. Most recently, he has taken on the mythology surrounding the historic 1927 Bristol Sessions, which gave rise to early country music recording stars Jimmie Rodgers and the Carter Family.[42] *Ashton* (2016) blends well-known Carter Family favorites, such as "Bury Me Beneath the Weeping Willow," with familiar Appalachian ballads such as "Fair Maiden in the Garden" and original songs that help to tie the narrative together.[43]

Adam Booth is many things creatively, and describing his musical work as "songwriting" might seem like a bit of a stretch, especially considering the many insights and influences that he draws from the realm of classical music. But, if songwriting is simply telling a good story with the aid of music, then Booth's work certainly fits the criteria. A masterful and award-winning storyteller, Booth knows that the key for telling a good story—like the epic poets of old—is balancing sublime details with a compelling form. And in *The Mountain Came Alive* and *Ashton*, he does just that.

———

DISCOGRAPHY

The Mingo Black, self-published (2012)
The Mountain Came Alive, self-published (2013).
210, self-published (2015).
Ashton, self-published (2016).

• • • •

Figure 12. Chelsea McBee
(photo by Brittney Butler, courtesy of Chelsea McBee).

• • • •

CHELSEA MCBEE

Shepherdstown native Chelsea McBee has almost always been drawn to the stage. Currently an integral part of the nationally touring Christian Lopez Band, a teenaged McBee had aspirations to take Broadway by storm. "I grew up in Shepherdstown, then I went to high school down in D.C. at the Duke Ellington School for the Arts," she recounted. "I was actually a theater major there and was going to maybe go to college in New York City and become a star of stage and screen. But that's not what happened at all!" she laughed. "Theater certainly helped me be aware of stage presence, and maybe it helped with things like character development [in my songwriting]."

McBee's early life was one filled with song, although she reflects that she "never really thought of myself as much of a singer." Her family was a musical one. "My stepfather is very musical," she noted. "He, you know, plays piano and bass. He's been in several bands as we grew up together, and he played the piano at church, which was actually where my mom met him. And she sang in groups and stuff when she was growing up, too." Her mother, particularly, encouraged Chelsea to find her voice. "My mom would make us sing," she recalled. "She taught us to sing harmonies on road trips. Like, we would all be singing along to, like, the pop-country songs of the '90s in the minivan, and I'm sure it was just because we were all terribly annoying and she was trying to get us to not kill each other in the car! But now I'm thankful for that because we all have decent ears and we can harmonize with each other. And, you know, with anybody."

After her high school studies at the Duke Ellington School for the Arts, McBee returned to Shepherdstown where, in 2002, she enrolled in undergraduate studies in photography at Shepherd University, eventually completing a Bachelor of Fine Arts there in 2006. It was during this time that McBee began to develop an interest in old-time string band music and the banjo. "I haven't really done anything with that [undergraduate degree] since then because my senior year of college is when I first started playing banjo. There's a man named Ben Townsend that is from Romney, West Virginia. It was 2005 when I was living with him in Martinsburg. And he had an extra banjo, and he would, you know, play old-time tunes around the house all the time, and one day, I asked if he would teach me. I had a favorite Gillian Welch song that I had just been listening and listening to ['My First Lover'], and there was a really cool banjo line in it. And I asked him if he could teach me that, and he said, 'Nope, I won't do that, but I'll teach you these old-time West Virginia tunes!' And so he did. I learned a handful of tunes from him, and then he ended up moving back home to Romney for a while, and I moved back to Shepherdstown. But I ended up with his old banjo."

The banjo provided an entrée into the world of old-time string band jams around Shepherdstown. "The first one that he taught me was 'Boil Them Cabbage Down,' which is a very simple tune," she recounted. "And then it was probably 'Angeline the Baker,' which is, you know, everybody knows that one if you go to any old-time jam. And 'Soldier's Joy.' So those were all the D tunes, but then he would do D tunes and A tunes, because you know, he played with old-time jams and with fiddle players, and so those were the two categories. And he started taking me to the old-time jams in Shepherdstown. I wasn't familiar enough with the instrument yet to really be able to just pick it up while we were there, so I would make notes. Like, 'Okay, I really like that song.' Try to remember what that was called. 'I really liked that one. Now show me how to do these.' So then we started to move on to A tunes like 'Old Joe Clark' and 'Cluck Old Hen' and 'Goin' Across the Sea.' So those are some of my favorite ones. They were my first ones."

One of the primary centers for these old-time jams was the Mecklenberg Inn on German Street in Shepherdstown where, when McBee was starting out, old-time musician and current member of Old Crow Medicine Show Chance McCoy led the jam. "If you've never been to the Meck," she observes, "it's this great old bar and right on the main street in Shepherdstown. It's like the 'townie' bar. You know, the place next door is, like, the pizza place with the college bar downstairs, but this is like the old people and the people that grew up in the town. It's really wonderful. But it's divided so that there's the front room that has the bar and some seating, and then there's a middle room that's just tables and chairs, and then a third room that is the dart room, and then a beautiful garden in the back. And there's a woodstove in the center room, so I would go to these jams in the winter. You know, everyone sits in a circle and calls out tunes and plays, and the woodstove is going. It's a magical memory for me because it was such a cool space."

The influence of old-time music is quite profound in McBee's original songs and selection of cover songs for her live performances and recordings. She has recorded such well-traveled Appalachian songs as "The Cuckoo" and "The Wind and the Rain," as well as the Scottish song "The Parting Glass." But, unlike many Appalachian songwriters who frequently trace the influence of Anglo-American song traditions to either local culture or recordings made by artists of the post-World War II folk revival, McBee came to some of this music through the work of contemporary Americana artists. "'The Wind and the Rain'—the first version that I'd heard of that was one that Gillian Welch sang on, and she's got such a, you know, great voice and delivery. Oh, that song is so haunting and tragic and beautiful. So I heard that and I thought, 'I want to create that same kind of feeling. And at that point, the only way that I necessarily knew how to do that was to use that song. Like just put our own spin on it and hope that we get that same kind of reaction." Recorded with her mother and sister for *The Whiskey Album* in 2013, the Chelsea McBee version echoed the sounds of the Wailing Jennies, a popular vocal group that made waves on the Americana charts around that time.

Around the same time that McBee picked up the banjo and began to learn about traditional Appalachian string band music, she also began to try her hand at songwriting. Finding a welcoming venue in an open-mic night hosted by Shepherdstown songwriter Bob Keel at the Mecklenberg Inn, McBee tested her singing, playing, and writing skills before a warm audience. "I was never going to be the best clawhammer banjo player in the world," she observed, "so I thought that I had better do something else with it. No, as much as I love old-time music, I really was interested in figuring out what else I could do with the instrument. Not necessarily, like, crazy stuff. Just, you know, how far can I push that traditional style and still have it be recognized as that traditional style? So, you know, the first couple songs that I wrote were really, like, the same kind of structure as an old-time tune. You know, AABB, and so my first couple of tunes were structured the same way. But then I started listening to more music that wasn't on the radio, and I started learning other peoples' songs that weren't old-time tunes. And like, okay, if I can learn this Bob Dylan song while still playing clawhammer banjo, I could probably write something else that's not necessarily in that same format but still use this clawhammer style. So then I started writing other stuff that was more of a contemporary song structure, I would say." Songs like "Bitter Root," "Miner's Minor," and "Mountain Girl," therefore, often sound as though they could be found in the pages of the Child ballad collections or in the discographies of early country music recording artists, but they are wholly original. At the same time, they channel the spirit—lyrically and musically—of McBee's Appalachian forebears.

"Bitter Root," for instance, captures the feminist spirit of songs by the Carter Family and Cousin Emmy by making a case for women's independence. "I certainly started out with those songs," she recalled. "That's the kind of person that I like to be. Certainly, I would love to see myself as a strong, fair, independent person. Not in a negative way. In just a very positive, I can do all of this on my own, and I have, and I do [kind of way]. But none of those songs are ultra-personal. You know, they are also what I would like to see from my sisters and from my female friends. None of the songs that I've written until more recently have been terribly personal. It's really just kind of creating the stories that I would want to hear or that I would expect from myself."

"Miner's Minor," too, draws on Appalachian history and culture to respond to the ongoing debate around mountaintop removal (MTR) coal mining practices in the state. Describing herself as "not necessarily the kind of person that would talk about my opinions, you know, especially in a group of people that I don't know very well," McBee became involved in the MTR issue when a friend of hers hosted an event at his house featuring a speaker from Keepers of the Mountains, an activist group based in Kanawha County. "There was this meeting going on at my friend's house," she recounted, "so I went over and sat down and listened. And it was the first time that I had really paid attention to a lot of what this group of people were saying. You know, I was like, 'All right. I get it.' And then I started doing a little more research on it and the history of mining in West Virginia." Another friend, a union organizer for the United Steelworks, introduced her to a wide range of labor songs, including the work of Utah Phillips and Florence Reece's "Which Side Are You On?" But McBee found that she could be persuaded by the binarisms of labor and environmental rhetoric. "I don't necessarily need to be on one side or another, but I could certainly take pieces from these other things and create a story based on what I've found out. You know, talking about the company store. Really these, at that point, men only, you know, dedicating their entire lives to this corporation to support their family. But really, it's not a win-win situation. But I'm also not from that part of the state, you know, so I also wanted to be careful. You know, here I live in the Eastern Panhandle, which is not the same. I try and be careful not to be too [much] one side or the other. And really, this is just a story based on the information I've had, inspired by what I was hearing at the meeting that was going on in my town."

McBee's understanding of the complexities around the anti-MTR movement grew even deeper when she traveled to Kayford Mountain in Boone County to play at a Keepers of the Mountains event. "The community pavilion is in the center, and then there's a mine on *this* mountain and a mine on *this* mountain," she recalled, indicating that the Kayford Mountain site is surrounded by MTR operations. "I cannot imagine living in this situation. So as the night goes on, you know, everybody's brought this potluck. There's all this food, families. Everybody is camping. It's really a wonderful, celebratory, fun place. And I play my set, and everybody is really supportive and wonderful. And, you know, people are dancing to the old-time tunes, and it's really great! It's such a wonderful space. And then it gets to be later in the evening, and pickup trucks are driving up and down the road right past the community center, and it's all the miners. They start throwing stuff at people, like throwing their beer cans at people, and at one point, a truck comes up to the community center and they just start, like, walking through the crowd being really aggressive. And so I left. I mean, we were supposed to camp and then do another show the next day as part of the whole weekend celebration, and I just went to the organizer and was like, 'I'm really sorry. I need to go. I'm not interested in being a part of this. I'm just not.' So I left that night, and everything was fine. You know, nothing super-dramatic happened or anything like that. I have a whole new perspective on this now just because I hadn't been there before. And I can really understand where the miners were coming from, too, because as far as they're concerned, this is their job and this is how they're supporting their family. And what do you know, supporting your family in a different way, trying to tell me that I'm not right?"

As a performing songwriter, McBee has made every effort to develop a fan base not just in the Eastern Panhandle and the surrounding D.C. and Northern Virginia area, but across the United States. With the support of Bob Keel, she developed a reliable thirty-minute set that she felt confident with, often alternating sets with Keel. It wasn't long before she was invited to join a tour with the group The Fox Hunt. "So I had almost finished recording my [first] album," she recalled. "I'd say we had like five songs finished and ready to go. So I printed out some, you know, homemade copies of the EP. They [The Fox Hunt] were going on this trip. They had booked a wedding on Vashon Island, which is just outside of Seattle, Washington. I think, if I remember correctly, the bride and groom had heard them busking in the subway in D.C. I kind of invited myself along on that trip. So, you know, I thought I would really love to experience [touring], to get some sort of idea of if that's something that I want to do. Because there are many different ways that I think you could choose to present your songs. Maybe being on the road all the time and going to new places, playing live music to people who have never heard of me before, maybe that's what I want to do. I don't know." Following behind the band in a vegetable oil-fueled car, McBee played across the nation's northern tier, visiting venues in Wisconsin, Idaho, and Washington, among other places. Unfortunately, her car's fuel filter failed as a consequence of her homemade biofuel, almost leaving her stranded with only a little bit of cash. "So I found this woman who ran a general store/nursery on Vashon Island," she recalled. "I had been asking around town [to find work to pay for the repair]. She said, 'Sure, you remind me of a young me. Come into the garden and pull these weeds.' And I did. For a couple of days, I would just go out there and pull weeds and talk with her, you know. Her story was very similar to mine in that she kind of just ended up there and then really loved it and just never left. And she wasn't really a musician herself, but she really loved music. So she was really happy to be supporting me. And then, at the end of those three days, she was very dear and paid me more than I deserved for those three days of weed pulling. But then I was able to take my car to the shop and get a new fuel filter and then be on my way."

After a decade of touring with her group The Random Assortment, as a soloist, and with a long-time member of the Christian Lopez Band, McBee still looks forward to returning home to Shepherdstown. "I've visited and played in a lot of really wonderful, beautiful places with wonderful people, you know," she reflected. "And I've really felt like, if I had to, these [places] would be an okay place for me to live. Like, I could be happy here. But it's never been so moving that I went home and packed up. Because I know what I have there." This sentiment is expressed most clearly in her song "West Virginia Line," which she describes as "very personal. It feels like the first time that I've really felt very personal about a song. And it's not about, you know, sneaking anywhere in the middle of the night or feeling one way or another about a coal mine. But that's really what my life is right now: being excited to go and travel and experience and play music for people who have never heard of me and hopefully win them over with, you know, the first couple songs. But I also feel real glad that my home is back in West Virginia and I get to go home and I get to be *at* home, even if it's for a couple days sometimes, you know? As long as I get to town before the bars close after a show, I always go down. I don't always have a drink, but just to go, 'Oh, this is my bar. These are my people. I feel good now. Now I can go home and go to bed!'"

DISCOGRAPHY

Don't Close Your Eyes (with the Fox Hunt), self-published (2008).
Bob Keel and Chelsea McBee, self-published (2009).
Put This In Your Jar (and Sip It), self-published (2011).
The Whiskey Album (with The Random Assortment), self-published (2013).

PART IV:
THE SOUTHERN COALFIELDS

THE
SPIRITUAL
HOME

ELAINE PURKEY[44]

"I don't consider myself a songwriter," Ranger, West Virginia's Elaine Purkey suggested. "I just happened along, and they needed me to do something when somebody needed something done." That attitude pervades Purkey's work, which has been focused on promoting the values of the labor movement and on organizing working people throughout Appalachia since the 1980s. A product of the United Mine Workers of America (UMWA), the Highlander Center in Tennessee, and the various grassroots movements that have emerged around issues of environmental rights in the coalfields, Purkey has been an important leader in the musical and political realms for nearly four decades. A reluctant but passionate leader, Purkey's songs have unified a diverse group of people around a variety of social justice issues.

Purkey's journey toward a life focused on social justice began, like those of Aunt Molly Jackson and Florence Reece before her, as a consequence of her domestic relationship. Although she was not raised in a union household, her interest/involvement in organized labor began in earnest when she married her husband, Bethel, in 1970. "My dad was a railroad laborer," she recalled. "They didn't have a union worth a dime. I mean, any union that will let the bosses be members of it ain't worth nothin'. I didn't get involved in union activity until I married Bethel in 1970. He's a third-generation coal miner, and I always left that union stuff up to him. I mean, I was at home having babies, raising them, you know—just doing what I thought I was supposed to. Bethel was the one who was out working, earning a living for us." But when the UMWA went on strike against Pittston Coal in April 1989, Purkey felt compelled to get involved.[45] "Pittston took that way of life away from us," she said. "I couldn't stay at home and just cook and clean and take care of the kids and all that anymore. I had to get out and work. That's when I started learning about the union and about union activity, and what it means to be union, *and* the difference between union and non-union. I didn't even know that."

The men at the mine where Bethel worked began gathering materials to file unfair labor practice complaints around 1984. "They had to do that and go before the Labor Board to get approval to file an 'unfair labor practice' lawsuit against the company before they could call a strike," Purkey remembered. "Bethel became one of the key people in that whole strike in West Virginia when they needed something done or the media needed someone to interview. We were all busy pulling people together and planning for when the international UMWA president called the strike." But despite her involvement in the activities leading up to the strike, she was discouraged by the limited roles that women were permitted to play on the picket lines. "Women could go [to the picket lines], and they could cook and serve things like coffee and donuts," she remembered. But many of her female friends and neighbors challenged gender bias and stood alongside the men. "That's not all we did," Purkey noted. "Many women actually walked the picket lines, too. We had [a group known as] Friends and Family of the UMW. And I told them when they asked me to organize the group, 'I'm not going to be a party to creating something for a group of women that's just going to carry coffee and donuts. If we're going to start something, we're going to work, and we're going to be there until one or two o'clock in the morning. We're going to be a part of this whole thing and let them see the whole face of this strike and what this company is doing! Ya know? It's not just about the men working and getting paid more."

Purkey soon found herself traveling around the state giving speeches and leading meetings to help mobilize support for the striking UMWA miners. "Most people thought that strike was just about higher wages," she observed, "but it wasn't! The miners had one of the best hourly rates of any job in the state and they knew it. That strike was about guaranteed retirement benefits, better, safer working conditions, and continued health care at least as good as what was in the 1984 contract. Yes, they were asking for higher wages but they would have let that drop if they could have gotten the rest of it. Their retirement was not even guaranteed and it should have been. That's what we were fighting for. So, that's what I did. I traveled all over the state telling the Pittston Strike story in my songs, talking to people—different groups such as college groups and community organizations, library groups, about what the strike was really about. That was a big, big step from where I was when I married Bethel, because I didn't know anything about anything then. Why, I didn't even know what a union was good for or what it was supposed to do."

Long before she became involved in union leadership, Purkey was a passionate musician who embraced the country, bluegrass, and gospel sounds that flourished around Harts Creek during the 1950s and 1960s. Music, she recalled, was always in the background during her youth. "My mom is from a family of fourteen kids, and every one of them sang and almost every one of them could play guitar," she noted. "Any time any of us got together—we didn't always have a guitar, but we always had the music. When the girls—Mom and her sisters—started getting old enough, my Grandpa Shelton made sure they started singing. My uncle Clifford Shelton loved music. He loved singing. He was a tenor singer, so he got the girls together and formed a gospel group. In the early years, my mom was one of the group. However, I was only about nine months old, and my mom would carry me on her hip and stand up and sing with my Uncle Cliff and my Aunt Dot and my Aunt Ruth. They'd sing at churches and Old Time Singing Conventions and stuff like that."

Particularly powerful, Purkey recalled, was harmony singing, especially that style of harmony that derives from the a cappella style observed in the Churches of Christ in Harts Creek and surrounding areas.[46] "I remember after our three girls were born, I'd take them with me to church, I always sat behind my mom. Now, I was a grown woman with three kids of my own, mind you, and here I was sitting back there behind her, and she decides that this day she was going to sing alto.

Now, that church house was full—and she started singing alto—and I started crying and I didn't know why. I thought, 'Why in the world?'" But then she recalled a story that her mother had told her. "There's an old preacher here in this area, Vernon Mullins. He traveled around the area holding revivals at the different Churches of Christ. Well, he would get my mom and her sisters to go with him to sing because they didn't have songbooks to give to people to do the congregational singing like the church was accustomed to. Most places didn't have songbooks then, and they couldn't sing from memory very well, so he would just have the girls to sing and invite everybody to sing along with them if they wanted to and knew the words. They would start to sing. I would start to cry and Mommy would have to give me to somebody to take me outside or to the back of the church away from her because I just couldn't stand to hear her sing alto. It's just like it broke my heart. She had that lonesome, soulful voice that so many of the older singers have and I loved her so much that I just couldn't take it." At that point, Purkey knew what to do try to keep from crying in church that day. "I poked her on the shoulder. I said, 'I wish you would sing something else. Sing lead or tenor or something because I can't sing. She looked back at me, and I was booger-bawlin', and she just laughed. She switched off to tenor, and I was just fine after that."

Purkey was confronted with an opportunity to merge her passion for music with her passion for union work during the Pittston strike. To launch the strike, the UMWA organized a large rally in Castlewood, Virginia, at the high school and Purkey was asked to perform. "God, I guess there was like ten thousand people down at that high school," she remembered. "They wanted to have it close to the Pittston office, so we went down there. It wasn't too far away from there, and those guys were in their offices that Saturday, too. It was wild. They were in their offices Saturday just looking. They knew what was going on. They [the unions] had song leaders. I mean, singers and songwriters and such down there. Long-time workers' rights activists Guy and Candy Carawan [from the Highlander Center] were down there, and I tried to get Guy to play banjo for me because I just play guitar, and not very well, and boy was I nervous.[47] I had *never* done this on my own, but it was something that needed to be done. So, I played a few songs, and that got the whole ball rolling. People started calling, wanting me to come sing for them. I never actually applied for a performance job. They all came knockin' at my door, which was unusual to say the least, and that just started the whole thing. A whole new world opened up for me. I had no idea it would last this long, though. I thought when the strike ended so would the phone calls. However, it wasn't just the message in the songs I was writing that they wanted. It was the mountain culture in my voice and my speech that they heard. One lady told me one time when I was going to Chicago Folk Fest that I didn't even have to bring my guitar and I didn't even have to sing if I didn't want to. She said they would just sit and listen to me talk and tell the stories I tell. Of course, I thought she was just a little bit out of it but when I got there, the people at the festival told me the same thing. Weird!"

Two significant compositions resulted from Purkey's involvement with the Pittston strike: "One Day More" and "The Jack Rock Song." The latter documented the often-controversial practice of throwing homemade spikes fashioned from bent nails under the tires of the coal trucks to prevent the transport of coal to market during the strike. Positing that the jack rocks were created by woodland elves, the song drew inspiration from a popular television commercial. "It's supposed to be a labor song," she reflected. "But it's also a fun song. I mean, we know that little elves in hollow trees didn't make those jack rocks. However, there was a commercial floating around about that at one time with the Keebler Cookies. They were made by little elves in hollow trees, and I just thought it was a good turn on words, and used it to connect with now." The former, on the other hand, was a song of solidarity. In it, Purkey warned the company bosses that, no matter how long they intended to hold out in their negotiations, the union would last "one day more." With a hooky melody and a chorus built around the repetition of the title phrase, the song lends itself to group singing and, like so many great labor songs, new verses can be added to address the issues and circumstances of a particular strike. As a consequence, the song has been circulated widely throughout the labor community.

Purkey's performance at the Pittston strike kickoff rally drew the attention to longtime civil rights and labor leaders Guy and Candy Carawan, who headed the celebrated Highlander Center in

Tennessee. Through the Carawans, Purkey became acquainted with a number of left-leaning folk musicians and scholars. "I went up there [to Highlander] several times," she said. "Again, more education. And they had a friend of mine come up with me one time. He had written a song about Buffalo Creek, and they had him come up with me and he sang that song and we did some stuff." Folklorist Archie Green, author of the landmark study *Only a Miner: Studies in Recorded Coal-Mining Songs*, was also struck by Purkey's singing and repertoire.[48] "Archie is the nicest man," she remembered. "I met him in North Carolina, and he came looking for me. He said, 'I've got to talk to you. I just want to sit down and talk to you.' I said, 'Well, that's fine with me.' I didn't know exactly who he was at that time. And then we got started talking about that book that he had written, and I knew that book existed, but I didn't know that was the same person that wrote it. He said, 'If I live long enough, I plan on doing another one.' He said, 'Where were you in 1973?' I said, 'I was around, but I wasn't singing. I wasn't doing any union stuff. I wasn't even on the radio at that time,' and I said, 'That didn't happen until the '80s.' And he said, Well, I want you to know if I'd known about you then, I'd just tell everybody else they would have had to wait because I would have come to you first.' Lord, have mercy! And you know, Hazel [Dickens] is in there. Jean Ritchie is in there. And it's like, he can't mean that, you know. And I said, 'I don't understand.' And he said, 'You really don't understand, and that's what makes it so special.' He said, 'You just do what you feel.' And I said, 'Yes, that's true!'"

Throughout the 1980s and 1990s, Purkey became increasingly active in local and regional politics, often drawing attention to issues of economic injustice in the southern coalfields. But, at the same time, her music was in high demand, and to meet that demand, she formed a band that included a young bluegrass musician named Scott Holstein, who became a powerful songwriter in his own right. During this time, Purkey performed not only at union rallies but at such august venues as the Chicago Folk Festival and the Smithsonian Folklife Festival in Washington, D.C. Through this work, she met and became friends with Hazel Dickens and Alice Gerrard, both of whom were outspoken supporters of organized labor and the feminist movement of the late twentieth century.

In recent years, Purkey has become a significant figure in the preservation and pedagogy of Appalachian song. She has been involved with Davis and Elkins College's Augusta Heritage Center, not only teaching but committing her songs to the vast folklife repository there. She has been documented by the state of West Virginia as a master of Old Mountain Vocals and Dance, an honor that allows her to teach people about the tradition of Appalachian song, dance, and storytelling. And, for many years, she has been involved in the production of the Wallace Horn Friendly Neighbor Show, a community radio program taped in Chapmanville, broadcast on local radio from Logan, West Virginia, and reaches four states with more than five thousand listeners. There, she sings the traditional gospel, bluegrass, blues, and country music that she loves, and creates a safe place for the region's musicians to perform. Finally, Purkey teaches Appalachian music, history, and culture to children from kindergarten age through high school students in after-school programs for the Step by Step program through a grant from the Lyell B. Clay Center for the Arts in Charleston.

For nearly four decades, Elaine Purkey has been using her music and her outgoing personality to build relationships, challenge the status quo, and find ways for underprivileged people to gain access to the resources they need for a better life. Although she is not the most prolific songwriter in this study, her songs have had a widespread impact not only within the region but across the nation, even providing encouragement for striking truckers during a work stoppage on the West Coast. Like such celebrated coalfield labor songwriters as Reece, Jackson, Dickens, and Ritchie, Purkey has made a significant contribution by placing her personal experiences in the coalfields into song, universalizing them and building solidarity with others as a consequence.

SELECTED DISCOGRAPHY

Mountain Music/Mountain Struggle!, self-published (1993).
Classic Labor Songs from Smithsonian Folkways, Smithsonian Folkways SFW CD 40166 (2006).

———

Figure 13. Shirley Stewart Burns
(photo by Matthew Burns, courtesy of Shirley Stewart Burns).

SHIRLEY STEWART BURNS

"I was literally ten years old before I realized that everyone couldn't sing," Shirley Stewart Burns recalled. This came as quite a shock to the Wyoming County native, who was raised in a family that was constantly singing. Her father, Neely Stewart, sang everywhere the opportunity presented itself, and the opportunity presented itself quite often. A coal miner whose life was cut short by black lung, Neely sang southern gospel music and songs like "In the Pines" and "Dark as a Dungeon" for his fellow miners, and he frequently sang southern gospel music at churches throughout "the state and the southern states." Burns noted that one song, in particular, stood out for its ability to reach sinners and convert souls to Christ, "Run On" (a song later made popular by Johnny Cash under the title "God's Gonna Cut You Down"): "He loved doing that song. He would do it in the churches, and it was so interesting to watch, even as a child. It hit people where they lived. Daddy and the groups, they prayed before they sang, and they would let the spirit move them. They had songs that they were going to sing, but they let what they felt was the spirit lead them to sing what that church needed to hear. And that one almost always showed up."

Neely Stewart's conviction and dedication are not far from the surface in Burns's work as a musician and as a scholar. A historian who earned a doctorate from West Virginia University, Burns has worked tirelessly on behalf of the people of West Virginia throughout her life. After earning a bachelor's degree in journalism and a master's degree in social work, she worked full-time as a social worker advocating for people with mental health issues for a decade, while also pursuing a PhD in history to document the impact of mountaintop removal (MTR) coal mining on communities throughout southern West Virginia. Her award-winning dissertation—published as *Bringing Down the Mountains: The Impact of Mountaintop Removal on Southern West Virginia Communities, 1970–2004*—speaks on behalf of people who, as she argues, have been victimized by the coal industry: "I still believe that MTR is part of the social injustices of being poor. If this coal was in the middle of where rich people live, it would be a lot different. We, being Appalachians, are part of a throwaway America that's linked to poverty."[49]

Scholarship, songwriting, and autobiography come together in many of Burns's musical compositions. "Leave Those Mountains Down," in particular, bears witness to the integrity of her vision. Sung as an a cappella call to action, "Leave Those Mountains Down" calls for coal companies to stop the practice of MTR and to honor the ancient presence of the mountains instead of exploiting them for short-term economic gain. As with many of her compositions, Burns reports that "Leave Those Mountains Down" came to her "in a dream": "I could hear that melody, and then I heard the words. And then I heard in my dream, 'Wake up.' And I woke up, and I wrote it down, and I went back to sleep. I thought, 'I'm supposed to get this out there. People are supposed to hear it.'" Burns debuted the song at an anti-MTR rally in the 1990s—a time that anti-MTR support was still relatively confined to those areas that were most directly affected by the practice.

As she worked on her doctorate in history, Burns became a leading figure in both the academic and activist communities, organizing the first session devoted to MTR at the Appalachian Studies Association conference and the first event addressing MTR at West Virginia University, as well as becoming a fixture at rallies throughout the state. After a rally hosted by the Ohio Valley Environmental Coalition, oral historians and traditional musicians Michael and Carrie Kline approached Burns to record an album, *Coalfield A Cappella*. To that point, Burns had kept her academic and musical lives fairly separate, but all of that changed during an Appalachian Studies Association conference in 2008, when Michael Kline asked her to sing "Leave Those Mountains Down" during the question-and-answer session; after a brief moment of shock, she consented, surprising her colleagues in academia and activism alike: "A lot of people came up to me afterwards, including Judy Bonds, whom I adored and miss terribly. She came up to me, and she said, 'My God, girl! I didn't know you could do that.' And I said, 'Yeah.' A lot of the academics later said, 'I didn't know you could do that.' And I said, 'Well, yeah, I can do that.' And I remember one of the men I admire most in the world, Dwight Billings. He just came up to me and hugged me and said, 'Is there anything you can't do?'" She also performed the song at Carnegie Music Hall in Pittsburgh, a hall named for famed steel baron Andrew Carnegie, during an award ceremony recognizing her dissertation.⁵⁰ In her speech that evening, she noted, "It's a long way from Coon Branch Hollow in Matheny, West Virginia to standing before you tonight." "That's one of the highlights of my life," she later observed, "because so many things happened that day. There I was, the offspring of a coal miner and his wife, singing a song about the exploitation of the poor people and the environment in this complete and totally utter opulence with this huge statue of Carnegie staring down at me. It was amazing. And they stood up and clapped and whooped."

Coal looms large in Burns's songwriting, which isn't surprising given the impact that the industry has had on her family and her community. In songs such as "No Friend of Coal," "There Goes Another Mountain," and "Pretty Mountains" (the latter two co-written with her husband, Matthew), she documents the ways that MTR has devastated the environment and economy of the southern coalfields, constantly challenging the coal companies to justify their methods. Yet, as a miner's daughter, she is deeply sympathetic to the men and women who work underground, as songs such as "Coalfield Blues" demonstrate. "Ode to a Miner (Song for My Father)" recalls a familiar coal mining song trope, as a miner begs the "young ones" to find another way to provide for their families because "if mining don't kill you, black lung's still around." Burns recounted that she wrote the song after looking at the cover of a book about industrial workers: "On the cover of it is this really handsome miner covered in coal dust. And he reminded me so much of my daddy with his big blue eyes, and I looked at that picture one day, and I said, 'What . . . you're trying to say something with your eyes.' That's what I thought. 'What would you tell us if you could?' And I looked at my picture of my daddy, and I said, 'What would you tell us if you could? What would you say if you could speak? What would you say?' And that song just came to me, and in five minutes, it was done. I really believe that if my daddy could speak again, that's what he would have said.'" She noted, though, that while her father's struggle with black lung was deeply personal, "I know this didn't just happen to my father. My daddy is one of so many that this happened to, and if I could give them a voice by giving him a voice, then I think he would be really, really proud and happy of that."

Burns's passion for telling the stories of West Virginians from the southern coalfields can be traced not only to her family's deep connections to the industry, but also to fact that her academic training as an historian has shown her that the official histories of her home community were deeply biased in favor of the coal industry. "Every time we would go to the grocery store, we would get stopped by the train carrying the coal, carrying the riches out of our county to God knows where. I didn't think a thing about it in seventh grade when I opened up my history text and it said 'Courtesy of Eastern Associated Coal' until I became an adult and realized this is wrong, that it is wrong for any industry to be sponsoring education." She recalls one particularly brave teacher who challenged the prevailing narrative when he taught his class about the Battle of Blair Mountain, a landmark event in the so-called "mine wars" that ravaged the southern coalfields in the 1910s and 1920s: "I grew up near Logan, and I grew up near Blair Mountain. It was not mentioned in classes. I did not know about it. I had one teacher that was brave enough to shut the door and actually tell us in seventh grade about what happened, because he said [that] he thought we had the right to know what happened just fifteen miles away. Plus, some of us had relatives that had fought there. And so he told us about it, and then he went back and he opened the door. It was such a taboo subject that he felt the need to close the door to tell the story."

Burns's singing voice is as unadorned as the truths that she discloses in her songwriting and scholarship. Although she often hears her songs with instrumental accompaniment, she does not play any instruments and has not had the opportunity to *record* her work with a full band. Fortunately, her a cappella singing evokes the sounds of generations of singers who came before her and lets her words stand for themselves. For instance, of "Leave Those Mountains Down" she observed, "I clearly knew this song should never be sung with music behind it. This song is powerful enough to be sung a cappella." In "The Ballad of Fisherman's Holler," a murder ballad that turns the familiar plot of so many traditional Appalachian ballads on its head by casting the female protagonist as a murderer, Burns's voice betrays a fast vibrato that is reminiscent of Dolly Parton, a singer-songwriter whose own work articulates the power of Appalachian women to control their own destinies. And in "Ode to a Miner's Wife," Burns's deep chest voice matter-of-factly speaks for her mother, Cora, who was a widow in her mid-forties. Burns remarked, "My dad was the love of my mom's life, and vice versa." The directness heard in Burns's voice—coupled with the brisk tempo that she used in her recording of "Ode to a Miner's Wife"—reveals the anger that comes with the unnecessary loss of a loved one. This is not just a song of loss, but one of resentment.

Due to ongoing health concerns, Burns has not been able to perform in public since 2014, but she continues to write songs with seemingly tireless ambition. Knowing that one of her greatest dreams was to hear her songs performed with a full band, I began to feature her original songs in the set lists of the West Virginia University Bluegrass and Old-Time Bands, which I direct. Witnessing their success with our audiences, I began to develop plans to get her songs to a still broader audience. In 2016, with the support of a research grant from the West Virginia University Faculty Senate, I brought several of the state's leading musicians together in a series of recording sessions to produce an album showcasing Burns's remarkable songwriting. Titled *Long Time on This Mountain: The Songs of Shirley Stewart Burns*, the album features such luminaries as Ginny Hawker, Tracy Schwarz, and Rachel Eddy, as well as a number of musicians featured in this book, including Scott Holstein, Clinton Collins, and Steve Smith, and WVU Bluegrass and

Old-Time alums Hillary Kay, Judith Meyers, and Sophia Enriquez. The album was released in May 2017.

In her conviction and commitment to finding and reporting the truth, Shirley Stewart Burns is as unstoppable as the coal trains that passed through the Wyoming County of her youth. And, as she recalls, personal integrity and perseverance have been essential character traits since she was a little kid, even if some of her dreams seemed impossible for a child of West Virginia's southern coalfields. "I just had such a yearning for learning from a young age. People would say, 'What do you want to do when you grow up?' and I would look at them and say, 'I'm going to West Virginia University. I'm going to be a writer. And I'm going to sing.' And they'd pat my head and say, 'Okay.' Except my mom and dad, who'd say, 'You do that, baby girl. You can do that.' I believed it."

———

DISCOGRAPHY

Coalfield A Cappella, self-published (2009).
Coal Country Music, Heartwood (2010).
Long Time on This Mountain: The Songs of Shirley Stewart Burns,
    no publisher (2017).

ROGER BRYANT[51]

Logan County native Roger Bryant has been immersed in music since he was a child. His grandmother, "Aunt" Jennie Wilson, was a widely celebrated traditional singer, banjoist, and storyteller. Bryant grew up taking her around the state as folklorists and participants in the folk revival movement of the 1960s and early 1970s became interested in her work. "I actually started out being Aunt Jennie's chauffeur, and I was traveling, you know, driving her around from place to place. She became quite popular back in the late '60s, early '70s with the folk revival," Bryant recalls. "And so, [English professor and Appalachian music scholar] Pat Gainer up at WVU was the one who actually got her started, like, on a professional level, if you want to think of it that way. How it came about, Adda Batton, who was the principal of the grade school, attended an extension course in Appalachian Studies taught by Pat Gainer. The students had to bring in a guest, and she brought my grandmother in as a guest. She didn't own a banjo at the time and borrowed one from her neighbor, Howard McNeely. She entertained the class, and, of course, Pat Gainer, he just went ballistic. She was the real thing. She had lived life." As a teenager, then, Bryant accompanied Aunt Jennie to festivals and fairs where Gainer had arranged for her to play, including the West Virginia Folk Festival in Glenville. As he recalls, "from that, her fame kind of spread. Actually, internationally. Her obituary appeared in the London newspaper. Seems like there

• • • •

Figure 14. Roger Bryant in the late 1970s
(photo by Lana Kelsey, courtesy of Roger Bryant).

• • •

was always somebody working on a thesis, some research project or recording."

Even before he was chauffeuring Aunt Jennie, though, young Roger was appearing in public and broadcasting periodically on a program called the "Saturday Night Jamboree" on station WVOW or WLOG. "The radio station at that time was on the second floor of the bus station," he remembered. "I can remember standing on a stool and singing 'My Bucket's Got a Hole in It' on that Saturday night radio show." Aunt Jennie had "been after me to learn" to play and sing. His father, a watchmaker and jeweler, "could play anything with strings on it, but didn't because the calluses on his fingers made it difficult to handle the tools needed to repair watches. In addition to selling musical instruments, they had a record department in the jewelry store. So I grew up with music all around me." But despite the prodding and his exposure to music, Roger abandoned his music in junior high because music "wasn't a very cool thing to do" at that age.

After graduating from high school in 1966, Bryant became more involved in music, playing not only with Aunt Jennie but also with famed West Virginia traditional musicians Frank George and Russell Fluharty. As a group, they played not only at fairs and festivals throughout the state, but as far away as New York and Colorado. By 1968, Bryant and Wilson "started doing the grandmother-grandson act," even as Bryant was serving in the United States Marine Corps and completing his undergraduate studies at Marshall University in Huntington.

Bryant's engagement with traditional music has led him to favor musicians who can tell a good story in their songwriting, most notably Merle Haggard, Tom T. Hall, and John Prine, all of whom also have exerted a strong influence on Bryant's singing voice. Furthermore, Bryant prefers to deal with the lives of real people in his compositions, as in the song "Queen of the All-Night Coffee Shop," which appeared on his first album. He often writes in a manner that avoids figurative language in favor of everyday directness. Traditional music, he observes was "woven in the fabric" of Appalachian lives before the national media infiltrated the region. "The only entertainment they had was the entertainment that they made for themselves," he reflected. "It was common for Appalachian musicians to have jobs or farm, and they did not view music as a vocation. They would work hard and then they would play music. Even the stuff I write now is based on that concept of living an everyday life with work and families and drawing on those experiences. I don't do it consciously, but subconsciously. I think it fits in with that ballad-type, old mountain ballad kind of structure because that's my experience."

By about 1970, Bryant was beginning to explore a new interest in commercial country music. During his time at Marshall, he had learned that people enjoyed hearing him sing and play. "My dad bought me a guitar," he remembered. "It was a Yamaha, I remember, and he showed me three or four chords, enough that I could second after her [Aunt Jennie] playing the banjo. And so I started doing that, and that's how the thing started. And then, of course, I was going to college at the time, so all of a sudden, you know, people were inviting you to parties and stuff. They'd say, 'Oh yeah, bring your guitar.' And then, you know, they'd call and say, 'I'll give you fifty bucks to play for this spaghetti dinner,' you know, and so, from that, it kind of grew to where I was doing road shows with country stars and that kind of stuff. I did that for, I guess, about six years."

One gig in particular stands out: the halftime show of a West Virginia University Mountaineer Week football game. Bryant recall, "They had a haywagon. They were going to wheel me out at halftime, and right before I started out, it kind of started raining a little bit. And then these big hail balls started falling. They were—'bang, bang, bang'—hitting the guitar, and by the time I got out on the haywagon, there was about a half-inch of snow! And I'll never forget, because they had a microphone on that haywagon that they had drug out, and I leaned up to hit a low note, and my lips touched that microphone, and my hair stood out, and I let out this squeal, you know, like a girl, I guess or something. But it really lit me up!"

In 1975, Bryant began a two-year stint as an artist-in-residence in Tucker County through the same National Endowment for the Arts–funded program that brought future *Mountain Stage* co-founder Larry Groce to the Mountain State. Bryant recalls that his position with the Tucker County Arts Council may have allowed him to work in the schools—where he remembers helping to write a play in honor of the

1976 Bicentennial celebrations—but it also conspired to give him a rare opportunity to relax after several years as a road musician. "It was the only vacation I'd ever had," he observed, "because I was working in the school system, and it was those two bad winters and they didn't have school from November until April, so I learned how to ski and ride snowmobiles and all that kind of stuff, you know, and played shows at the ski lodge. And that was my residency when I was up there."

One of Bryant's most powerful early compositions, "Valley of Canaan," is set in the Tucker County ski country, but it actually pre-dated his residency there. The song was written in response to a proposed hydroelectric project that threatened the biologically diverse and aesthetically engaging valley. But, as Bryant remarked," At the time I wrote that song, I had never been to Canaan Valley. I had only seen it through [my friend] Bill Gehold's paintings. He kept telling me about Canaan Valley. And he had told me about the Davis Power Project. The residency probably came as a result of that song, 'Valley of Canaan.'"

At the conclusion of his Tucker County residency, Bryant had amassed a sizeable catalog of original songs and was hoping to break into a wider commercial market. Although he had recorded an eponymous album in Bill Carpenter's basement studio in Sutton, he did not have a professional-quality recording that would be suitable for radio airplay. With financial backing from the Kelsey family, friends of Bryant's, he traveled to Nashville to record his 1978 album *Allegheny* at Hilltop Studio. Roger grew up with Bradley's Barn engineer Vic Gabany, who engineered the album and, along with Jimmy Helms, produced it, as well. Featuring the contributions of Nashville session guitarist Jimmy Capps, fiddler Johnny Gimble, and steel guitarist Hal Rugg, *Allegheny* met with some success, with the single "Valley of Canaan" reaching the regional country charts.

Allegheny also featured a powerful pro-labor coal mining song, "Stop the Flow of Coal," which Bryant reissued on his album *On the Banks of Old Guyan* in 2002. Told from the perspective of a union miner who is traveling to Kentucky to stand in solidarity with fellow UMWA strikers, the song does not romanticize striking or the coal-mining life. Rather, it channels the rhetoric of solidarity to provide musical encouragement for the men and women standing on the front lines of the strike. "What I was trying to do with the song," Bryant reflected, "was document the nation's longest coal strike. I think it was '75, '76 at Rawl Sales, over the Kentucky border.[52] And I'd been reading in the newspaper, you know, where [the strikers] were going back and forth across the state line. That's the strike that's credited with busting the UMWA, incidentally. I was trying to document it through the eyes of a coal miner. My grandfather was one of the original UMWA members [in West Virginia] and was killed in a slate fall in '37. So my grandmother [Aunt Jennie], you know, got a widow's pension, so I was very UMWA-oriented in my thinking and in my life. You know, most of the people I cared about were coal miners and that sort of stuff. And so basically, I was trying to depict what that coal miner in that particular era, you know, what his life would be like. And I was trying to depict that in a song, kind of a mental video picture, if you would."

Among the UMWA rank and file, "Stop the Flow of Coal" was a juggernaut hit. Bryant remembers his surprise when he found his song referenced in a newspaper article about the strike. "My dad was having bypass surgery in the hospital over in Lexington, and so I was there with him. And I walked down in the lobby, and I picked up a newspaper, the Lexington paper. And on the headlines—I can't remember exactly what it said—but it said, you know, 'Song Strikes Violence in the Coalfields' or something like that. And I remember the first line because it said, 'Roger Bryant, a little-known folk singer from Logan, West Virginia, recorded a song that's getting a lot of airplay in the coalfields. However, requests for this song are offset by threats to blow up the radio station if they play it.' I'm sitting there reading about myself, and, of course, you know, people around me, they were reading the newspaper, and they had no idea that it's me sitting there in the lobby of this hospital!" In an effort to generate further support for the union, UMWA leaders "sent me all over the country singing that song." Unfortunately, Bryant remarked, the reception of "Stop the Flow of Coal" was not exactly what he had intended, as some people saw the song as a more overt political statement than he had hoped it to be. He observed, "The left-wing folks kind of grabbed ahold of that song, but really, my intent with the song was not so much a political statement as it was trying to paint a picture of what the coal miner's life was like during strike times."

Although *Allegheny* was received very well throughout Appalachia, Bryant found himself at a major turning point as he approached his thirtieth birthday. He had recognized early on that the work of maintaining an active performing career and teaching school full-time simply were not compatible activities, so he quit his teaching gig to pursue music full-time and promised himself that he would return to non-musical work when he turned thirty. But, due to *Allegheny*'s success, he delayed his return to non-musical employment to his thirty-first year, a year that happened to coincide with the birth of his daughter, Tressie. In 1979, he began working for the newly established Logan County Emergency Ambulance Service Authority, providing much-needed emergency medical services to the large coalfield county. "My first year's budget was $35,000, and I had to buy three ambulances, and I had to pay my salary and my secretary's salary." With his guidance, the Logan County EASA has grown exponentially, and Bryant is understandably proud of the role that his organization plays in the local community and its economy. "We're probably about a six-million-dollar-a-year business now, and we've got seventy-five employees and six stations." But even through the 1980s and 1990s, he still maintained his musical interests as time permitted, even as he dealt with the grief of losing his eldest daughter, Dawn Ann, in a car accident. As he recounted, "I really went through a bad spell. Grief sometimes inspires some people to write. It had an opposite effect on me. For years, I had no interest in writing. Performing was often painful."[53]

When celebrated old-time musician David O'Dell suggested that he and Roger work together on a new album in 2002, Bryant was still working through the grief. "I don't think I ever got over it," he reflected, "but I acclimated, at least to the point where I enjoy it [music] again."[54] The new album, *On the Banks of the Old Guyan*, paid tribute to many of the great songs that people had written about Logan County over the years, including Aunt Jennie Wilson's prisoner song that lent its title to the album. "I wanted to do that song," Bryant recalls, "and Dana Dorsey was a good friend of mine. Dana was a music teacher, bandleader, that sort of stuff. We'd get together, and we'd talk about songs that were native to this area, you know, like 'Vance's Confession.' To the best of my knowledge, those had not been collected, so I thought, just for no other reason, just for posterity's sake, we needed to get those down, and we need to get those recorded somewhere." In addition to the traditional songs recorded for *On the Banks of the Old Guyan*, Bryant included an original song based on historical research that had been published in the *Logan Banner*. "The Vixen of Stratton Street" tells the story of a real-life Logan County murder mystery. The song later grew into *Mamie*, a musical dealing with the case which was performed by the Aracoma Story as part of their summer theater series. Bryant wrote the soundtrack for the production.

Bryant has received numerous awards for his contributions to the people of Logan County and the state of West Virginia, including the prestigious Vandalia Award, which he received in 2014.[55] But when asked to describe his impact on musical life in the state, he points to the widespread growth of old-time jams across the Mountain State. "I hear a lot of the songs and a lot of the stuff that I did on stage thirty-five years ago. I hear those same things, you know, coming back at me from a lot of the younger folks. They say imitation's the highest form of flattery. I'd like to think I had an impact on that. I think if you go back and you look at those 4-H programs that Jane George and Frank George and Russell Fluharty and my grandmother and I did, I think you see a real influence, particularly if you go to places like Vandalia and the Appalachian String Band Festival. You know the folks who go on and they play publicly and that sort of stuff, but you don't know how many people that you've influenced that don't want to play publicly and never played in front of anybody except at the house, you know?" But as anyone who has shared a tune with him will tell you, his influence runs deep.

DISCOGRAPHY

Allegheny, self-published (1979).
On the Banks of Old Guyan, self-published (2002).
Mamie (Original Soundtrack), self-published (2015).

SCOTT HOLSTEIN

Bluegrass singer-songwriter Scott Holstein was raised in an environment that steeped him in the traditional bluegrass sounds of the Stanley Brothers and the lore of the southern coalfields. A native of Boone County, Holstein writes contemporary bluegrass songs that channel what Bill Monroe—the so-called "Father of Bluegrass"—described as "ancient tones," but with an ear toward modern recording practice and production techniques. These modern updates make his messages about coalfield deindustrialization, systemic multi-generational poverty, and environmental devastation all the more powerful. His 2011 album *Cold Coal Town*, featuring a band of Nashville studio hotshots led by dobroist Randy Kohrs, reveals a strain of bluegrass songwriting that eschews romantic tropes about Appalachian life and instead promulgates a harshly realistic, yet sympathetic, view of a region that remains a touchstone of Appalachian postindustrial abjection.

Holstein's view of life in the coalfields was indelibly shaped by his family's long involvement in the coal industry. His grandfather, Omer Holstein, fought at the Battle of Blair Mountain. Omer, Holstein notes, "was my dad's father. After he came back from World War I, there was another battle going on. It was in the coalfields, and the Battle of Blair Mountain happened. They took up arms and fought the coal thugs. A lot of things, you know, get swept under the rug of true history of what really went on, but quite a few people got killed in that. And when they

· · · ·

Figure 15. Scott Holstein
(photo courtesy of Scott Holstein/Coal Records).

· · · ·

were forced to lay down their arms—my grandfather had borrowed his rifle from his uncle, so he knew he couldn't return back home without that rifle—so he kind of hid his in the train car that was heading out, that they carried the bodies in. So once he got back near Camp Creek down there, he kind of got off the car, and they never got his rifle. That's how he got away with his. I'd love to have that rifle."

Early on, Holstein realized that music could provide an opportunity to follow a different path than his ancestors had, one that would allow him "to stay out of the coal mines," as he recollected. He recalled that his childhood and adolescence were filled with music, especially bluegrass music. "My parents played bluegrass gospel music when I was growing up, and I've been around that. It kind of led to instruments always being around. So, next thing you know, you're picking them up and playing them," he remembered. The bluegrass gospel groups featured Donald Ray White, who emceed their shows. "Donald Ray was actually the spokesman in the gospel group they had," Holstein recalled, "and he would do recitations, and they [his parents] would do the background music. I remember those the most, you know, because even then it'd just make you cry listening to that stuff." In the late 1970s, the group also performed a live radio program, which was broadcast over Madison radio station WWBB. "They done it live out of my Uncle Joe Turner's church in Camp Creek," he remembered, "which was one of the first snake-handling churches out those parts." His mother occasionally wrote songs, as Holstein reflected. "I would see her sit around and pen stuff down," he said, "and she'd have books of different songs she'd written. And I guess it all just came naturally."

Scott was but a kid when he made his public debut, playing with his parents' group at a Labor Day rally in Racine, West Virginia, in 1978 or 1979. "Senator Robert C. Byrd was there, and they got me onstage, and we played a set with him. I guess the feeling I got from the crowd, it probably got in my blood, you know?" His debut was documented in the *Coal Valley News*. "I had a little miniature guitar, and I had a little cowboy hat on, and I had a little badge on. I remember the little pin said, 'I Love Coal.'"

As Holstein became more interested in expressing himself musically, he found mentorship in a powerful labor songwriter and

traditional musician, Elaine Purkey. "You know, I never really took lessons, so I guess being around [music] and watching them, I learned
more that way. My parents started taking me out to the radio shows,
and one in particular, WVOW in Logan, *The Wallace Horn Friendly
Neighbor Show*. I ran into Elaine Purkey. She was an activist singer, and
she did a lot of music about coal and coal mines, protests, unions. She
kind of took me under her wing, and I started doing a lot of shows with
her." Purkey's songwriting struck him as direct and powerful. "Elaine,"
he recalled, "she was just a very poignant person and straight to the
point. And just the power she had with those words. It seemed like she
transcended a lot of boundaries. It may have made some people mad,
but most people got it." Together, Holstein and Purkey performed at the
National Folk Festival, where Scott had one of his first opportunities
to play for a large national audience and to show off his guitar, banjo,
and mandolin skills. He reprised his role with Purkey in 1997, when
she performed for the Smithsonian Festival of American Folklife as a
representative of Appalachia.[56] As Holstein observed, "She represented
the voice of Appalachia. And she made sure they heard her."

After graduating from high school, Holstein set out to build a
career in bluegrass music. In 1992, at Purkey's suggestion, he joined the
Gillis Brothers, a brother duet from Georgia that performed songs with
a Stanley Brothers-influenced sound, a sound that had been popular
for decades in the Boone County communities where he had grown
up. "It's pretty much like Boone County transplanted into the swamps,
you know?" Holstein remarked of the south Georgia home of the Gillis
Brothers. "I hooked up with them in the summer of 1992, and that was
at the Summersville festival," the august bluegrass festival that has been
staged in Nicholas County for the past four decades. "I'd graduated high
school," he recalled, "and Elaine had told me, she said, 'I met these boys
[at the Chicago Folk Festival].' She said, 'They're right up your alley.'
She says, 'They don't have a mandolin player with them.' She said, 'You
might want to check into that.' So I knew they were going to be close
at the time, and I packed the suitcase and a mandolin, and when they
showed up and the bus door opened, I was the first one they saw with
my hand out. I introduced myself and told him I was the man for the
job." Apparently, the Gillises were impressed with Scott's playing and

his eagerness, so "they hired me, and I think I went eight days and never seen a bed."

With the Gillis Brothers, Holstein toured the United States "from Florida to Maine, you know, to California" for most of the 1990s, all the while building a professional network and occasionally "trading off with other bands." By the early 2000s, Scott had left the group, which eventually broke up. He rejoined Larry Gillis in 2004, spending a two-year stint as a lead singer and allowing Larry to build an act so that, "if his brother wasn't interested in doing it, he didn't have to lay it down. So he kept the tradition going, I guess, as Ralph Stanley did," when his brother Carter died.

One of the musicians that Holstein came to know toward the end of his tenure with the Gillis Brothers was Dave Evans, a legendary bluegrass singer and banjoist whose powerful voice is one of the most raw and emotionally charged voices ever heard in the genre. "I started out playing mandolin with him," Holstein noted, "and later he moved me to lead guitar and singing lead for him. So yeah, that has always been a dream of mine, too, to get that job. We traveled many a mile together ourselves, you know? Dave offered me the full-time position if I'd take it and a partnership with him. And we did it as much as his health would hold up." Holstein notes that, "if it could be taught, I guess everyone would want to be able to sing like" Evans, who he describes as singing with high "heart and soul into it and you sing it like it's your last, you know? It comes from his toes all the way out."

After more than two decades as a bluegrass sideman, Holstein began to pursue a career as a solo artist around 2009, thanks in large part to the encouragement of two Nashville heavyweights: Randy Kohrs and Jim Lauderdale. "I spent a lot of time down in the South with the Gillis Brothers," he recalled, "and I met a lot of good people down there. They had a festival outside of Macon there. It was around Cochran, Georgia, I believe it was. Scott Brown had me down there as a guest and let me stay at his beautiful house there, and they had a beautiful festival going on. A couple of guys came in by the name of Randy Kohrs and Jim Lauderdale. Out of meeting Randy later on that evening, you know, we had a chance to do a few tunes together, and he said, 'Man, you need to be in Nashville. You get down there, I'll record you,' you know? So I made the point to try to get down there as quick as I could, you know. It took me a few more months to get things together, and once it did, you know, Randy was the first one I looked up. That led to *Cold Coal Town*, which is an album I've been wanting to do for quite some time, and it just couldn't have worked out any better."

Cold Coal Town, released in 2011 on Holstein's own Coal Records label, marked not only his first significant appearance as a lead vocalist on records, but as a songwriter, as well. The album is notably devoid of the heartache songs and testaments of religious faith that one typically finds on a contemporary bluegrass album. Instead, Holstein favors tales of "hard hit people" in the vein of Purkey and her friend and mentor Hazel Dickens. The album's title track, for instance, addresses the boom and bust cycles of the coal industry and the impact that they have on the people who live in coal towns throughout southern West Virginia. Holstein reflects that the song has its origins in his Boone County roots. "You know, my father never encouraged me to be a coal miner," he observed. "He always said that there's no future in it, you know. So it's good one day, and then it goes bad. And then if you study it, it's a history pattern of it, you know? It just seems that once they tell you you've got a forty-year job, it seems like all the young boys, they go in debt, and they buy 'em a house and have a family and the next thing you know, they don't have a job and they lose it all. That's just a recurring theme, I guess, throughout my life, and I've seen it too many times. I guess the thought of, you know, having to go back to the mines and fight in that whole spirit about it, you know, probably led to that song, you know? 'I'm trying to leave this cold coal town.'"

Holstein works hard to depict the experiences of his friends and family as he documents life in coal country. One such example is "Roll, Coal, Roll," a rhythmically pulsating bluegrass driver that explores the experiences of the truck drivers who haul coal from the mines. "Well, you know, it's trying to speak for my boys," he remarks. "You know, I've got a lot of friends that's in the mining business in some form or fashion. Or, if they're not in that, they're hauling coal. There's somebody somewhere, you know, that's in the coal mining industry that is effected by this. And I had an old boy who asked me, he said, 'You know, why don't you write a song about us truck drivers, you know?' So that always stuck in my head, you know?"

Perhaps the most moving song on *Cold Coal Town* is "Black Water," an a cappella ballad that recounts the devastating failure of a slag dam on Buffalo Creek that destroyed several Logan County communities, including the town of Man, in 1972.[57] Added to the album as an after-thought, "Black Water" matter-of-factly recalls the torrent of sludge water that powered through the valley below, bringing "death and destruction" to the area. "We had all the instrumentals done," Holstein remembered. "We did that in one session, one rainy night session, you know. It was just going so smooth, and I knew I had that song in my head, you know. I thought it would go perfect with the album. You know, it was everything about where I come from, and I just thought, 'Maybe that's the one we do without any instruments,' you know? So Randy Kohrs and Don Rigsby, they came in to sing harmonies with me." Buffalo Creek was more than the site of an historic disaster to Holstein, however; it was also a place where he developed as a young musician. "That goes back to the days of when I was learning the music as far as finding a mentor. His name was Virgil Osborn. Virgil lived at the head of Buffalo Creek, and I would cross over from the Wharton side of Boone County and cross over into the head of Buffalo Creek. I did that quite a while to hear this guy pick, because he could play anything. He wasn't, you know, much educated, but as far as instrument-wise, he couldn't be beat. So I spent a lot of time up there talking with his father, and they kind of explained a lot of the stories and a lot of the family that was lost and explained to me how devastating that was, you know, in those days. You know, I always had those stories in my head, and I remember I was down by the river later after that. This was after his father had passed, and Virgil, unfortunately, has already passed. I was kind of down and out on myself, you know, and I was there down by the river where I was baptized, and that song just came to me like it was water rushing over me. And I never forgot it, you know? It kind of sends chills thinking about that, too, you know, just the way it came to me."

Although his music is often critical of the coal industry, Holstein is careful to point to the mutual respect that he and coal miners have for one another. He describes his music as being "on the verge of being controversial. You know, it might make some people mad." Discussing a particularly powerful line in "Black Water"—"never . . . trust a company man"—Holstein reflected, "I know a lot of company men, too, but it's not pertaining to the working company man. It's pertaining to, you know, the guy who owns the coal that's never been in the coal mine. He's not worried about what it takes to get it out. He just wants it out. You know, it still bothers them when I sing that verse, but hey, it is what it is. If it bothers you, there must be something wrong." Holstein notes that, in southern West Virginia, those messages are well-received: "You know, it's been amazing. My music is on all the jukeboxes all over the land in this country, and there is nothing better than to go back home and walk in a Moose Club or a club downtown—there's not many left where I'm at anyway, you know—but if they're playing your music, that means they're thinking about you. So it must be something, you know, that kind of hits home with them. They like it."

———

DISCOGRAPHY

Cold Coal Town, Coal Records (2011).

PART V:
THE TAMARACK SCENE

BECKLEY, BLUEFIELD, LEWISBURG

• • • •

———

Figure 16. Doug Harper
(photo by Jon C. Hancock, courtesy of Doug Harper).

• • • •

DOUG HARPER

The tired travelers passing through Beckley's Tamarack have come to appreciate the well-advertised arts and crafts gallery for its convenient location to the West Virginia Turnpike, the delicious food served at the Greenbrier Resort's cafeteria, and the exceptional variety of pottery, sculptures, woodcrafts, and foodstuffs available for purchase. Juried artists and crafters can be found offering close-up views of the techniques and practices that define their art, and visitors can walk away with a souvenir of their time in the Mountain State.

Hidden from view in a Tamarack conference room—but no less vital to the state's creative landscape—is Songwriters Circle, a monthly gathering of southeastern West Virginia's songwriters led by Beckley native Doug Harper. Held monthly since February 2015, Songwriters Circle seeks to create a positive environment for songwriters of varying experience levels to improve their craft. "I thought, 'Let's try the Songwriters Circle,'" Doug reflected, "and make it not so much a critique kind of workshop, but a non-clinical workshop where we play and tell each other how we did it rather than bring these songs to be shredded." Harper, who "always wanted a music scene" in Beckley, has cultivated a community that is committed to mutual improvement, constructive criticism (when requested), and confident songwriting: "You either build someone up, or you shut up," Harper observed. "You help, but it's only if they ask you to." And unlike major music industry centers like Nashville and Los Angeles, where constructive feedback can lead to lawsuits over ownership of ideas, the Tamarack Songwriters Circle eschews obligatory co-writing credits in favor of a spirit of sharing. "We sign a waiver that says, 'I won't attach myself to anyone else's song just because I gave them an idea. I'm not going to claim co-authorship.' But now I've said, however, if someone gives you an idea that turns your song around, you *should* invite them as co-writer and offer them that." Drawing songwriters from Lewisburg, Charleston, Princeton, and beyond, Songwriters Circle has helped to transform a formerly scattered group of songwriters into a single unified community that seeks to improve everyone involved.

Harper's interest in community building is evident in his songwriting as well as his efforts to establish the Songwriters Circle. With the exception of the four years that he attended West Virginia University (where he studied landscape architecture), a three-month stint in Hickory, and six years in Greensboro, North Carolina (1987–1993), Doug has spent his entire life in Beckley. In songs such as "City Bus Station" (*Travelogue*, 2003) and "Do You Remember" (*Seasons*, 2004), Harper presents his bustling hometown at the height of the Winding Gulf and New River coalfields' postwar production. The Beckley of Harper's memories is one of almost Mayberry-esque simplicity, full of specialty stores for clothes, shoes, and hardware, and people who, although unfamiliar, weren't "strangers." Always optimistic, Harper notes but doesn't lament the societal and economic changes that have come to the area. In "Do You Remember," for example, the coming of "shopping malls and superstores that had it all" wasn't a death knell for the "model for Small Town, USA," but a temporary blip in the town's long historical narrative. "I hope one day it'll all turn around, / the shops and restaurants will move back down. / We'll have an uptown once again. / I'm looking forward to the day the streets bustle again," Harper sings in a tuneful major-key bounce.

It was during this Beckley heyday that Harper—born in 1954—was infected by the music bug. Like many kids of his generation, the transistor radio brought the exciting sounds of mainstream popular culture to Doug's open ears. "It started with a Motorola radio when I was in the fifth grade," he remembered, "so all of these influences started to come in mass media. I'm listening to pop songs on the radio, The Beatles and Dave Clark Five and all that, when I go to sleep. Mom or Dad bringing in records of country, Ray Price and Johnny Cash and all that. Then I've got Ed Sullivan." In junior high, Doug began to learn to play the banjo—despite the fact that the "squawky" sound of bluegrass initially turned him off to the genre—when his cousin Bobby Harper offered him lessons. Bobby had played with bluegrass pioneer Bill Monroe in the 1960s and could offer firsthand insights into the Scruggs style of playing.

"A fish out of water" musically, Doug made his debut at a junior high concert, where he awkwardly performed a Bob Dylan song. "I humiliated myself," he recalled. "When you're trying to imitate someone who's a weird singer anyway, and you're not a singer. That was my first crash and burn." Undeterred, he continued developing his banjo and guitar skills, especially after hearing some early recordings by the California country-rock group, Eagles. "I backed into [bluegrass] when I went to college because I heard the Eagles, and when I heard a banjo in a rock song, I went ballistic. I mean absolutely crazy," he remembered. Upon graduating from Beckley's Woodrow Wilson High School in 1973, Harper moved to Morgantown, where he "majored in parties" for his first year. It was during that time that he formed a group with Pete Parish called the New River Group, a country-rock band featuring Doug's banjo prominently. Playing in a group, however, was not particularly enjoyable for Harper because, as an instrumentalist, "I always felt like I was wearing somebody's clothes." Instead, he longed for an opportunity to write his own songs and to share the stories of the people he cared about most.

Although he is quick to downplay his talents as an instrumentalist, Harper's recordings and live performances reveal him to be a strong fingerpicker with an expansive harmonic vocabulary and a thorough knowledge of the fretboard, and his songs have a way of drawing listeners into his private world. His 2004 recording of the instrumental "A Quiet Place," for instance, demonstrates his strong rhythmic sense and a sensitive touch. Moreover, "I'm Like a Letter" (*Keepsakes*, 2007) showcases Harper's devotion to the fingerpicking styles popularized by Merle Travis and Doc Watson, steadfastly supporting his wife Shelley's mesmerizing vocal performance.

Describing his guitar playing as "more sculpture than . . . music," Harper seeks the best musical support for his lyrics, which he builds around a striking poetic conceit or broad idea. "I call [my approach to songwriting] 'from the inside out,'" he described. "I don't just take a hook and build a story around it. What I do is have a concept or a story or something I want to express. So I most often sit down and write things out in prose first. Then I'll start shrinking it down, and then I'll brainstorm and write down every little flash of an idea that has anything to do with the lyric. I fill a page full. I might have three pages of just brain droppings before I ever get started, and I fight the urge to make a verse or make a melody until my thoughts are complete."

Such was the case in two songs written in honor of Doug and Shelley's two children: "Princess Erin" and "Sir Douglas." On a long drive to Shelley's home state of Missouri, Doug found himself reflecting on his twelve-year-old daughter's personality traits: "Her personality and her wittiness. I started to think of things like her birthstone, diamond. And I thought, 'old world, new world.' Her name is Erin, which is Irish. Well, I thought, 'I'll 'Irish' this thing up,' so I kind of made it the Irish girl from New World ancestors." Douglas's song, written when he was eight years old, attempted to import character lessons to the young boy. "Douglas's song is more like a medieval knight," Harper recalled. "He liked animals, so I kind of used animals to talk about character. I lectured a whole lot more in his."

Family and friends are always at the center of Doug Harper's musical activities, and they form a solid foundation upon which his entire life is built. They appear as characters in his songs, as in "Ghost Fiddler," which portrays his grandfather, Oliver "Cherokee" Harper, a Raleigh County fiddler who was recorded by noted West Virginia University folklorist Patrick Gainer. Since the late 1990s, Doug has played music with a three-piece band composed of his wife Shelley, who sings and plays percussion, and boyhood friend Dave Fondale on electric bass. A gentle man who works ceaselessly at his family-owned nursery and as an office building custodian, Harper has become an important figure in the southern West Virginia songwriting community not simply because of the strength of his original compositions, but because he strives to support those around him and to provide opportunities to celebrate the unique qualities of his hometown and his family.

When, in 2016, he was diagnosed with multiple myeloma, Doug's community rallied to provide support—both financial and spiritual—to someone who had given them so much. Benefit concerts were organized in his honor, raising a significant amount of money for his treatment. And a never-ending chorus line of fellow songwriters and other musicians stayed with him almost non-stop during his weeks-long treatments in Morgantown. As a fly on the wall during many of those visits, I can attest to the great admiration that his peers and mentees feel for him; many of them credit Doug as the inspiration to write their own music in the first place. Through his support of family, friends, and neighbors, Doug Harper has succeeded in spurring growth in the music scene he so desperately wanted to see develop in the Beckley area, and, in the process, he brought a fragmented community together through creativity and mutual affection.

AUTHOR'S NOTE: After a more than two-year fight against multiple myeloma, Doug Harper passed away on January 22, 2018. His final hours on earth were filled with music, as many of his friends gathered at his home to share songs, stories, and fellowship. That day, he also charged Charlestonian Tony Wegman to preserve the Songwriters Circle in his absence, showing his trademark mentorship all the way to the end. His love, compassion, and friendship will be felt in this community for decades to come.

SELECTED DISCOGRAPHY (WITH SHELLEY HARPER)

Scrapbook, Hybrid Folk (2000).
Travelogue, Hybrid Folk (2003).
Seasons, Hybrid Folk (2004).
Keepsakes, Hybrid Folk (2007).

• • • •

Figure 17. Clinton Collins
(photo by Beni Holley, courtesy of Clinton Collins).

• • • •

CLINTON COLLINS[58]

Every August for the past eight years, Mercer County resident Clinton
Collins and his wife Sanette hold ClintFest, a gathering of songwriters from across the state as well as a few nationally successful guest
writers. Performing in sixty-minute "rounds," these songwriters share
their favorite songs on a custom-built stage nestled in the trees behind
their house near Bluefield. Drawing dozens of by-invitation-only guests
and providing a chance for songwriters of all levels—from relative
beginners to chart-toppers—to share their songs with appreciative
listeners, ClintFest plays an important role in maintaining the southern West Virginia songwriter scene, and Clinton Collins, in his gentle
and good-natured manner, enjoys creating a space for musicians and
listeners to gather together in low-stakes fellowship, complete with a
potluck dinner.

Music has always been a tool for Collins to connect with others
throughout his life, whether his family, church community, classmates,
or co-workers. His father, a second-generation coal miner, and his
mother were both very interested in music, Collins recalled, "especially
country music." "I couldn't be his son if I didn't love Flatt and Scruggs,"
Clinton said of his father. "In the evenings, we had a local channel, what
is now WVVA but at the time was Channel 6 [WHIS]. And they had
evening broadcasts of Buddy Pennington and Mel Street. So we would
watch those shows, and obviously the *Grand Ole Opry*." A singer in her

own right, Clinton's mother cared for Clinton and his siblings while his father mined coal during the evening shift at a mine near their home in the McDowell County community of Panther. "I thought she was a prolific songwriter. It turns out that they were Carter Family songs."

If his parents introduced him to country music, it was his older siblings who opened his ears to the rock and pop sounds of the mid- to late 1960s. "My sister, who was ten years old than me, she loved Brenda Lee, the Beatles, Gary Lewis and the Playboys, and all that kind of stuff, you know." His brothers, on the other hand, brought the exotic sounds of soul and hard rock back to Panther when they returned from their respective homes in Chicago and Brockton, Massachusetts. "When they came back," Collins remembered, "the brother from Chicago brought Wilson Pickett, Sam and Dave, all that Motown music. My other brother brought Led Zeppelin, The Beatles' *White Album*, Jimi Hendrix. And they just collided in my brain. All this came to me, man. I was just like, 'I love *this* music. I love *this* music.' So that's pretty much how music came into my life: in a roundabout way. And then, you know, I just started hunting it myself. I started finding my own artists I liked."

As a teenager in the early 1970s, Collins had a lot of music to choose from. "I would go to a place called G.C. Murphy's," he recounted, "and they would have albums. As I got a little bit older, my brother brought a lot of music. Leonard and I was more connected on a musical level and liked the same things. He introduced me to J.J. Cale. And I've loved J.J. my whole life. And then he brought the *Best of Eric Clapton* in, and I thought, 'Oh, my God! I've never heard this guy.' I didn't like Cream until I heard this. Because it was Delaney and Bonnie, and it was the *Layla* album, and I'd never heard those things. It just really influenced me."

Church, too, was an important musical gathering place for Clinton. Raised in a Church of God that was "more like a Baptist" church, music was always a key part of every service, especially the shape note traditions that remained popular in the region throughout the twentieth century. But still more moving was the music of a nearby church, located near his home in Panther. "There was a church," he recollected, "an Old Regular Baptist church, probably three hundred yards from my house. And on Sunday, man, that wailing"—the unaccompanied chant-like hymnody of the Old Regular Baptists—"went. And that stays with you forever. I was recently down at Folk Alliance. And Hazel Dickens's partner, Alice [Gerrard], she was there. They're singing those songs, and I just want[ed] to weep, because it was home. I was back home. I could hear it. It came through my valley, those songs, and it was just incredible."[59]

Collins made his first foray into music-making when he was twelve years old. His parents "had some cheap guitar, some cheap acoustic where the strings were that high off the bridge," he remembered, as he makes a gesture indicating unplayably high strings. "And mom and dad couldn't finally recognize that, 'Hey, he's learning how to play.' And I had a cousin who had a Martin and a Gibson. He even let us have those for a while to play. I'm thinking, 'Man, very generous.' But my brother came home one day and had bought me my first guitar that was mine. It was a Silvertone hollow-body electric. And I had the nice Silvertone amp with the two Jensen speakers on it, tremolo and reverb. That was it. I loved this thing. It had a Bigsby on it. I still have it and play it. It's got that vintage sound." The guitar—as well as his father's frustration with its loud amplified sound—forms the subject for "Silvertone," which appears on Collins's 2016 album *Around the Sun*. Layering dark tremolo with vintage tube crunch, the song recounts his efforts to learn to play while his father shouted for him to "turn down that boom, boom, boom!"

By high school, Clinton's reputation as a guitarist was beginning to grow among his peers in the Panther area, and it wasn't long before he was asked to play with others. "I was invited . . . on a New Year's Eve to join a band at a party. It was 1975. I had a friend that we had a guitar class together. I think I was in the tenth grade. We had guitar class together, and he told them I was a good guitar player. I knew these guys. I'm thinking, 'Hmmm, you know, that's a rich band.' They had amps, PA systems. I went on a New Year's Eve night, and I played with them, and I was pretty good at this time. And they let me join the band. Very cool." The first band that Collins was a regular member of formed with childhood friends Dennis and Billy Bailey when he was still in junior high.[60] "They had a Kay guitar and an amp. And we would play like two instruments through that thing, taking turns. So we decided we were going to form this band. It was called Revolutionary Three. I'm thinking, 'What is that even about? I don't know what a revolution is.' But that was our name. We thought, 'Hey, that's cool!' And the only people we played for was us."

Collins's first experiences with songwriting came in the tenth grade when he formed a new group with Tony Vance called Nickel Plate Road. "There used to be a railroad company called Nickel Plate Road. And we stopped at a railroad crossing one day. We're thinking, 'What are we going to name our band?' And there it comes across, you know, on one of the coal cars: Nickel Plate Road." The group was very interested in the singer-songwriter movement that was filling the radio airwaves of the early 1970s, and it wasn't long before Nickel Plate Road started to develop their own material in the same vein. "I met these guitar players, and they were songwriters in high school. This was tenth grade, and I'd never met any songwriters. And those guys were really good. Did a lot of Bread, a lot of mellow stuff. But they were really good. Their harmonies were great. And they started writing their own songs. So once I got in this band, we would have one whole set of original music. I was the George Harrison of the band." A club band, Nickel Plate Road persisted for several years until Vance converted to Christianity, followed by Collins, as well. "It changed me," he said. "I mean, I got converted and became a Christian. And that changed our music. They started writing about the Gospel, and I would throw something in there on occasion. And then when that band dissolved, I just started writing. You know, I learned from those guys. I was probably about twenty-three years old at that time."

As is often the case with aspiring musicians, family pressures and the need for consistent income made it difficult to maintain a single-minded focus on music. Clinton found work in a U.S. Steel coal mine and fell in love with the woman who would become his wife, Sanette. "We had gotten married and ended up with two children, and that kind of curbed my music a lot, because of my family. Nothing wrong with it. I don't regret it. I ended up as a wage-worker for years, what they call a fire boss, which was pretty much an inspector. I did that for a number of years, and then I went salary and became a safety auditor," a position he held until December 2014, when he retired from the mines.

Although music couldn't be a priority during those years, Collins still made time for music in his church community. He recalled that, "while [Tony and I] were playing Christian music, I made a friend named Chris Vanover, and he was in another band. We would play festivals and churches together and different places. And once that dissolved, his band had dissolved, and we started us a band. But we needed a drummer. [Chris] said, 'I know a drummer.' So we go down to Richlands, [Virginia,] and Randy [Fielder], my drummer today, was working at Little Caesar's. Chris said, 'We need a drummer. Would you like to try it for us?' He said, 'Sure!' So he came up and played Chris's drums, and he didn't even own a drum kit. He had quit playing music. And then he started playing with us. Borrowed a drum kit, and he and I have been playing music ever since."

This new configuration was in great demand around southern West Virginia and southwestern Virginia. "You know, we ended up playing battles of bands. We would play in churches of any color and shape and size, man. It didn't matter. Anywhere someone invited us, we would go. And I think that's an attitude that stayed with me. That I would not try to turn down anybody if it was reasonable. Now I've gotta cover these guys. I want them to get paid. But if it was reasonable and it's a place nobody was going to throw a knife at me or shoot me or something, I would go play. And I've never stopped from being like that. Back then, we were kind of staying in the Christian circles, and that didn't make no sense to me. If we had a message of hope, then we needed to get away from the Christians who said that they had it already."

By the beginning of the twenty-first century, Collins was ready to devote even more of his creative energies toward songwriting. Inspired by a variety of roots music styles as well as the Christian-oriented songwriting of Bob Dylan and the spirituality of Bruce Cockburn, Collins wrote a variety of new songs that obliquely address his faith and his deep commitment to Appalachian life. "I wanted to find a way that I could express who I am as a person and at the same time, you know, I could sing for anybody," he observed. "I could connect with any person out there is what I want to do as a human being. And I didn't have to be preachy or none of that. And I don't like it when it is preachy or religious." One such song is "Ain't Never," which appeared on his 2016 album *Around the Sun*. "Man, it's just a rocking gospel, upbeat kind of style," he smiled. "And anybody can like that. An atheist—non-religious or religious. A song of worship, in my opinion, you don't really know what it's about. You know, it's taking some biblical scenes. I'm putting them in there as anybody, you know. Talking about Babylon. Talking about, you know, 'I was naked and thirsty,' and, you know, all those things that Jesus said. That's the story we give unto other people. So I want to write songs like that, but I try to twist it to where it's about me today. You know, it's about my life. It's not about biblical times. It's about now."

In 2005, Collins entered the contest at the New Song Festival in Shepherdstown with a composition inspired by his domestic life. "I wrote a song called 'Home and Garden,'" he recounted. "[Sanette] comes in one day. She's got these chimes. She says, 'I bought you some chimes.' I'm thinking, 'I don't need chimes. Why are you buying me chimes?' She just, well, she wanted them, but they're for me. She loves those home-and-garden shows, and I thought of all of her influence on my life, to build decks and all the flower gardens and all the other crap around the house. So I wrote a song called 'Home and Garden.' Very humorous song. We played a gig one night. I played it for my two band-mates at the time. They said, 'Oh, man, we've got to do that tonight!' So we put a dobro and a bass and a guitar and that was it. And it was a hit. So people said, 'You need to enter it in a contest.' So I found out about the New Song—I think through Doug Harper or somebody like that—and I entered it in, and it got knocked down on the state level. I went to Charleston, played the song, didn't make it. So I went to the festivals. I said, 'I'm going to enter it again.' And I won at the festival, the main festival."

Collins's work is focused on life in the southern coalfields of West Virginia. For more than a decade, his band took its name from the area where he grew up. "Well, when we were growing up, all these guys were from these different little creeks, little tributaries. So we decided, 'Hey, we're all Creek Boys.' So that was kind of—whenever there was a group of us, we called ourselves the 'Creek Boys.' So that stuck with me. And probably about 2001, I won a songwriting contest, actually here [at Tamarack]. 'The Appalachian Way' was the song. And I took that money, went to Bristol, and recorded an album called *Creek Boy Blues*." Collins describes that album as "a southern coalfield album."

In his retirement years, Collins has no plans to slow down. In fact, in 2016, he released a new album of original material called *Around the Sun* and has been touring widely, both around the region and as far away as the Chicago area. House concerts, coffeehouses, song-writer circles, and festivals fill the books, and, as he travels from place to place, he is an outspoken advocate for the Mountain State and its people. "When people find out where I'm from, in a lot of places, you know, you've got that stigma. I think for me with my music and trying to be artistic and creative about trying to say, 'You know, maybe you're mistaken. Or maybe you're mistaken about my home state or where I'm from or who I am.'" With more musical energy than a person half his age, Collins continues to write several songs each month, and he maintains a home studio where he has recorded a number of other artists. With a new album in the works at the time of this writing, it doesn't look like he has plans to stop any time soon.

DISCOGRAPHY

Creekboy Blues, Lost Cauz Records (2006).
Junebug (with the Creekboys), Hollowcreek Songs (2009).
This Day is Mine, Creekboy Records (2014).
Around the Sun, Creekboy Records (2016).

MARK SPANGLER

Lewisburg's Mark Spangler presides over an intensely musical family. With his children, Spangler is the lead vocalist and guitarist of The Spanglers, a rock and Americana group that plays venues along the I-64 corridor. Son Josiah and his partner Abigail Reynolds constitute the Charleston-area folk-rock band Marguerite. And, as a soloist, Spangler presents a stylistically varied and lyrically evocative body of original material that explores the intersections of everyday life and spirituality.

Spangler's interest in music was cultivated from his earliest days, thanks to parents who were passionate fans of the diverse musical styles promulgated by the post-World War II recording industry. His father—a union construction worker from Monroe County—did as so many men and women of his generation did and moved to Ohio (where Spangler was born in 1963) and to western Pennsylvania in search of employment. Entering into the postwar middle class, Spangler's parents sought to fill their home with good music. "We always had music in our home," he recalled. "My father played harmonica at the house all the time, but I remember my mother always singing, and she would sing hymns and she would sing folk songs. Old folk songs. My dad, although he was a West Virginian, he didn't like country music or anything. He said, 'That's hillbilly music.' In our home, he would be playing Johann Strauss, Beethoven. They both loved big band, and they both loved western swing." Furthermore, his mother introduced a deep love of poetry into Spangler's life. "My mother loved poetry," he noted, "and I remember as a child my mother having poetry books laying around the house, and I can remember her saying, 'Listen at this one! Listen at this one!' And she would read it to me, and I would ask her what it meant."

As Spangler grew into his teens, his parents' musical tastes grew along with those of their children, much as his own current musical interests have been profoundly influenced by his children's tastes. "I had a lot of older siblings," he observed, "and it was the '60s, the '70s. So we had a lot of rock and folk and all of that playing in our home, and my parents liked it, as well. So it was interesting because, even though my folks were old folks—or, in my mind—I would still jump in the car, and all of a sudden, my mother would have a James Taylor eight-track in or, you know, listen to the [Rolling] Stones or something like that. Dad would listen to the Stones, as well."

When Spangler was fifteen, his family moved back to Monroe County, which was something of a culture shock for him. "I left the greater Pittsburgh area and came to Monroe County," he remembered, "and I was used to going to concerts. You know, I was going to see Kansas, Nazareth, Blue Öyster Cult on the weekends. Then I came to Monroe County, and we had one television station if the antenna was turned just right and the neighbors' electric fence wasn't on [laughs]. And as for radio, there was not much there." With a lack of mediated options at his disposal, Spangler turned toward creating his own musical entertainment, first learning chords on a hand-me-down Harmony guitar that hurt his hands, playing in rock cover bands, and later joining an after-school program that taught young people about traditional Appalachian string band music. Spangler recalled that, "at our local little high school, there was a guy named Bob Martin in the [musicians'] union who was from Massachusetts, and Bob was a musician, singer-songwriter, and played jazz music. But Bob made friends with a lot of these senior citizens around Monroe County that played old-time fiddle music and mountain music. He got these guys together and actually recorded an album with them. Then he found some federal grant money to bring these guys into the school every Thursday afternoon to teach kids—any kid that wanted to learn—either a mandolin, a fiddle, or a guitar, banjo, whatever, and he also had some basketweavers teaching basket weaving. He had quilters working with kids, teaching them to quilt, but I signed right up, and these guys took an interest in me. I did what they said. I practiced, and these guys poured life into me." Learning such songs as "Sally Goodin," "Soldier's Joy," and "Under the Double Eagle," Spangler quickly distinguished himself among his peers as an excellent guitarist, and, when federal funding for the program ended, he joined his teachers at dances around Monroe and Mercer Counties, as well as nearby Giles County, Virginia. As Spangler's guitar playing improved, he began to explore ways to use his developing musicianship to support the long-standing passion for wordplay that his mother had cultivated in him. "I like playing other people's songs," he reflected, "but to me, learning other people's songs—even the standards—was just a segue into figuring out how to tell the world what I want to say through music."

One of the most significant things that Spangler wanted to communicate through song was his Christian faith. Encouraged by his pastor while he was still in high school, he slowly agreed to play at his church. "Our pastor of the church we attended visited our home and heard my playing and singing," he remembered, "and he started asking me, 'When are you going to play at church?' And I was very, very hesitant to do so. Now, I don't know where this thinking came from, but I thought I was good enough to play these [social] events and dances and community events, but I wasn't good enough to play in the church." After persistent reminders that he should use his talents in the church, Spangler finally consented: "I sat on the piano bench. I was afraid to stand. I sat on a piano bench, and I sang." Before long, Spangler was regularly performing the so-called "Jesus freak" music of artists such as John Michael Talbot and Keith Green at his church, and trying his hand at a career in the emerging contemporary Christian music industry.

In 1988 or 1989, Spangler recorded his debut album, *Shelter*, at a studio in Big Stone Gap, Virginia, and hit the road to support the tours of Christian artists The Imperials and Dallas Holm. His music was quickly met with some success—he "had some songs that charted on the Contemporary Christian charts"—but he soon found that his songwriting approach was something of a liability to his long-term sustainability in the music industry. "I've never been ashamed that I'm a Christian who writes and plays and performs," he observed, "but I've never seen myself as just stuck in that genre. I like to think that I write about my experience in life, both the struggle and the accomplishment and the victory. I never really bought the whole idea that, if a song doesn't completely fit some specific pre-expectation in our genre, that it's not valid." Moreover, the music industry's—Christian or otherwise—tendency to typecast artists made it difficult for Spangler to break into the mainstream of the contemporary Christian market. "I remember when Sparrow Records listened to some of my stuff," Spangler recalled. "Our guy from Sparrow Records [Peter York] called me up at home and says, 'Hey, I listen to your cassette to and from work all of the time. I really want to encourage you. I love it! I like it a lot.' And I'm thinking, 'Great! They're going to sign me, right?' But he said, 'We just signed a singer-songwriter named Steven Curtis Chapman, and we don't have room for two singer-songwriters to play guitar on our label.'" Yet, in an era in which Contemporary Christian groups such as Jars of Clay found success on secular radio stations, Spangler's debut album did enjoy some top-forty airplay on the West Coast. Unfortunately, Spangler was unable to capitalize on this development with a tour.

In 1992, Spangler and his young family moved to Lewisburg, where he began working as a licensed counselor at Davis-Stuart, a multi-site facility that cares for abused and neglected adolescents; he remained in this position until 2017, when he became the executive director of the West Virginia Board of Medicine.[61] Music played an important role in his efforts to care for and empower the children in his care. "The work that I do has been really a great fit for me as a musician," he observed. "Some people say, 'This is my day job, and then music's my [main thing],' but it's all my gig, man. Our main campus [at Davis-Stuart] in Lewisburg is on a five hundred and fifty acre farm there, and we have forty-five kids, and we do music with them, too. I play music in the chapel there, and I teach kids guitar sometimes, and when I get out and do shows, I oftentimes drum up support for our non-profit organization, as well."

Lewisburg proved to be a very welcoming community for Spangler and his family's musical efforts, in large part due to the

eclectic back-to-the-land movement that shepherded educated creative urbanites and suburbanites into the area during the 1970s and
1980s.[62] Spangler notes that Lewisburg, especially, has welcomed creative people to a variety of venues, especially its Carnegie Hall: "The
Lewisburg area has been very distinct for being a town with a Carnegie
Hall. One of only three in the country, I think. An operating Carnegie
Hall, an operating full-time theater, and the community has embraced
that. As a result, there's a lot of opportunity for young people. My wife
and I decided early on that we would raise our children in that community because of the opportunities it would provide for them artistically
and educationally. So we have kids involved in theater and dance and
music that they would have never had in many other communities."

The creative spirit and eclecticism of the Lewisburg area fits
Spangler's artistic vision, which constantly eschews classification. As
an active creative artist in a small community, Spangler listens carefully to the world around him and responds to the needs and challenges
of the people with whom he lives and the environment in which he
lives. This tendency shows up most obviously in his decision to write
music using different instruments, rather than writing with an acoustic guitar. Spangler is particularly responsive to the voices of the instruments that he plays: "Sometimes I will write a song on the mandolin, or
I'll try to write a song on a dobro. This sounds really weird, but I believe
that instruments have songs in them, just like your voice. So I'll switch
up instruments frequently, and I'll go to instruments I can't play very
well sometimes, and I'll find a song in them, and I'll translate the song
back to a guitar that I'm comfortable with."

Spangler's 2008 album *Transition* reveals the many ways that his
eclectic tastes and willingness to embrace different stylistic vocabular-
ies filter into his work. The album features Spangler in two principle
vocal types: 1) progressive rock belter, and 2) sincere folk singer-songwriter. In the latter voice are such songs as "New England Lady" and
"To See You Smile," which also draw upon acoustic guitars, mandolins,
and the restricted harmonic vocabulary of American folksong. But
Spangler's songwriting and performances really shine on the modal
and minor-key songs that evoke the quieter moments of his adolescent
musical favorites. For instance, "To Be With You," the album's opening

track, offers a Rumi-esque mediation on the deep spirituality of loving relationships, much as progressive rock of the 1970s was also cloaked in mysticism and explored deep spiritual truths.

Mark Spangler has carved an important niche for himself in the southern West Virginia music scene. Like so many of his neighbors, he chose to build a life in the Greenbrier Valley because of its potential to both support his creative pursuits and to accept the love he has to give back to the community. As a songwriter, Spangler responds to the community he lives in by writing songs that speak to the potential for a more peaceful and loving world. At the same time, he does not become pedantic or preachy. Rather, he casts himself as a lone individual trying to make sense of the confusing world in which we live while providing a model for how we might live more kindly, lovingly, and peacefully.

SELECTED DISCOGRAPHY

AS A SOLO ARTIST:
Shelter, no label (1989).
Transition, Lost Cauz Records (2008).

WITH THE SPANGLERS:
The Spanglers, self-published (2016).

• • • •

———

Figure 18. Andrew Adkins
(photo by Candace Evans, courtesy of Andrew Adkins).

• • • •

ANDREW ADKINS

If Texas singer-songwriter Guy Clark were a West Virginian, he'd probably sound a lot like Summersville native and Fayetteville resident Andrew Adkins. His rough-hewn baritone voice reflects a wisdom beyond his years, and his songs convey powerful emotions through the economical use of poetic language and an uncanny ability to find the beautiful narrative in everyday objects. Echoes of Clark's "Randall Knife," which uses the eponymous blade to describe the complicated relationship between father and son, can be heard in a recent unrecorded Adkins song that traces a similar relationship through a vintage car. The Clark influence is strong in Adkins's working method, as well. He recounted a tale about co-writing with Clark that he heard from a fellow writer: "You know, you'll be fighting over a line, and Guy Clark is like, 'What are you trying to say?' And then you say it, and then he's like, 'Well, then just say it like that.'" Like Clark, Adkins is also a master woodworker and luthier, transforming old barnwood into beautiful furniture and discovering the musical qualities in the grain of the hardwoods of central West Virginia. And finally, Adkins's output is prolific, both as a soloist and a co-writer, much like Clark, who wrote or co-wrote hundreds of songs through his more than four decades as a professional songwriter in Nashville.

Adkins was raised in a home that valued musical storytelling. Growing up in Summersville, where his father helped run his grandfather's sawmill, young Andrew was immersed in the music of Harry Chapin, whom he still cites as one of the zeniths of American songwriting. During family trips to Florida, for instance, the Adkinses would sing Chapin songs to pass the time. "I don't sleep much and I never have," Adkins said, "so my dad used to drive us to Florida, and we would leave at seven o'clock at night, and I would stay awake with him and I would sit in between the seats without a seatbeat on—obviously, because it's the '80s. We didn't believe in safety then—and we would sing Harry Chapin songs all night long all the way to Florida."

Another key influence on Adkins was the musical community that flourished alongside the summer tourism season along the New and Gauley Rivers. "We always went to the Summersville bluegrass festival," Adkins recalled, "and my dad was into whitewater rafting. He was a CPA, and he worked as a CPA for all of the rafting companies, so we always went rafting for free. And back in the day, all of those old raft guides were out playing guitars on the porch, and I just always had a love for it, you know?" These early formative experiences led him to begin writing songs while he was still in elementary school. "I started writing at a really young age, and they [my parents] just kind of encouraged it, so I did," he remembered. "But I just wrote songs starting when I was about nine. I was writing full songs, but they had no sense of time, rhythm, or meter. And it wasn't until I was probably thirty to where somebody took one of my songs—it was a fiddle player—and taught me about crooked tunes. And they were basically like, 'You write crooked.' And so they sat me down and explained it to me. And another friend of mine would pat his foot for me and show me what I was doing wrong. My head just exploded, and I was like, 'I wish someone would have told me that a long time ago.' I wrote more songs from thirty to forty than I wrote from nine to thirty because I just got it at that point. Plus I think, as a writer, you want to find out what kind of writer you are, and I didn't know that. I wanted to be Harry Chapin, so all of my songs were nine minutes long and told this epic story that—in the end, when Harry Chapin does it, you're disappointed when they're over, and my songs are nine minutes long, and you're disappointed that they were still going."

Although Chapin loomed large in his upbringing, Adkins was interested in an eclectic array of music growing up in Nicholas County, especially the heavy metal and hip hop that was hitting record stores throughout the late 1980s. "I start out with Harry Chapin and the Beatles and Kenny Rogers and stuff like that," he recounted, "and then my friends were all into Guns 'n' Roses, which I didn't think was very good, and Bon Jovi and that first Skid Row album. But I wasn't into that, so I got into the rap part of it. The Easy E and Slick Rick and NWA and KRS-1 and those kind of folks. And that led me to Public Enemy. I came from a very liberal family, so Chuck D was right there in my wheelhouse. I heard my dad say all that stuff for all of those years, just not with the profanity and not with a hype man. That would have been awesome! But Public Enemy led me to Anthrax, because they did a couple of songs together with Anthrax. Then Anthrax played with Slayer, and Slayer led me to heavy stuff. Then I hated Metallica. I thought they were terrible, so I got away from the heavy stuff and went to the more punk rock stuff. And then punk rock stuff led me to X's *Los Angeles*, which is probably the greatest punk rock album of all time, in my opinion. And then X led me to Sonic Youth, and Sonic Youth led me to Townes Van Zandt. Then Townes Van Zandt led me to Steve Earle and Guy Clark and Rodney Crowell, Kris Kristofferson, and those types of songwriters."Upon graduating from high school, Adkins moved to Fairmont to pursue his undergraduate studies at Fairmont State College (now Fairmont State University), where, for a brief time, he played football for the Falcons. He arrived in the Friendly City at an opportune time for an aspiring musician, because the Marion and Monongalia County music scenes were thriving in the early 1990s. Groups like the Joint Chiefs (led by Charleston native Michael Pushkin) and Karma to Burn were performing around the region and drawing a great deal of support from the local pool of college students. Adkins found a way to make certain that he could stay abreast of the happenings in the musical community while continuing his studies in criminology. "All of my good friends from high school went to WVU," he recalled, "so I would schedule my classes to where I didn't have class on Friday, and Thursday night, I would head to Morgantown and party at their house or go out and listen to music or do whatever, and go up to Cooper's Rock the next day or down on Decker's Creek or whatever we were doing that night." The I-79 corridor between Fairmont and Morgantown was a dynamic musical environment, Adkins recalls. "I dug Fairmont. The Davidson Brothers were starting right around then. I was probably a senior when they started hanging out in the bar scene there. The Joint Chiefs and all of those guys would come down to Fairmont to play, and some other bands would come around. There were some other bands that would come around. There were some bands that would sprout up here and there, but, you know, they were awesome, but they would break up a week later."

After his brief football career at Fairmont State ended, Adkins found solace in his songwriting. Influenced in part by the work of Ani DiFranco, he focused his efforts upon improving his guitar playing and using it to communicate his observations and emotions. He soon decided to debut his creative work at Fairmont's College Lunch, which hosted an open mic on Wednesday nights. Unfortunately, his work met with decidedly unfavorable responses. "I would always go, and I would try to get up the courage to do it. And then I remember the first time I did. I got up there and did a fifteen-minute-long story song, changing chords whenever I wanted to. No refrain. No turnaround. No chorus. Just words. And afterwards, it was like the high school movie slow clap, and that destroyed me. I retreated to my apartment and only played for myself. I did that for years."

When he graduated from Fairmont State, Adkins moved to Fayetteville, where he began hosting an open mic event for raft guides and tourists. Although other musicians frequently took the stage, he always needed to be prepared to play. "Some nights, I would have to play because nobody was there," he remembered. "So I did that, and it gave me more confidence because everybody was kind of into it." Before long, Adkins wanted to expand his act from a solo singer-songwriter to a full band, but he struggled to find musicians who were willing to work with him because his sense of musical timing was underdeveloped. But in 2008, after a decade in the New River Gorge, Adkins joined with banjoist and guitarist Alan Sizemore and bassist Clint Lewis to form The Wild Rumpus, a group playing what they described as "stompgrass" music.[63] The group performed widely along the East Coast, at times booking as many as one hundred fifty performances each year. Fronted by Adkins, who also played guitar and mandolin, the Wild Rumpus released three

albums, each of which features a number of Adkins's original compositions. 2008's *Love, Trains, Home* includes "These Mountains," a paean
to the Appalachian Mountains and the traditions of music, dance, and
moonshine that make the work week more bearable. "For Grandpa"
channels Guy Clark's "Desperadoes Waiting for a Train," reflecting on
the important mentorship that his grandfather offered him and celebrating his role in showing Adkins how to be a man. In 2011, The Wild
Rumpus released *304*, drawing its title from the statewide telephone area
code. *304*'s "Logan County Line" is a first-rate murder song, telling the
tale of a man running from the law after committing an act of violence
in the state's southern coalfields, while "Moonshine and Crossroads"
offers a conversion story that draws freely from Hank Williams, Robert
Johnson, and Old Crow Medicine Show. And 2013's *Shake Yer Rumpus*
showcases traditional numbers such as "Shady Grove" and "Columbus
Stockade Blues" alongside the humorous breakup song "I Never Loved
You" and the melancholy "Last Time I Saw You."

In 2014, Adkins released his debut solo album, *The Long Way to
Leaving*. Unlike his work with The Wild Rumpus, which frequently
veered toward the good-time Appalachian hill-party vibe, the work in
The Long Way to Leaving finds Adkins exploring emotional complexity
and hewing closer to the work of Van Zandt, Clark, Earle, and Crowell.
"Sweet June," for example, is a tuneful yet wistful sensory exploration of
the warmth of an early summer day. Refraining from cliché, the song
skillfully connects familiar pastoral imagery with poetic care. "I'll Cry,"
which features Summersville's Chris Stockwell on the resonator guitar,
discusses a heartache that has grown tiresome as the speaker tells the
wandering lover that "I'll cry for you this time / But this time'll be the
last time that I cry." And "Thinking About Leaving" could easily be sung
by current Americana superstar Chris Stapleton, the speaker soulfully
reconciling his desire to roam and his realization that he "can't live
without" the person he considers leaving.

2016 found Adkins continuing this work in his album *Wooden
Heart*, which offers still more exploration of loss and love. "80 Acres,"
for instance, examines the Appalachian diaspora from the perspective
of the man who was left behind with his farm and no family to continue caring for it. The speaker—a veteran of military service, illicit

moonshine running, and the decline of rural America—speaks matter-of-factly about the way that "the American Dream passed me by," despite his best efforts to work hard. "Hardest Thing" picks up where "I'll Cry" left off; a lonesome man left behind by a former lover sits alone reflecting on "the hardest thing I've ever done," which is "watching you fall out of love with me." In late 2016, Adkins released a second album, this time a duet with singer-songwriter Annie Neely, titled *Appalachia*.

Andrew Adkins continues to make great strides as a songwriter and promoter of the West Virginia music scene. He mentors aspiring writers, frequently participates in the Songwriter Circle at Tamarack, and is quick to talk of the success that his neighbors and friends have had in their creative endeavors. During the 2016 flood that devastated much of central and southeastern West Virginia, he worked tireless to help his neighbors, even providing entertainment for them while he was involved in cleaning up the damage that was done to his family's property in Nicholas County. And, at the same time, he is always busy writing, recording, and performing.

DISCOGRAPHY

WITH THE WILD RUMPUS:
Love, Trains, Home, self-published (2008).
304, self-published (2011).
Shake Yer Rumpus, self-published (2013).

AS A SOLO ARTIST:
The Long Way to Leaving, self-published (2014).
Wooden Heart, self-published (2016).

WITH ANNIE NEELY:
Appalachia, self-published (2016).

PART VI:
MORGANTOWN

SONGWRITING
IN THE UNIVERSITY
CITY

····

———

Figure 19. Maria Allison
(photo by Wes Ornick, courtesy of Maria Allison).

····

MARIA ALLISON

———

"That's a goal, to get on *Mountain Stage* one day," Monongalia County songwriter and West Virginia Hitchers frontwoman Maria Allison remarked during a conversation on a hot July day in 2015. The St. Mary's County, Maryland, native has been an active contributor to the Morgantown music scene for more than a decade, and the Hitchers, her most recent project, is the most roots-oriented group she's been with thus far, making it all the more likely that she could appear on the august public radio program. Roots music was not, however, a part of her musical upbringing. Rather, Allison has made a careful study of it as an adult. "As a teenager, I was growing up in the '90s. Appalachian music was the last thing on my list," she recalls.

Born in Charleston in 1982, Allison was adopted by a family in St. Mary's County, Maryland, when she was three days old. As a child along the shores of Chesapeake Bay, Allison was involved in music through school and community programs, participating in the elementary school chorus—an experience that she continued to enjoy throughout her high school years—and, by high school, she was also heavily involved in the local theater community, where her ability to sing and dance proved to be especially advantageous. Living a short drive from Washington, DC, Allison's mother made certain that her daughter had the opportunity to see professional productions of Broadway musicals, including *Cats* and *Les Miserables*, both of which inspired her to develop her expressive toolbox. "I was totally a theater geek," she laughed.

Despite her love of Broadway, however, Allison found that, in the middle of the grunge revolution of the 1990s, her love of such overt sentimentality marked her as different, a difficult blow for most middle schoolers. "The only negative response I've ever had [to my music], which almost stopped me, was when I was thirteen in middle school, and I sang 'Memories' from *Cats* at a talent show. If I would talk to those kids again, they would still remind me of how embarrassing that was for everyone. I did great. I got a standing ovation, but the kids at school, they didn't want to hear 'Memories' from *Cats*. In the '90s, they were very, very harsh. They did not approve of that, so I couldn't live that down. That's the only negative response I've ever really had that made me question music, and it took me a couple of years to get over that because you're vulnerable as a kid."

Summer for Allison meant a return to the place of her birth, where she stayed with her aunt and her grandmother. One of the highlights of her time in the Kanawha Valley was Camp Nathan, a summer arts camp held at the University of Charleston. "I was enrolled in that every summer, she recalled. "It was a lot of fun." Among this community of musicians, dancers, and "theater geeks" like herself, Allison found peers who, unlike her Maryland classmates, came from a similar sensibility. At the same time, South Charleston summers also allowed her to connect with her Appalachian roots as she learned about small-scale farming from her grandparents. "Whenever I came in from Maryland, all I wanted to do was be out in the chicken coop with my Papaw or be out helping my Mamaw peeling potatoes for dinner or in the garden pulling weeds. So I just wanted to be near them."

Allison's interest in songwriting emerged alongside her childhood interest in the performing arts. "I actually started writing songs when I was six. On the piano. I started piano at six. I just begged them [my parents] for a year to get me a piano, then they got me lessons. And I hated lessons, but I stuck to it just so I could get the chords down. Then at home, all the time, if I wasn't outside playing, I was in there on the piano, noodling around and writing little notations as best as a six-year-old could, and that just progressed up through elementary school." As her musical and theatrical interests expanded, Allison also began to draw inspiration from the hits of musical theater, which encouraged her to develop more music that suited her voice. Still today, live performances reveal Allison to be a strong vocalist with a broad expressive range.

In 2001, Allison left St. Mary's County to move to Morgantown, but she didn't journey to the city to pursue her formal education as so many others do. Rather, she followed a friend's tip about the University City's music scene and decided to try her hand there. "I came here to try and start my folk singer-songwriter career, and I had a friend who was going to school here, and I just wanted out of Maryland. I was like, 'Well, I really love West Virginia, so why not go back? I want to learn more about where my family's from.' I heard from my friend who had lived here that there's always a good music scene. Lots of local artists. The community supported local artists." Furthermore, she was already somewhat familiar with the north-central West Virginia music scene—which also includes artists and bands from western Maryland and southwestern Pennsylvania—through Sunshine Daydreams, a Preston County festival space that Allison visited during her high school years and that would later be a valuable site in her professional development.

In a town that has built a lively environment of open mics and jam sessions, Allison—whose musical interests were profoundly shaped by Tori Amos, Ani DiFranco, Sarah McLachlan, the Smashing Pumpkins, and Alice in Chains—quickly found venues that were willing to give her a space to share her music with others.[64] The Morgantown Brewing Company, known locally as the "Brew Pub," was one such friendly venue. On Thursday nights, Maria performed a mix of covers of songs by Bob Dylan and Joni Mitchell, as well as traditional folk songs. Over time, she became more willing to share her original compositions during what came to be termed "Viva la Maria," a name bestowed to her show by her friend Celeste. "I had just started writing on the guitar, so I started filtering in my stuff," she recalled. "No one really noticed at first, but liked it regardless. As I grew, I just started pushing out the covers, and the core of my repertoire became original."

Allison's sojourns to Terra Alta's Sunshine Daydreams also turned into a regular gig playing covers of a different sort. Catering to a young counterculturally oriented crowd presented an opportunity to explore the music of the Grateful Dead. "I was going to the Sunshine Daydreams festival grounds just as a fan," she remembered, "and I became friends with the owner, Kevin MacClenney—'Trip,' as everyone knows him— and I imported some friends from Maryland to come up. Then I met some friends here [in Morgantown], and we all combined together and we created the Sunshine Family Band." Through the Grateful Dead and Jerry Garcia Band covers that formed the backbone of the Sunshine Family Band's repertoire, Allison also gained a deep appreciation for a wide range of American roots music, which continues to exert a strong influence on her music-making today, as exemplified by her continued performance of such songs as the Memphis Jug Band's "Stealin.'" But unlike her current performances of such classic blues, jazz, and country numbers (which she describes as "slowed down, jazzed up a little, bluesed up a little"), the Sunshine Family Band's takes on these songs were more in line with the standards of the outdoor festival space, especially in terms of volume: "It was fun. They were loud. I've never been in a louder band in my life." With the Sunshine Family Band, she had the privilege of playing on the same bills as progressive bluegrass musicians David Grisman and Tony Rice, among many others.[65]

After five or six years with the Sunshine Family Band and three or four more with the Family Outlaws, a splinter group from the Sunshine Family Band, Allison decided that it was time to move on to new creative endeavors. Partnering with Keyser-area songwriter Harold Liller (whose 2016 EP *Harold Liller Is Sick of Being Used* deserves a much wider audience) and Andy Tuck, former member of the Greens, Allison formed Big Shiny Gun in 2011. From a promising open mic performance, the three decided to form a group, for which Allison immediately had a name: "It just popped in my head, because Harold is a big guy, and I'm shiny, apparently, and Andy's the gun because he's rock and roll."

The group coalesced around their mutual admiration for alternative country/Americana lightning rod Ryan Adams (who, Allison is quick to point out, "was the only young new musician that the Grateful Dead ever covered") and the Americana superduo Gillian Welch and David Rawlings. "Harold and I were obsessed with [Adams] and Gillian, as well, because they work together sometimes," Allison observed, implying a similarity between the creative relationship of Big Shiny Gun's constituents and that of their musical heroes. "Her, David Rawlings, and Ryan, they all get together and swap songs and sing their music for each other." Their songs suited the vocal prowess of the trio's members, especially when they sang together. "We were all about harmonies," she reflected, "so we wanted to pick stuff that we could easily transition into dual vocals, or even with Andy sometimes a third vocal in there. Something simple, but effective." Their songs also explored themes that were significant to Liller, Tuck, and Allison. "We talked about the themes [of their compositions] and what we were all interested in. Like, we were really into the Appalachian hard life, hard times, thinking like your grandparents did kind of experience. So those songs just seemed natural to sing."

Although the members of Big Shiny Gun boasted serious songwriting talents, Liller was the dominant songwriter for the group. "I didn't really put my two cents in," Allison remarked. "I just wanted to sing with Harold and Andy. It was like, 'I'm going to sing, and you guys play the instruments. Take the pressure off.'" After a couple of years together, which included a tour that took the group to Boulder, Colorado, Big Shiny Gun disbanded in 2012 when Liller left the Morgantown area and Tuck's growing family made it difficult for him to perform in public as regularly as the band needed to.

Without a band and eager to take charge as a songwriter and a bandleader, Allison formed the West Virginia Hitchers in 2013. After Big Shiny Gun disbanded, she recalled, "I was kind of left by my lonesome, and I sat for a year and kind of pouted. And then I was like, 'Okay, it's time to pull yourself up from the bootstraps and do something. You've been building up to this for ten years now. You need to do something that's solely for you, solely original, and try to find members of a band that will back you on it and have as much confidence as I have in you sometimes, which is surprisingly not enough.'" Allison found those musicians in steel guitarist Chuck Snider, drummer Dan Vellaso, and bassist John Creed. The Hitchers, Allison describes, is the result of the things she learned during her earlier experiences as the lead singer in three bands. "The Hitchers," she observes, "is kind of what I've been culminating, building towards, learning stage presence, learning how to do harmonies. All the little things I have picked up from the other bands has led up to the Hitchers. So in the other bands, it was all covers a lot. I never really did my solo songwriting thing except every now and then at an open mic. You know, I didn't have a show like I did when I first got here because I kind of got distracted. But, with the Hitchers, I see it as my way to give back to all the hard work that I've put in, to where I come from, to my grandparents, to my parents, to my culture, to West Virginia."

Armed with her new vision and a bachelor's degree in creative writing that she earned during her years as a journeyman musician, Allison has crafted several impressive songs that reflect her understanding of West Virginian culture and history and that often add nuanced shading to familiar Appalachian stereotypes. Her songs reveal at once the vital role that Appalachian stereotypes play in shaping identities within the region and the constant battle that its residents undertake to redefine and overturn them. Nowhere is this approach more obvious than in "Coal Miner," a stunning narrative that interrogates the ongoing place of coal extraction in West Virginia through the lens of a devastating mine roof collapse. Surveying the extensive coal song repertoire, one would have comparatively little difficulty locating songs that address the sustainability of coal, warn young men of the dangers that could befall them underground, and memorialize the noble yet deceased miner. But Allison's "Coal Miner" artfully combines these elements in a manner that amplifies ambiguity, reflecting the uncertain positions held by many people throughout the region. But, at least initially, Allison "thought that was the one [song] that was going to ruffle the feathers" of her audiences because "coal mining is a touchy issue for a lot of West Virginians. It feeds people. It's been a way of life. It's how people make their living. On the other hand, it's a horribly dangerous thing that is kind of hurting the earth, in a sense. You know, we're taking something that's been there for millions of years and just picking it out and putting guys in the line of fire, in a sense, of many accidents. So I kind of wrote it from two perspectives. Respect and caution. I wanted to tell it from the father and the son having the conversation, and be able to reflect those two points of view without being too controversial and too abrasive."

As she notes, her songs often "tie old-timey themes and ways of life into what's happening now in a way that people in the twenty-first century can relate to the stuff that's happened a hundred years ago." For Allison, who lives on a small farm near the boundary between Monongalia and Wetzel Counties, these continuities are important and often appear in her original material. "There are still people who live like that [the 'old-timey' ways] now, and a lot of people don't understand that. We truly live Appalachian culture the way it was back in the 1920s now, and the road I live on is a prime example. You've got big old farm houses that's just put up, and then people living in shacks. Literal shacks. And you see a bunch of kids and cats in the yard, and everybody has the best garden, and people are self-sustaining. They have manners. They're community friendly. The type of people that will help their neighbor if they need anything. They depend on themselves and their family. They're never looking for a handout." These neighbors might hear their own lives and attitudes reflected in "Farmer's Life," a song Allison wrote about her Charleston grandparents: they "used to say, 'It's just a farmer's life for me. / It's the simple things that make the most sense to me.'"

Surveying Allison's songs, one is struck by the dark emotions that often hover around her characters or, in some cases, envelops them entirely. During her studies at West Virginia University, she identified strong poetic influences in the work of Emily Dickinson and Sylvia Plath, as well as the more melancholy passages by Walt Whitman, and the strong influence of Adams and Welch on her musical education undoubtedly exerted similar influences. "That's what people have said to me. I'm like, 'Pain writer?' Like, 'Yeah. Your songs are sad.' And I'm like, 'Well, I try to write happy stuff. It just doesn't work out.' I can write kind of fast and kind of happy, but a lot of my life has been tough—and a lot of what I have observed in life [has been hard, too]. I've kind of noticed the tough stuff, and it's much easier to write about it like that, so of course, I'm drawn to the dark poets and melancholy stuff."

This melancholy and sadness can be heard in "Quiet," an adjective she used to describe herself during our conversation. The song traces an autobiographical arc from her "angsty" and "cynical" teen-aged years to her current, more mature self. "As a teenager, I was loud.

I was opinionated. I was boisterous. I was rebellious. I was mouthy. I was ornery. And then now, who I am is like [a] 360 [*sic*]. I mean, I'm still cynical, but I look at life different. Before, I didn't really like life so much. Now, I'm like, 'Woo, life! Let's live this!' So it took the time for me to be quiet to get that. It took a time to reflect on things that have happened in my life."

Maria Allison has a promising future as a songwriter who blends the interpretive "confessional" songwriting that was so popular during the 1990s with the narrative traditions of folksong and balladry. Having written more than one hundred fifty songs, she continues to find new ways to capture the world around her in word and tune; as she noted, "the music just kind of flows out of me like water. I spend time absorbing the world around me, and then all of a sudden these songs come rushing out in full reflection of my experiences."[66] The West Virginia Hitchers' 2016 debut album, *Ghost in the Room*, reveals a solid creative vision and a songwriting prowess that can only be further refined as she continues to reflect on the world around her. And with an ambitious attitude, she will likely find herself on the airwaves as a featured *Mountain Stage* guest soon.

DISCOGRAPHY

AS A SOLO ARTIST:
　　Out of the Shadows, self-published (2003).
　　Into the Light, self-published (2003).

WITH THE WEST VIRGINIA HITCHERS:
　　Ghost in the Room, self-published (2016).

PAM SPRING

The Mountain State has a rich and colorful history that most residents of the state hold dear. It is this common history of Native American hunting grounds, pioneer settlements, Civil War battles, and industrialization that forms a narrative that unites people in a state that was forged in the furnace of civil war and that remains sectionalized still today.[67] Although informal means of passing this history along abound in storytelling, festivals, literature, and song, children who are raised in West Virginia also undergo a rigorous formal education in the state's history. Fourth- and eighth-graders across the state take West Virginia history as part of their social studies curriculum, and it is here that most students become aware of the significance of the Wheeling Suspension Bridge, Chief Logan, and the New River. Culminating in the prestigious Golden Horseshoe Award ceremonies at the State Capitol every spring, these experiences leave an indelible mark on the students who participate in this education, from the most studious to the least engaged.

Not surprisingly, then, classroom teachers across the state play a critical role in ensuring that each generation understands the state's history. Pam Spring, a native and lifelong resident of the Taylor County seat of Grafton, was one such teacher. In her fourth-grade classroom at Anna Jarvis Elementary—a school named for the Webster resident who established and fought to preserve the sanctity of Mother's

· · · ·

———

Figure 20. Pam and Lloyd W. Spring III
(courtesy of Pam Spring).

· · · ·

Day—Spring always tried to use music to engage her students, especially in social studies.[68] "Grafton is a very patriotic town because of the National Cemetery [located there]. So I taught lots of patriotic music to go along with my social studies. I taught 'Fifty Nifty United States' to teach the kids. Of course, on the different holidays, like Christmas holidays, we always did programs, all the time. Taught square dancing to the kids."

The incorporation of music into her classroom pedagogy came naturally to Spring, who has been musically active in the community since her youth there in the 1950s and 1960s. From the very beginning, she recalled, the radio played a key role in her development, as she internalized the pop hits played by local radio personality Bernadine Waters. Her parents were members of Grafton's middle class, her father—a former prisoner of war during World War II—established a Nationwide Insurance agency, where Spring's mother served as his assistant, and they made every effort to provide music instruction for their children. Shortly after her sixth birthday, her parents enrolled Pam in piano lessons with Mrs. Nicola, who instructed her in the rudiments of musical notation, harmony, and keyboard, skills that allowed her to play the music she heard on the radio. As Pam's sister Connie told me, Pam quickly advanced beyond Mrs. Nicola's studio, so she began "special lessons [with Morgantown pianist and composer Ralph Federer] because she's the only one that was really interested [in music].[69] Some of us were forced to do it. Some of us loved it. And so Mom would bring her over here once a week to Morgantown for lessons." Piano lessons also granted her access to the music of her Baptist church, which Pam describes as "pretty conservative," hewing close to the treasured hymns of the Broadman hymnal. Her passion for church music persists to the present day, as she serves as the choir director at Beulah Baptist Church in nearby Pruntytown. School choir and band—Pam was a clarinetist at Grafton High School—also played a central part in her musical development.

Despite the central role that music played in her personal and social life, Spring was, for the most part, content with playing the music that other people composed. But, as West Virginia history began to figure more prominently in the state social studies curriculum around the

year 1980, she found that music could prove very useful in augmenting
the pedagogy she had developed during her undergraduate studies at
Fairmont State College (now University) and her prior experiences at
Hepzibah and Anna Jarvis Elementary Schools. The state, she recalls,
"wanted us to do a whole semester [of West Virginia history], so I incor-
porated music with everything I taught." With few resources available
for teachers like herself, Spring resolved to create her own. With her
husband, Lloyd, a local attorney, she wrote several compositions to
help her students develop an understanding of the state's history and
geography, as well as to develop a sense of pride in the place they called
home. "When I needed something for West Virginia history, Lloyd and
I sat down, and we wrote the song 'Proud of West Virginia.' The main
idea of it was to teach important facts about the state in a fun way. And
then we [wrote another that] included the fifty-five counties, and then
we also wrote one about Grafton."

Soon, the Springs were writing songs for civic occasions and
organizations, as well. "We wrote this school song for Anna Jarvis
[Elementary], the *alma mater* for Anna Jarvis, and then an elementary
school in Taylor County was consolidating, so we wrote the school song
for West Taylor Elementary School. And we even wrote a little song for
the 4-H camp [Camp Towles]." Perhaps even more important than supporting a community they loved, though, was the opportunity to share
creative time with one another. As Spring remarked in her rather suc-
cinct manner, "He and I, we really enjoyed working on all that music
together."

The Springs' musical creations were quite popular in the city as
generations of students learned about their home in Spring's classroom. Her sister Connie remembered one young student who even won
a radio contest by singing one of them for a live audience: "She had a
student at one time. It was some kind of contest. If you could stand up
here in front of the DJ and 'sing a song that I didn't know,' then she got
some kind of a prize. Maybe it was at the fair. I don't remember. But this
little girl got up and sang 'Grafton, My Hometown.' Or else she sang
'Proud of West Virginia,' and that DJ did not hear know that song, so
she got something for singing a song this DJ did not know."

Spring's West Virginia history compositions were popular not only with her students, but with her colleagues, as well. Aware of the potential her songs had in the classroom, Spring forwarded them David Bice, who was the head of Jalamap, the firm that published the state history textbook. "Somehow, I found out about the textbook, and I sent them a copy of everything, and they called me and were interested in them. [Lloyd and I] met with them and did that," Pam recalls. "The Fifty-Five County Song" and "Proud of West Virginia" were easily published because of their universal applicability throughout the state, but "Grafton, My Hometown" required some minor modification to reach everyone. "The idea of it," Spring observed, "was for other kids in the state to substitute their hometown for Grafton and then sing and learn facts about their hometown." The Springs' songs remained fixtures in West Virginia history textbooks until recently, and from this platform, the songs began to take on a life of their own. A middle school band director named Matt Le Barber arranged "Proud of West Virginia" for middle school band—no doubt in response to the eighth-grade state history requirement—and premiered the arrangement during a concert in Charleston. The arrangement is now in the Taylor County Middle School band library, bringing it back home where it all started.

Spring, who was a fourth-grade teacher for four decades, worked diligently to keep her students involved in music and civic participation, not only in her classroom but through her work with the Anna Jarvis Singers, a special choir of third- and fourth-graders who sang in the community. In partnership with the school's music teacher, Spring auditioned this special group of dedicated musicians: "It was kids in third and fourth grade who were interested in just singing. You know, they tried out, and then we performed for the schools. Sometimes we performed out of the school for different community groups." One such community group was the people of Philippi in nearby Barbour County. When the town's historic covered bridge burned in 1989, members of the community fought to have the bridge replaced.[70] In 1991, the replica was opened to the public, and Spring was offered an opportunity to share her music with her neighbors to the south. "My students and I always went to the Kid's Day in Philippi, and we became friends with the coordinator. So I took my group, the Anna Jarvis Singers, to the rededication." There, they presented a new song, and they sang it for the town; "we presented the song from the people of Grafton to the people of Philippi," Spring remembered.

Pam Spring has written songs, along with her late husband Lloyd, for the past three and a half decades, but she seems reluctant to consider herself a songwriter. Rather, she repeatedly insists that she is a teacher who was simply trying to develop novel ways to get her students interested in West Virginia history. Yet, thanks to textbooks, band arrangements, and the Anna Jarvis Singers, her music has been performed throughout the state. For her dedication as a teacher, the West Virginia Division of Culture and History named her an honorary member of the Order of the Golden Horseshoe in 2000.[71] The honor was well deserved in light of the many Golden Horseshoe winners who fell under her pedagogical influence, whether directly or indirectly.

CHRIS HADDOX

Live in the Morgantown area long enough, and chances are that your life will intersect with Chris Haddox's. An active community leader who has served as the Executive Director of the Monongalia County Habitat for Humanity and who has been at the forefront of efforts to transform the abandoned Woodburn Elementary School into a vital community resource center, Haddox's good-natured attitude and baritone chuckle bring people together. A rare musician who can play anything with strings, Haddox can be found singing and playing guitar at community picnics and block parties, fiddling in an old-time jam session, or accompanying a monthly FOOTMAD dance at Morgantown's Marilla Park. A professor of sustainable design in West Virginia University's Davis College of Agriculture, Natural Resources, and Design, Haddox is also an engaging songwriter whose work explores the rich veins of Appalachian folklore, traditional music and, occasionally, parody and satire.

Haddox's musical journey began in Logan, where his father worked with songwriter Roger Bryant to establish an emergency medical service there in the 1980s. Born in 1960, Chris recalls that his father was a musician and encouraged the kids to play and sing, too. "My dad was a singer and played a little guitar. Played baritone uke, which was what was around the house most of the time. He was from Clendenin, and he was a thespian and he loved acting. They did their own plays in a

• • • •

Figure 21. Chris Haddox
(photo by Susan Eason, courtesy of Chris Haddox).

• • • •

community play group and all that in Logan. So he was always singing this, that, or the other. Show tunes and everything else." Haddox also remembered that his uncle, Jim, "was the real guitar picker and singer. I play his 1953 Gibson LG-1 now."[72] And his neighbor Danny Harrison was a somewhat successful songwriter, scoring at least one album cut by Nashville recording artist Jim Reeves, who taught Chris that the best way to write a song was to limit it to "three minutes and a hook."[73] But it was probably his brother and sister's interest in music that really prompted him to give it a go. "My brother and sister took piano, and I was really drawn to it. They're older than me, and so I just kind of showed an inclination to the piano and started playing on my own and later took lessons." By second or third grade, Chris was also playing the guitar—"an old Silvertone that was kind of murder on the fingers"— and by high school, he was learning to play covers of John Denver, Neil Young, and John Prine songs with his older brother.

Upon graduating from high school, Haddox moved to Morgantown to study at West Virginia University. Living in the dorms, he soon found that his guitar playing helped him make friends and that he still had a lot to learn about the instrument. "I got to college," he recalled, "and the guy down the hall from me was from Boone County, and he was a dobro player. And so I had my guitar, and he heard me playing, and he's like, 'Hey, do you do any flatpicking on there?' And I said, 'I don't even know what flatpicking is.' So he's like, 'You need to come down here.' So he got his dobro out, and I was mesmerized by the dobro. And it turns out his dad was a really good flatpicker. His brother lived in a trailer up here in Morgantown, so they would all come up and visit his brother. And they'd have these big picking parties. And so it was Joe Toler, who was my friend, and his dad, his name was Vaughn. Vaughn had a Gallagher guitar, and he played Doc Watson-style picking, and so I was just kind of like, 'Holy smokes! I've got to get me some of that!' So Joe gave me a Tony Rice album, and that was it. It was like, 'All right!' So I went home that summer and saved up money and bought myself a Martin guitar and kind of went at it from there."

Inspired by the rise of great singer-songwriters like Prine, Dan Fogelberg, and other songwriting stars of the 1970s and early 1980s, Haddox began to work on his own songwriting during his early twenties, continuing a practice that had begun to fascinate him during junior high. (He does recall having written a song as part of a second-grade poetry assignment, for which he "stole the first two lines from a poem my friend wrote!")[74] At the same time, he was busy preparing for a career as a veterinarian. Admitted to veterinary school at Ohio State before he had finished his undergraduate studies at WVU, Haddox found himself torn between his interests. With an armload of original material, enthusiasm, and talent on his side, he made several attempts to establish himself in Nashville, first during his studies at Ohio State and later after he dropped out of vet school and returned to WVU to complete his undergraduate degree. Chris went to Nashville in 1982, 1984, and 1987, staying for extended periods of time with each trip. "I was down there in three different stints," he recollected, "just meeting people, kind of seeing what it was like. Made some really good connections. Demoed a few songs here and there and tried to get some stuff out and about. Looking back on it, it's kind of amazing the people that I did meet. I was kind of running in the right circles. I worked in a store in Green Hills, which is kind of the ritzy end of town. A lot of music people live there. So there were a lot of people in the store, and Guy Clark would come in there, and Even Stevens, who was Eddie Rabbitt's producer, writer. Super nice guy, you know. I pitched some stuff to him. He gave me feedback. He was real encouraging, saying, 'Hey, send me anything any time. I'm always looking for stuff.' I had the classic 'go to Music Row and play for ASCAP folks,' and they'd give you about twenty seconds of their time. They're listening, answering the phone, writing, talking, and listening to songs."

While in Nashville, Haddox lived with a talented group of musicians who were employed at the Opryland theme park, where they provided musical entertainment for tourists. Jeff Smith, Chris McDaniels, and Jim Whiteside formed Palomino and played for many of the city's recording artists in addition to their Opryland work. Chris, too, auditioned for road work with a group that was backed by legendary Nashville session pianist Floyd Cramer. He remembered, "They were looking for a guitarist. They came over to the apartment. They just sang these three songs, and so I played. And they didn't go anywhere. It was kind of funny. It was like a demo or audition type of thing." He also recalls meeting "Garth Brooks before Garth was Garth. That was neat. We were at the Bluebird Café, and he was demoing somebody else's songs, just singing for somebody who didn't sing. I never got to play the Bluebird. Never was able to swing a showcase down there or anything."

Despite some of the challenges he faced, Haddox remembers that he learned how to think of a particular singer's style and write for their strengths, a valuable skill for a commercial songwriter to develop. When writing for someone else's voice, Haddox observes, there are many factors to consider: "Topic. You know, what kind of stuff are they singing about? Is it the structure of the song? Is it a straight verse-cho-rus-bridge thing? So I try and study them and think about them along those lines. Try not to be chasing a winner. I'm not going to write their next [version of] that same song, you know, which is a temptation. You can go back and look at folks and certainly find that their next two or three songs after their hit has a very similar flavor, same beat." Chris also learned that Nashville songwriters have a rich folklore about how to pitch songs to potential artists. "You know, you heard these kind of hard-and-fast rules, and one of the funniest rules that I always heard when I was in Nashville was don't take sad songs to anybody. And I'm like, 'Okay, but that's kind of what country music is. You're not going to sit there and tell me it's all happy, 'Yay, we did it' kind of songs. So how do they get there? It's kind of like you're pitching one thing, but what gets these heartfelt emotional [songs on the radio]? That's what country music's all about. It's a raw emotion kind of thing, and all of those emo-tions aren't all kind of happy emotions. And so that was always kind of baffling to me."

Nashville didn't work out for Haddox, and after his last trip to Music City, he returned to Logan to regroup and decide what to do next. By the early 1990s, he found himself back in Morgantown, where he began to get involved in the old-time music scene. One particu-larly strong influence in his life was Leo Herron, an old-time fiddler from Barbour County who had worked as a professional musician on Fairmont radio station WMMT in the 1930s and 1940s. Many of the tunes in Haddox's repertoire come from Herron, who taught him these works through the assistance of an Augusta Heritage Apprenticeship. Playing one of Herron's fiddles, Chris maintains a rich repertoire of

Herron's tunes, including "Middle Fork Splash," a jaunty tune that may allude to the river that runs through the middle of Barbour County. Haddox also occasionally writes his own fiddle tunes because, as he notes, "the fiddle's an awfully easy instrument to noodle around on."

In Morgantown, Haddox has become a go-to songwriter for special events and projects. Recently, he contributed songs to a compact disc project produced by WVU School of Art and Design professor Eve Faulkes that documents the cultural diversity of Scott's Run, a Monongalia County watershed that was home to numerous coal camps in the early and mid-twentieth century. *The Songs of Scott's Run* showcases Haddox's ability to channel the traditional coal mining songs of Merle Travis and newer originals songs by Roger Bryant and John Prine. His "Come All You Young Miners"—for which I provided harmony vocals—evokes the lilting waltz feel of Travis's "Dark as a Dungeon," as well as its sentimental tone. "Poor Folks Ready for a Better Day," on the other hand, uses a snappy melody and a catchy, up-tempo rhythm to capture the hopefulness of those members of the Scott's Run community who were relocated to the Preston County planned community of Arthurdale as part of Franklin Delano Roosevelt's Resettlement Administration.

Chris Haddox is not the kind of songwriter who goes around touting his own abilities. In fact, more often than not, he is quick to deflect attention to others rather than to claim the spotlight for himself. And, as I've learned from making music with him over the years, that's what makes him such a valuable contributor to the Morgantown community. Like many of the people profiled in this book, Chris wants to reflect the life of his family and his neighbors through his art. And all of us who know him are grateful for that.

———

DISCOGRAPHY

Songs of Scott's Run Museum and Trail, no publisher (2016).

STEVE SMITH

On a Friday night in April 2016, country music fans from at least three states filled the Lyell B. Clay Concert Theater at West Virginia University's Creative Arts Center to witness a live broadcast of one of the nation's great country music programs, *The Wheeling Jamboree*. The program—which was celebrating its 83rd anniversary that night—featured a wide array of country styles, from a high-school-aged boy singing Tim McGraw and Alan Jackson covers to a female singer invoking the countrypolitan sounds of Lynn Anderson and Jeannie Seely and the WVU Bluegrass and Old-Time Band playing the hits of Cousin Emmy and Wilma Lee and Stoney Cooper. But the star of the show was a banjo-playing natural gas pipeliner hailing from nearby Garrett County, Maryland, named Steve Smith. A member of the Wheeling Jamboree since 2014, Smith kept the audience on the edge of their seats as he played his hand-crafted five-string banjo at blazing speeds in a "Dueling Banjos" battle with the house band's lead guitarist, drew laughs as he talked self-deprecatingly about his ignorance of the ways of love, and even convinced the audience to join him in a moving communal singalong to West Virginia's newest state song, "Country Roads."

A native of Roane County, West Virginia, Smith developed his remarkable showmanship through a lifetime of serious devotion to making meaningful musical connections to other people. When he was eleven years old, he got his first guitar—a Sears and Roebuck Global

· · · ·

Figure 22. Steve Smith
(photo by Chelsie Warnick and Addie Glotfelty,
courtesy of Steve and Katie Smith).

· · · ·

model—for Christmas, and he "jumped out of the gate wanting to be serious about it." Although there weren't musicians in his family—"no one in the family even knew how to tune it," he recalled of his first instrument—music did serve an important role in community build-ing. "I got [my first guitar] for Christmas, and then that following June, my grandpa thought that people didn't sit around and visit enough or talk enough. And he's like, 'I need to have me a get-together or some-thing at least once a month where people can sit around and talk.' And music was how he did it." At the first of these gatherings, Smith felt the power of music firsthand: "When I heard my first set of bluegrass pickers, I jumped off that bale of hay—that's what everybody had to sit on—and I danced. And I danced for probably two or three months. I knew that music stirred me so deep, even though I couldn't figure out why at that point."

Throughout the early and mid 1980s, Smith soaked up as much music as he could. His uncle James "Early" White taught him to play "The Boogie," a simple three-chord song that helped him learn to play with strong rhythm. Church provided access to the deep vein of American hymnody thanks to the do-re-mi shape note hymnals they used, and high school music classes—including guitar class and choir—offered some formal music instruction, although Steve's well-developed musi-cal ear made written notation relatively superfluous for him. "In Guitar 1, the thing we had to do was learn how to play [notated] music. So the first couple of times, Mr. Vineyard [the music teacher] would go ahead and play the song, and it was just single-string stuff. And he would play it, and I'm looking at this thing, and he would tell us what those notes are. And I didn't have a clue, but if I could hear him play it, I could play it. It didn't take very long for him to realize that I didn't know how to read music. Long story short, I passed Guitar 1 and 2 with flying colors, and I was teaching him to play 'The Wildwood Flower.' But I never did learn how to read music."

The blazing banjo style of bluegrass legend Don Reno was particu-larly inspiring to the young Smith, who saw Reno's claim to possess "the fastest five alive" as a personal challenge. "Don put out an album, *The Fastest Five Alive*," Smith remembered. "I don't know when the album was put out, but I heard it in the '80s. So whenever I heard that, it was my goal [to play at those speeds] at that point. If Don Reno is the fastest five-string picker alive, I'm going to be as fast as Don Reno." Struggling to develop the three-finger approach, Steve adopted Reno's signature licks to a two-finger picking style, which proved sufficient for a while. But a sledding accident that left Smith with a severely broken hand and wrist ultimately helped him develop the technique that he needed to play like Reno. During his recuperation, "one of the old fellows I played with, Johnny Harold, he came up to the house and he said, 'Hey, Steve! Now would be a good opportunity to get that banjo out and just lay it across your lap and just sit there and start working that third finger in.'" Twisting his arm in the cast to give his hand the range of motion it needed, he practiced constantly and, as he recalled, began "to develop the smoothness" that both the Scruggs and Reno style require.

At the age of thirteen, Smith preached his first sermon at his family's Baptist church, a location that also nurtured his music-making. "I just played acoustic guitar along with the hymns that we'd sing in church. Now, if they'd done 'I'll Fly Away' or 'Over in the Glory Land' or 'There's Power in the Blood,' I'd pull the banjo out," he remembered. From the age of fifteen until he graduated from high school, Smith was also the bass singer in a southern gospel quartet called Revived that traveled throughout central West Virginia. It was here that Smith developed his showmanship: "Jackie Burks, she played the piano, and in between the songs, I was the emcee." When he turned eighteen, Smith decided to enroll at Liberty University to pursue his calling to the ministry while, at the same time, he began touring with the Camp Family, a southern gospel group from Hendersonville, North Carolina.

Infused with passion for his faith and a desire to merge music with his evangelical activities, his songwriting reflected his religious fervor from the very outset. His first song, "Who Holds Tomorrow?," was written when Smith was just twelve years old. He recalls that the song came to him during a solitary walk through the woods. "During the summer," he recounted, "I loved digging ginseng, and I could dig ginseng on a seven-mile stretch of road, and I could go on both sides of the mountain in or out or wherever I wanted to go. So this one particular day, I was ginsenging on my uncle's farm, which was about a mile away from my house. And coming off the point, Zion Hill Baptist Church sits right off the end of a point, just right above the road. So I came down past our family's graveyard and walked into the church. Churches were never locked back in that time. And whenever I walked into that church, they always had, on the pulpit, one of the big family Bibles. It was nice and cool, shade trees all around it, and I just kind of went in there to cool down a little bit. And opening up the Bible, there was a bookmarker in there that said, 'I may not know what tomorrow holds, but I know who holds tomorrow.' And I thought, 'Man! That is a really, really good saying. So I had to walk a mile back up the road, and I was trying to think of some words in my head and then, you know, I had a guitar in my hand, and I just kind of had this little melody, and that's the first song I ever wrote." He still performs it regularly today.

By his twenty-sixth birthday, Smith decided to give up music altogether, as marriage and the birth of a daughter changed his priorities in life. Working as a pipeliner in the natural gas fields of West Virginia and Pennsylvania, Steve found little time to continue his craft. Divorced at thirty-seven, he moved to Uniontown, Pennsylvania, where he joined a crew with Columbia Gas Pennsylvania. A friend and co-worker, Randy Breakiron, owned a horse barn in nearby Hopwood, Pennsylvania, and many of the people who boarded their horses there would stop by to hang out and share a good time. Breakiron learned that Smith played music and invited him to join in the festivities. "I just sat around, and I would sing songs," Smith said. "Older country songs like 'Here's a Quarter' and maybe 'Friends in Low Places' or maybe some of Keith Whitley's older stuff, just kind of exploring my country roots along with it, too." The horse barn quickly led to his first paying gig as a solo artist at Mahoney's in Uniontown. "People came out. All my friends supported me, and then that got my confidence up enough to where I wanted to start writing other songs again. So there came 'Don't Blame My Heart,' and there came 'Another Beer.' There came all these songs because now I had my confidence up."

Smith's reputation grew rapidly as venues in West Virginia, Pennsylvania, and Maryland sought out his interpretations of country hits from the 1980s and 1990s and, increasingly, his original compositions. In 2014, Smith's commitment to "traditional" country music— which he describes as "a Telecaster, a pedal steel, a keyboard, a set of drums, and an acoustic guitar—was recognized by Dave Heath, the president of the *Wheeling Jamboree*, who contacted him to play on the historic program as a cover artist. Smith's wife, Katie—who handles all of Smith's business operations—encouraged him to give it a shot: "She said, 'Now listen, you're going in as a cover band. Just go there and do the cover songs, and if you feel like the audience might like some of your original stuff, then throw one of them on 'em.'" After a successful debut, he was invited back "once every two months or so," slowly expanding his performances to include banjo features and more original compositions. In October 2014, he was officially initiated as a member of the *Wheeling Jamboree*, a position he carries with great pride.

Following on the heels of his *Jamboree* membership, WVU's Mon Hills Records—a student-run venture housed in the WVU School of Music—signed Smith to a record deal. At the time, he was the only artist that they had signed without a previous affiliation with the university. In spring 2016, his debut album *Then and Now* was released, representing the full breadth of Smith's musical creativity. Leading off the album in his first gospel composition, "Who Holds Tomorrow," followed by such traditional songs as "The Old Rugged Cross," "Wildwood Flower," and "I'll Fly Away." Steve's banjo playing is on full display in such songs as "Foggy Mountain Breakdown." Original compositions "The Brave" and "Thought Away (Dylan's Song)" explore the sounds of Tim McGraw and Kenny Chesney, with a resonant vocal style and tasteful accompaniment. "'Til I Saw You" speaks to new love, reflecting the life-changing presence of his wife Katie and her encouragement of his dreams.

At home in bluegrass, gospel, and mainstream country music, Steve Smith reflects the highlights of the past half-century of West Virginian country music. He maintains a high standard of musical performance, and his songwriting would easily be at home in the Nashville of a decade ago. Working tirelessly to promote his vision of traditional country music, Smith—currently living just a few miles across the West Virginia-Maryland line and actively shaping the country music community of northern West Virginia—offers a valuable model for the ways that local and regional country musicians bring life to our communities.

SELECTED DISCOGRAPHY

Then and Now, Mon Hills Records (2015).

· · · ·

———

Figure 23. Dan Cunningham
(photo by David Traugh, courtesy of Dan Cunningham).

· · · ·

DAN CUNNINGHAM

Morgantown singer-songwriter Dan Cunningham's music is steeped in the legends and lore of some of the Mountain State's most iconic folk heroes, from John Henry to Sid Hatfield. Describing his music as "New Appalachian," Cunningham—a stellar guitarist who can play traditional tunes and harmonically rich accompaniments—explains that his songs often respond to his deep feeling for the state and its people. "It's in your blood or something," he reflected, "and writing is the same way. I just can't escape the imagery and the feelings. West Virginia's reputation is not very good. There's some things to be said about that reputation, except there are just some tremendous things about living here and being part of the culture, you know? I just can't escape it."

Cunningham's fascination with the Mountain State began early on during his childhood in the Wood County town of Washington Bottom. Born in 1952, he was raised in a musical family. "I started playing because my father played upright bass in a jazz band at one point," he recalled. "And, in fact, I still have his bass. My mom played a little bit. I started playing cello when I was young. And later, I learned to play the guitar and later on was a professional musician, as a bass player mostly around Parkersburg. Of course, the [musicians'] union was strong then, and they used to call me for jobs. They'd say, 'A country band needs a bass player tonight. Will you go and try and learn those songs in a quick fifteen-minute jam session?' Or 'A polka band needs a bass player.'" Upon graduating from high school, Cunningham moved to Morgantown, where he spent two semesters as a music education major before returning to the Parkersburg area to play for a while. Eventually, Cunningham found his way into a couple of regional bands, including one that he described as "a show band that traveled around, did dance steps, and wore uniforms. You know, learned shows from beginning to end."

In 1975, Cunningham decided to leave the Ohio Valley and move to Freeville, New York, where he joined a Jesus Community called the Love Inn, located in a dairy barn. "I went there because a man named Scott Ross had a syndicated radio show out of there," he recalled, "and this place just drew artistic people from everywhere for some reason. And it was into the hippie culture, and I ended up playing in a band there." Also in that band were future Nashville producer Lynn Nichols, Nashville songwriter Phil Madeira, and Phil Keaggy, who has built a distinguished career as a Christian recording artist. "The Phil Keaggy Band was what it was called," Cunningham remembered. "We played in Canada, New York, Connecticut. All through the South. Just about anywhere east of the Mississippi, and then Washington and a few places west." After a three-year stint running from 1976 to 1979, the Phil Keaggy Band "fell apart," with the rest of the band moving to Nashville and Cunningham returning to Morgantown in 1986.

Finding it difficult to maintain a band while also working odd hours at a day job, Cunningham moved from one group to another for many years, including a brief stint with some of the state's more progressive traditional musicians. "I used to play traditional music with Robert Kessinger, Roy Clark, Jr., and Danny Kessinger. Jenny Allinder. We had a little group together, except they didn't want me to play guitar or bass, although I did play bass for a little while. They wanted me to play cello, which was kind of weird. I never got adapted to playing traditional music on the cello." To accommodate his schedule, Cunningham played solo at social events, often teaming up with his wife Julie, a Celtic harpist, for weddings and receptions.

By the late 1990s, however, the songwriting bug bit him, and he decided to make a concerted effort to capture interesting stories in song. Beginning around 1998, Cunningham began to develop a regular circuit of venues around the Morgantown area that would allow him to present his songs and encourage patrons to listen to what he had to say. "One of the earlier places was the Black Bear [on Pleasant Street], which was a great opportunity because they had a lot of live music. They booked regularly. They don't pay much, but they give a chance for people to get out and play and sometimes feature people who haven't been doing it much at that point, you know." Before long, he was producing albums of his original music—releasing albums featuring many members of the Morgantown musical community as backing musicians—and submitting material for the New Song Contest, which flourished in the Mountain State during the late 1990s and early 2000s, where he earned recognition as a regional finalist.

A skilled multi-instrumentalist who is largely self-taught on most of the instruments he plays, Cunningham's albums often reveal him to pay particular attention to the ways that instrumental textures can support his storytelling. Listening carefully to his guitar style, for instance, one will hear delicate fingerpicking that makes idiomatic use of the guitar's open strings to create shimmering textures. "There are so many people that are better than me," he observed, "and they ask me, 'How do you do that?' Well, part of the secret—I almost feel like I'm cheating—is when I was in high school, a guy came my senior year and demonstrated classical guitar, and I said, 'Wow! That looks neat.' So I took some lessons afterward, and the thing I got out of that was technique. So adapting things I hear to the guitar has been so much easier because I don't have to fight myself." Freed by this technical mastery to play up and down the neck of the guitar, Cunningham often creates harmonically advanced accompaniments that would be much less effective if he were to simply strum the guitar. "I have just been fascinated with other people fingerpicking," he noted, "and that was my original thought when I was doing that—and why I didn't strum. I just want my own little orchestra so I can do moving lines." His 2001 album *Into the Flow* features many of these skills in such original numbers as "River Flow" and "Nothing I Intended," which resonates with some of internationally renowned guitarist Leo Kottke's mellower work.

Many of Cunningham's songs address life in the Mountain State head on, but they just as frequently turn on his wry sense of humor.

"Nelsonville 1970," from his 2006 album *Wayfaring Stranger*, tells of an encounter between a young hippie (probably Cunningham himself) and a rural resident of nearby Nelsonville, Ohio. Reminiscent of the work of the New Riders of the Purple Sage, "Nelsonville 1970" is filled with silliness and ironic confrontation. But Cunningham is quick to dismiss such songs. "I played that in the house," he recalled, "and she [Julie] said, 'You need to quit writing silly stupid songs.' So I quit. I pretty much quit. It took me a while to figure it out. My mind is like a cartoon, and writing stupid silly things is easy. I could sit down and write it in an hour, but writing real songs is an effort. So I kind of try to shut off the stupid songs. So I'm a little embarrassed by those things."

Cunningham's more serious repertoire engages with many of the core issues of life in late twentieth- and early twenty-first-century Appalachia, as well as the region's folklore and history. His 2003 album *I Think of Home*, for instance, features songs addressing the experiences of Appalachian migrants as well as the powerful draw of the region's natural beauty. "Breeze at Eventide," for example, uses the Celtic harp to create a meditative mood as Cunningham discusses the spiritual refreshment that he feels in the evening breeze. Nature is "one of the things I love about West Virginia," he observed, "and it's the same for a lot of people. There's nothing that cleans my mind like going and walking in the woods, and the further back, the better. My wife had convinced me that I was too old to be wandering in the wilderness areas by myself. But I'm getting back to it. I say the heck to it." Similarly, "Have I Been Away Too Long?" from *Wayfaring Stranger*, and the title track to *I Think of Home*, deal with Cunningham's own experiences watching people leave, and his personal journey to New York. "I left West Virginia in '75, and the tug was always there to come back," he noted. "I Think of Home," then, "is kind of half made-up, but I thought about the people that left West Virginia to work, and, in fact, I knew some of them or their families. They went to Akron to work in a tire factory or in a gear factory, or they went to North Carolina to work, but this was still home. Vacation time? Come back here."

Cunningham's most ambitious solo project, released in 2013, is the concept album *Appalachian Song*, which he describes as exploring "the turmoil, tragedy, beauty, and humor of those remote Appalachian

Mountains."[75] Drawing well-known traditional songs such as "John Henry," "Angel Band," and the Hazel Dickens classic "West Virginia, My Home" into a dialogue with original songs dealing with the Mine Wars of the 1920s, *Appalachian Song* captures the essence of the "New Appalachian" style that Cunningham has developed. "I like writing about things that are real," he observed. "There's so much illumination to be done. Like 'Out of My Mind.' It's not just about the Mine Wars, but it's kind of the backdrop for it. And you know, when I play out and I just explain that history to people, some are just amazed. You tell them, 'Well, you work for the mine. They owned your house. If you did something like union organizing, you may lose your house. You may be evicted. If you die, they would probably evict your family.' Sometimes people are very surprised that they didn't know that."

Now in his sixth decade, Cunningham is pleased that he is able to share his original compositions with audiences around north-central West Virginia and southwestern Pennsylvania. Today, he plays many of the same venues that he played when he was developing as a songwriter, but with a loyal following that has come to expect a good show and thoughtful songs. "I've had the privilege of music and getting to play with some great folks. I don't consider myself a seasoned songwriter because I haven't done it that long, but I intend to keep doing it. But, you know, you always have these hopes of something big happening to a song. I'm a little more realistic now, but I still plug away. Whatever happens now is okay."

SELECTED DISCOGRAPHY

Into the Flow, Pickndawg Music (2001).
I Think of Home, Pickndawg Music (2003).
Wayfaring Stranger, Pickndawg Music (2006).
Back to Morgantown, Pickndawg Music (2008).
River Flow, Pickndawg Music (2011).
Appalachian Song, Pickndawg Music (2013).

NOTES AND INTERVIEWS

NOTES

1. Sowell offered a number of revisions to the quotations here in an e-mail to the author, 28 March 2017 (in author's possession).

2. Mickey Raphael is probably best known for his work as a member of Willie Nelson's band, of which he has been a member for more than forty years.

3. For more on the progressive country music scene, consult Jan Reid, *The Improbable Rise of Redneck Rock*, new ed. (Austin: University of Texas Press, 2004); Barry Shank, *Dissonant Identities: The Rock'n'Roll Scene in Austin, Texas* (Middletown, CT: Wesleyan University Press, 1994); Kathleen Hudson, *Telling Stories, Writing Songs: An Album of Texas Songwriters* (Austin: University of Texas Press, 2001); Travis D. Stimeling, *Cosmic Cowboys and New Hicks: The Countercultural Sounds of Austin's Progressive Country Music Scene* (New York: Oxford University Press, 2011); Jason Mellard, *Progressive Country: How the 1970s Transformed the Texan in Popular Culture* (Austin: University of Texas Press, 2013); Craig E. Clifford and Craig Hillis, *Pickers and Poets: The Ruthlessly Poetic*

Singer-Songwriters of Texas (College Station: Texas A&M University Press, 2016).

4. Carter Taylor Seaton, *Hippie Homesteaders: Arts, Crafts, Music, and Living on the Land in West Virginia* (Morgantown: West Virginia University Press, 2014), esp. 100–118.

5. For more information on the Putnam County Pickers, consult "The Putnam County Pickers," accessed April 11, 2017, http://www.mywvhome.com/seventies/pickers.htm.

6. Groce offered a number of revisions to the quotations offered here in an e-mail to the author, 12 March 2017 (in author's possession).

7. For more background on the Helvetia Star Band, consult David H. Sutton, *Helvetia: The History of a Swiss Village in the Mountains of West Virginia* (Morgantown: West Virginia University Press, 2010), 74–81.

8. For further background on the Currence Brothers, consult Jack Waugh and Michael Kline, "The Currence Brothers: 'The Spark to Play Music,'" in John Lilly, ed., *Mountains of Music: West Virginia Traditional Music from* Goldenseal (Urbana: University of Illinois Press, 1999), 196–207.

9. Information drawn from Discogs.org, "Larry Groce," accessed April 12, 2017, https://www.discogs.com/artist/419143-Larry-Groce.

10. Julie Adams contributed to the editing of this chapter—both the quotations and the text—in a letter to the author, 30 March 2017 (in author's possession).

11. Julie Adams, letter to the author, 30 March 2017 (in author's possession).

12. Julie Adams, letter to the author, 30 March 2017 (in author's possession).

13. Julie Adams, letter to the author, 30 March 2017 (in author's possession).

14. Expanded by Julie Adams, letter to the author, 30 March 2017 (in author's possession).

15. Expanded by Julie Adams, letter to the author, 30 March 2017 (in author's possession).

16. Expanded by Julie Adams, letter to the author, 30 March 2017 (in author's possession).

17. For more information, consult "John Lilly's State Songs," last accessed April 12, 2017, http://pages.suddenlink.net/ johnlillymusic/StateSongs/index.html.

18. The Green Grass Cloggers, "History," last accessed April 18, 2017, http://www.greengrasscloggers.com/History.html.

19. John Lilly, ed., *Mountains of Music: West Virginia Traditional Music from* Goldenseal (Urbana: University of Illinois Press, 1999).

20. Virginia Lad, *Sodom and Gomorrah of Today, or the History of Keystone, West Virginia* (no place, 1912), http://www.wvcul- ture.org/history/communities/historyofkeystone.pdf.

21. Many of Jolly Gargoyle's recordings and other materials are archived by Chris Ramey at http://www.chrisrameymusic. com/jollygargoyle.cfm (accessed April 11, 2017).

22. A number of the Joint Chiefs' live shows and other materials have been archived by Chris Ramey at http://www.chris- rameymusic.cm/joint-chiefs (accessed April 11, 2017).

23. For additional insights about "29," consult WestVirginia- Ville, "Song of the Day: 600LBS of Sin!," March 11, 2011, ac- cessed April 11, 2017, http://westvirginiaville.com/2011/03/ song-of-the-day-600lbs-of-sin/.

24. See, for instance, Ri J. Turner, "West Virginia Jews Join En- vironmental Push after Charleston Chemical Spill," *Forward*, February 16, 2014, accessed April 11, 2017, http://forward. com/news/192773/west-virginia-jews-join-environmen- tal-push-after-c/.

25. For more background on Cabin Creek Quilts, consult Carter Taylor Seaton, *Hippie Homesteaders: Arts, Crafts, Music, and Living on the Land in West Virginia* (Morgantown: West Vir- ginia University Press, 2014), 65–77.

26. Colleen Anderson, *Missing Mrs. Cornblossom* (Charleston: Quarrier Press, 2012).

27. Todd Burge, e-mail to author, 15 March 2017 (in author's possession).

28. Todd Burge, e-mail to author, 15 March 2017 (in author's possession).

29. Todd Burge, e-mail to author, 15 March 2017 (in author's possession).

30. Ivan Tribe, "Doc Williams: A Half-Century at the 'Wheeling Jamboree," in John Lilly, ed., *Mountains of Music: West Virginia Traditional Music from* Goldenseal (Urbana: University of Illinois Press, 1999), 147–55.

31. "I-40 Paradise," Wikipedia, accessed April 17, 2017, https://en.wikipedia.org/wiki/I_40_Paradise.

32. *Billboard*, "Lionel Cartwright," last accessed April 17, 2017, http://www.billboard.com/artist/307439/lionel-cartwright/chart?f=357.

33. *Billboard*, "Lionel Cartwright," last accessed April 17, 2017, http://www.billboard.com/artist/307439/lionel-cartwright/chart?f=357.

34. "Reporting stations" are stations that report their playlists to *Billboard* and, therefore, have a direct impact on chart positions.

35. "Lionel Cartwright," last accessed April 17, 2017, https://www.discogs.com/artist/1158643-Lionel-Cartwright.

36. Jim Savarino, e-mail to author, 14 March 2017 (in author's possession).

37. For more information on Jack Hardy, consult Michael Kornfeld, "Jack Hardy, Singer-Songwriter and Fast Folk Founder, 1947–2011," AcousticMusicScene.com, March 11, 2011, last accessed April 19, 2017, http://acousticmusicscene.com/2011/03/11/jack-hardy-singer-songwriter-and-fast-folk-founder-1947-2011/.

38. Jim Savarino, e-mail to author, 12 March 2017 (in author's possession).

39. For more background on the Kerrville Folk Festival, consult Dyanne Fry Cortez, *Hot Jams & Cold Showers: Scenes from the Kerrville Folk Festival* (Austin: Dos Puertas Publishing, 2000); Craig Clifford, "Too Weird for Kerrville: The Darker Side of Texas Music," in *Pickers and Poets: The Ruthlessly Poetic Singer-Songwriters of Texas*, eds. Craig E. Clifford and

Craig Hillis (College Station: Texas A&M University Press, 2016), 17–26.

40. Jim Savarino, e-mail to author, 12 March 2017 (in author's possession).

41. Adam Booth, e-mail to author, 9 April 2017 (in author's possession).

42. For more information on the Bristol Sessions, consult Charles K. Wolfe and Ted Olsen, eds., *The Bristol Sessions: Writings about the Big Bang of Country Music* (Jefferson, NC: McFarland, 2005).

43. Adam Booth, e-mail to author, 9 April 2017 (in author's possession).

44. Purkey contributed to the editing of this chapter—including both the quotations and the text itself—in an e-mail to the author, 19 April 2017 (in author's possession). For additional background on Purkey, consult Paul Gartner, "'One Day More': Activist Songwriter Elaine Purkey," *Goldenseal* (Summer 2006).

45. For more background on the Pittston Strike, consult Richard A. Brisbin, Jr., *A Strike Like No Other: Law and Resistance During the Pittston Coal Strike of 1989–1990* (Baltimore: Johns Hopkins University Press, 2002).

46. For more information on religious practices in the region, consult Howard Dorgan, *Giving Glory to God in Appalachia: Worship Practices of Six Baptist Subdenominations* (Knoxville: University of Tennessee Press, 1990); Deborah Vansau McCauley, *Appalachian Mountain Religion: A History* (Urbana: University of Illinois Press, 1995); Bill J. Leonard, ed., *Christianity in Appalachia: Profiles in Regional Pluralism* (Knoxville: University of Tennessee Press, 1999).

47. For more background on the Highlander Center, consult John M. Glen, *Highlander: No Ordinary School, 1932–1962* (Lexington: University Press of Kentucky, 1988); *idem*, "Like a Flower Slowly Blooming: Highlander and the Nurturing of an Appalachian Movement," in *Fighting Back in Appalachia: Traditions of Resistance and Change* (Philadelphia: Temple University Press, 1993), 31–56.

48. Archie Green, *Only a Miner: Studies in Recorded Coal-Mining Songs* (Urbana: University of Illinois Press, 1972).

49. Shirley Stewart Burns, *Bringing Down the Mountains: The Impact of Mountaintop Removal on Southern West Virginia Communities, 1970–2004* (Morgantown: West Virginia University Press, 2007).

50. This performance can be viewed at https://www.youtube.com/watch?v=pFJNtvTg_1w (last accessed July 27, 2017).

51. Bryant edited some of the quotations here for clarity and added some new material to provide additional detail in an e-mail to the author, 16 March 2017 (in author's possession).

52. For more information on this strike, consult Ben A. Franklin, "Miners Ratify Contract to End Longest Strike; Work to Resume Monday," *New York Times* 25 March 1978); Paul J. Nyden, "Rank-and-File Rebellions in the Coalfields, 1964–80," *Monthly Review: An Independent Socialist Magazine* 58, no. 10, March 2007, accessed April 13, 2017, https://monthlyreview.org/2007/03/01/rank-and-file-rebellions-in-the-coalfields-1964-80/.

53. Roger Bryant, e-mail to author, 16 March 2017 (in author's possession).

54. Roger Bryant, e-mail to author, 16 March 2017 (in author's possession).

55. Liz McCormick, "2014 Vandalia Award Goes to Logan Native," *WV Public Broadcasting*, 27 May 27, 2014, accessed April 13, 2017, http://wvpublic.org/term/roger-bryant.

56. The program for this festival is archived at https://archive.org/stream/festivalofameric00festival/festivalofameric00festival_djvu.txt (last accessed April 18, 2017).

57. For more background on the Buffalo Creek disaster, consult Gerald M. Stern, *The Buffalo Creek Disaster: How the Survivors of One of the Worst Disasters in Coal-Mining History Brought Suit Against the Coal Company—and Won* (New York: Vintage, 1977).

58. Collins requested a few changes to the quotations found here in an e-mail to the author, 14 March 2017 (in author's possession).

59. For more background on Old Regular Baptist singing, consult Beverly Bush Patterson, *The Sound of the Dove: Singing in Appalachian Primitive Baptist Churches* (Urbana: University of Illinois Press, 1995).

60. Clinton Collins, e-mail to author, 14 March 2017 (in author's possession).

61. Jake Jarvis, "WV Board of Medicine Names New Executive Director," *Charleston Gazette-Mail*, December 13, 2016, last accessed April 18, 2017, http://www.wvgazette-mail.com/news-health/20161213/wv-board-of-medicine-names-new-executive-director.

62. A number of the figures profiled in Seaton's *Hippie Homesteaders* spent significant time in the Greenbrier Valley.

63. Lydia Nuzum, "Stompin' with The Wild Rumpus," *WVLiving*, March 28, 2013, last accessed April 17, 2017, http://www.wvliving.com/WV-Sound/Spring-2012/Stompin-with-The-Wild-Rumpus/.

64. Maria Allison, e-mail to author, 13 March 2017 (in author's possession).

65. Maria Allison, e-mail to author, 13 March 2017 (in author's possession).

66. Maria Allison, e-mail to author, 13 March 2017 (in author's possession).

67. For more on the sectionalization of West Virginia, consult Louis H. Manarin, "Sectionalism and the Virginias," in *e-WV: The Encyclopedia of West Virginia*, October 29, 2010, accessed April 11, 2017, https://www.wvencyclopedia.org/articles/229.

68. For more on the history of Mother's Day, consult Katherine Lane Antolini, *Memorializing Motherhood: Anna Jarvis and the Struggle for Control of Mother's Day* (Morgantown: West Virginia University Press, 2016).

69. Much of Federer's music is held at the West Virginia and Regional History Center, West Virginia University Libraries, Morgantown, WV ("Music Research Resources in the West Virginia and Regional History Collection," *West Virginia and Regional History Collection Newsletter* 20, no. 1 [Fall 2004],

6, accessed April 11, 2017, https://wvrhc.lib.wvu.edu/news/ newsletter/1995-2004/v20n1.pdf).

70. West Virginia Department of Transportation, "Philippi Covered Bridge," accessed April 11, 2017, http://www.transportation.wv.gov/highways/bridge_facts/covered-bridges/ Pages/PhilippiCoveredBridge.aspx.

71. West Virginia Department of Education, "221 Students Receive Golden Horseshoe Award," May 19, 2000, accessed February 1, 2017, https://wvde.state.wv.us/news/166/.

72. Chris Haddox, e-mail to author, 13 March 2017 (in author's possession).

73. Chris Haddox, e-mail to author, 13 March 2017 (in author's possession).

74. Chris Haddox, e-mail to author, 13 March 2017 (in author's possession).

75. "Appalachian Song by Dan Cunningham," accessed April 13, 2017, https://www.cdbaby.com/cd/dancunningham4.

INTERVIEWS

Adams, Julie. 27 July 2015. Charleston, WV.
Adkins, Andrew. 3 June 2016. Beckley, WV.
Allison, Maria. 30 July 2015. Morgantown, WV.
Anderson, Colleen. 30 April 2014. Charleston, WV.
Arcuri, Mike. 4 March 2016. South Charleston, WV.

Booth, Adam. 15 July 2014. Morgantown, WV.
Bryant, Roger. 17 July 2015. Logan, WV.
Burge, Todd. 4 November 2014. Parkersburg, WV.
Burns, Shirley Stewart. 31 October 2014. Morgantown, WV.

Cartwright, Lionel. 16 July 2015. Telephone interview.
Collins, Clinton. 26 July 2015. Beckley, WV.
Cunningham, Dan. 21 July 2015. Star City, WV.

Groce, Larry. 19 January 2015. Morgantown, WV.

Haddox, Chris. 10 September 2014. Star City, WV.
Harper, Doug, Shelley Harper, and Dave Fondale. 7 November 2015. Beckley, WV.
Holstein, Scott. 23 June 2014. Marlinton, WV.
Hornbaker, Dina. 27 July 2015. Charleston, WV.

Lilly, John. 13 December 2014. Kingwood, WV.

McBee, Chelsea. 7 August 2014. Thomas, WV.

Purkey, Elaine. 4 June 2016. Chapmanville, WV.
Pushkin, Michael. 31 July 2015. Telephone interview.

Rabalais, Roger. 24 March 2016. Charleston, WV.

Savarino, Jim. 20 April 2016. Star City, WV.
Smith, Steve. 7 July 2015. McHenry, MD.
Sowell, Ron. 1 August 2015. Charleston, WV.
Spangler, Mark. 15 August 2015. Bluefield, WV.
Spring, Pam, and Connie Price. 22 July 2015. Star City, WV.
Stanley, Patrick. 17 July 2015. Huntington, WV.

Thomas, Taryn. 16 July 2015. Telephone interview.